T0158971

MITCHELL'S
Big Book Concordance

WILLIAM P. MITCHELL

Inspiring Voices®
A Service of **Guideposts**

www.bestbibleconcordance.com
wpmitchell7@sbcglobal.net

For information contact:
W. P. Mitchell
8135 Bunkum Road
Caseyville, IL. 62232
618-698-1948

Inspiring Voices books may be ordered through booksellers or by contacting:

Inspiring Voices
1663 Liberty Drive
Bloomington, IN 47403
www.inspiringvoices.com
1-(866) 697-5313

ISBN: 978-1-4624-0281-6 (sc)
ISBN: 978-1-4624-0282-3 (e)

Library of Congress Control Number: 2012914718

Printed in the United States of America

Inspiring Voices rev. date: 9/24/2012

This concordance covers the portion of the "Big Book" starting with the chapter called "The Doctor's Opinion" beginning on page xxii.
It continues through the next 164 pages, and takes in the first story titled "Doctor Bob's Nightmare".

In the back of the book are "teachings from the Big Book". And on the last page is a poem that tells who we are.

Dedicated, in memory of the three sponsors I outlived, who loved me through all my craziness and never got to see the finished book. Cowboy Jim, Emmet E. and Roy B.

And to my daughter Lisa, who stood by me, and encouraged me through the whole process from inception to publishing.

How To Use The Concordance

The concordance is the most basic tool for study. It enables the user to quickly locate any line in the Big Book even when you just know one key word in that phrase. Every significant word in the first 164 pages is arranged alphabetically in the concordance followed by the phrase reference where it can be found.

For example, if you were looking for the phrase. "Abnormal action of alcohol", you would look under A and scroll down to abnormal where that is listed. It will have the chapter title, page number and line number. Like this:

Abnormal
To Emp 140-31 **abnormal** action of alcohol on his mind
You would then turn to page 140 in the chapter To Employers and scroll down to line number 31.

Unfortunately, to have the lines numbered on each page of your Big Book, you have to mark it yourself. As yet no one has printed the Big Book with the page lines already numbered. Perhaps now that we have our own concordance someone will do that. I numbered each page by hand in my book. I skipped the first line and started at line 2 with the number two and counted by twos on every other line all the way down on each page. Takes 10 or 15 minutes, works like a charm.

Knowledge is Power

The more you learn and understand the Big Book and how this program works, the more powerful it becomes in your life.

MITCHELL'S
Big Book Concordance

A

Abandon
Ho It Wo 63-22 **abandon** ourselves utterly to Him.
A Vi Fo You 164-21 **Abandon** yourself to God
Abandoned
We Ag 48-5 This sort of thinking had to be **abandoned.**
Aberrations
To Emp 140-25 understand the **aberrations** of the alcoholic.
Ability
We Ag 54-2 have confidence in our **ability** to think?
To Emp 143-24 confidence in his **ability** to recover?
Abnormal
Doc's Op xxiv-13 body of the alcoholic is quite as **abnormal** as
Th Is A Sol 23-28 these drinkers are **abnormal**
To Wives 114-11 mental condition too **abnormal** or
Th Fam Af 122-21 a highly strained, **abnormal** condition.
To Emp 140-31 **abnormal** action of alcohol on his mind.
A Vi Fo You 155-11 aware of being somehow **abnormal,**
Above -board
To Emp 140-29 a seemingly **above-board** chap
Absence
A Vi Fo You 160-30 the **absence** of intolerance of any kind,
Absolutely
Doc's Op xxiv-4 You may rely **absolutely** on anything they say
To Wives 120-26 Make him feel **absolutely** free
Abstainer
To Emp 139-16 than a total **abstainer** would be.
Abstinence
Doc's Op xxviii-31 have to suggest is entire **abstinence.**
Dr Bob Ni 181-9 two and one half years of **abstinence.**
Absurd
Mo Ab Al 37-28 Our behavior is as **absurd** and
Absurdities
To Emp 140-16 Can his past **absurdities** be forgotten?

Abundantly
Th Fam Af 133-20 God has **abundantly** supplied
Abused
Dr Bob Ni 181-14 I had **abused** it so frightfully that it
Accept
Th Is A Sol 25-32 to **accept** spiritual help.
We Ag 47-28 But I cannot **accept** as surely true
We Ag 47-32 inability to **accept** much on faith,
Wo Wi Ot 97-28 Should they **accept** and practice
Accepted
To Emp 139-5 he **accepted** the principles and procedure
To Emp 145-8 if he has **accepted** our solution
Acceptance
We Ag 48-23 Why this ready **acceptance?**
Accepted
Doc's Op xxvi-25 we have **accepted** and encouraged
We Ag 47-24 unless we **accepted** many things on faith
Accepting
Doc's Op xxv-1 **accepting** what we have to offer.
Accomplished
To Wives 118-30 has **accomplished** in a few weeks
Th Fam Af 128-20 that God has **accomplished** the miracle
Acquaintance
A Vi Fo You 161-2 for some stricken **acquaintance**
Act
To Wives 112-20 If you **act** upon these principles
To Wives 113-12 stumbling convinces him he must **act,**
Action
Doc's Op xxvi-5 the **action** of alcohol on these chronic
Bill's Story 9-30 a practical program of **action**
Th Is A Sol 17-24 brotherly and harmonious **action**
Mo Ab Al 42-22 and program of **action**
Mo Ab Al 42-25 program of **action** though entirely sensible
Ho It Wo 63-32 on a course of vigorous **action,**
Into Ac 72-8 This requires **action** on our part,
Into Ac 76-15 Now we need more **action,**
Into Ac 80-1 Before taking drastic **action**
Into Ac 80-28 His **action** met widespread approval,
Into Ac 85-13 the spiritual program of **action**

Into Ac 85-31 and that means more **action.**

Into Ac 87-32 ask for the right thought or **action.**

Wo Wi Ot 93-26 unselfish, constructive **action.**

Wo Wi Ot 94-4 Outline the program of **action.**

Wo Wi Ot 94-31 had you not taken **action.**

Wo Wi Ot 98-5,6 when such **action** is warranted.

Wo Wi Ot 98-28 principles into **action** at home.

To Wives 113-25 They can urge **action** without arousing

To Emp 140-18 **action** of alcohol on his brain?

To Emp 140-31 abnormal **action** of alcohol on his mind.

To Emp 142-32 you may suggest a definite course of **action.**

A Vi Fo You 157-31 the course of **action** they carried out.

Actions

Ho It Wo 61-24 And do not his **actions** make

Into Ac 83-7 our own **actions** are partly responsible.

Into Ac 87-6 in all sorts of absurd **actions**

Active

A Vi Fo You 156-18 they must keep spiritually **active.**

Activities

To Wives 120-14 he must redouble his spiritual **activities**

Activity

Th Fam Af 131-16 developing new channels of **activity**

Th Fam Af 131-23 but this **activity** should be balanced.

Actor

Ho It Wo 60-30 Each person is like an **actor** who wants to run

Into Ac 73-12 He is very much the **actor.**

Ho It wo 61-28 Our **actor** is self-centered-ego-centric,

Acute poisoning

A Vi Fo Yo 157-18 was told of the **acute poisoning**

Acutely

To Emp 144-14 while **acutely** depressed,

Addiction

Doc's Op xxiii-9 alcoholic and drug **addiction**

Doc's Op xxv-6 those afflicted with alcoholic **addiction.**

Doc's Op xxv-9 treating alcoholic and drug **addiction.**

Admire

Th Fam Af 123-25 But the wise family will **admire** him

Admit

Doc's Op xxvii-26 must **admit** we have made little

Doc's Op xxviii-13 who is unwilling to **admit** that he cannot

Mo Ab Al 37-22 to **admit** that our justification for a spree

Mo Ab Al 38-27 We **admit** we have some of these symptoms

Into Ac 81-22 we should **admit** our fault.

Wo Wi Ot 93-28 **Admit** that he probably knows more

Wo Wi Ot 99-6 may see their own defects and **admit** them.

Th Fam Af 135-17 He had to painfully **admit** that

A Vi Fo You 164-22 **Admit** your faults to Him and to

Admits

Into Ac 78-6 **admits** his own fault.

To Wives 109-16 He **admits** this is true, but is positive

To Wives 110-4 He **admits** he cannot drink like other people,

Th Fam Af 127-27 begins to see his shortcomings and **admits**

Admitted

Doc's Op xxix-8 He frankly **admitted** and believed that for him

Bill's Story 11-18 he had **admitted** complete defeat.

Bill's Story 13-18 these individuals, **admitting** my wrong.

We Ag 46-25 As soon as we **admitted** the possible

Ho It Wo 59-9 We **admitted** we were powerless over alcohol-

Ho It Wo 59-5 **Admitted** to God, to ourselves,

Ho It Wo 59-28 when we were wrong promptly **admitted** it.

Ho It Wo 67-23 We **admitted** our wrongs honestly

Into Ac 72-4 We have **admitted** certain defects

Into Ac 72-9 that we have **admitted** to God,

Into Ac 76-4 all the things which we have **admitted** are

Into Ac 78-29 have already **admitted** this in confidence

Wo Wi Ot 93-1 not have entirely **admitted** his condition,

Th Fam Af 135-10 He **admitted** he was overdoing these

Admitting

Mo Ab Al 39-24 Far from **admitting** he was an alcoholic,

Mo Ab Al 40-3 a long way from **admitting**

Ho It Wo 61-16 **Admitting** he may be somewhat at fault,

Into Ac 72-16 have done well enough in **admitting** these

Into Ac 77-22 not too keen about **admitting** our faults.

Into Ac 79-28 We suggested he write his first wife **admitting**

Wo Wi Ot 92-30 soon have your friend **admitting** he has

A Vi Fo You 155-23 to his family by foolishly **admitting**

Admonish

Th Fam Af 135-9 wife commenced to **admonish** him about it.

Adopt
To Wives 114-27 women **adopt** a spiritual way of life
To Emp 143-26 can you **adopt** the attitude that
Adopted
A Vi Fo Yo 153-26 have **adopted** this way of life.
Adopts
Th Fam Af 130-26 wife who **adopts** a sane spiritual program,
Adventures
Ho It Wo 60-14 our personal **adventures** before and after
Advice
Ho It Wo 70-4 We avoid hysterical thinking or **advice.**
Into Ac 73-28 nor have we followed their **advice.**
Wo Wi Ot 96-19 can give him much practical **advice.**
To Wives 121-2 much direction and **advice.**
Th Fam Af 133-33 depending upon a doctor's **advice.**
Affair
Th Is A Sol 28-26 an entirely personal **affair**
Into Ac 81-10 a secret and exciting **affair** with
Th Fam Af 124-32 would unearth the old **affair**
Affairs
Ho It Wo 60-4 practice these principles in all our **affairs.**
To Wives 105-14 retaliatory love **affairs** with other men.
To Wives 120-24 guide his appointments or his **affairs**
Th Fam Af 124-28 have had love **affairs.**
Affected
Th Fam Af 126-6 The family will be **affected** also
Affection
To Wives 104-15 bound by ties of blood or **affection**
Affections
Th Fam Af 128-19 a God who has stolen dad's **affections.**
Affectionate
Th Fam Af 126-13 not gay and **affectionate** as the family
Affections
Into Ac 82-26 **Affections** have been uprooted.
Afflicted
Doc's Op xxv-5 those **afflicted** with alcoholic addiction.
To Wives 116-20 we were **afflicted** with pride

Dr Bob Ni 180-25 terrible curse with which I was **afflicted.**

Afraid

Into Ac 78-18 Nor are we **afraid** of disclosing our alcoholism

Into Ac 78-25 drink if we are **afraid** to face them.

Into Ac 85-10 nor are we **afraid.**

To Wives 116-5 **afraid** your husband will lose his position.

A Vi Fo Yo 157-13 I'm **afraid** to go out the door.

Age of miracles

A Vi Fo Yo 153-13 The **age of miracles** is still with us.

Age-old

To Wives 116-18 If God can solve the **age-old** riddle

Aggrieved

Th Fam Af 124-31 the **aggrieved** one would unearth

Agnostic

Th Is A Sol 28-32 addressed to the **agnostic.**

We Ag 44-10 who feels he is an atheist or **agnostic**

We Ag 44-23 we were atheists or **agnostic**'s

We Ag 45-18,19 Here difficulty arises with **agnostic**'s.

We Ag 46-13 Yes, we of **agnostic** temperament

We Ag 49-17 **agnostic**s and atheists chose to believe

We Ag 52-31 We **agnostic**'s and atheists

Ho It Wo 60-14 the chapter to the **agnostic**

Wo Wi Ot 93-5 if the man be **agnostic**

Agnostically

We Ag 53-7 We **agnostically** inclined would not

Agony

Bill's Story 6-23 endured this **agony** two more years.

Agree

Mo Ab Al 31-4 **agree** there is no such thing as

We Ag 50-11 Whether we **agree** with a particular approach

Into Ac 73-24 psychologists are inclined to **agree** with us.

Wo Wi Ot 93-6 he does not have to **agree** with your conception

To Wives 117-30 that you have to **agree** with your husband

Th Fam Af 129-27 does not fully **agree** with dad's spiritual

Agreed

Mo Ab Al 35-29 He **agreed** he was a real alcoholic

We Ag 50-17 men and women are strikingly **agreed.**

Into Ac 76-25 Remember it was **agreed** at the beginning

To Wives 108-1 dangers were pointed out and they **agreed,**

A Vi Fo Yo 163-23 the doctor **agreed** to a test among his patients
Agreement
Th Fam Af 131-9 and comes to a friendly **agreement**
Ailments
Th Fam Af 135-22 more serious **ailments** were being
Ails
To Emp 139-8 as to what really **ails** the alcoholic,
Al-Anon
To Wives 121-11 The fellowship of **Al-Anon** Family Groups
Alarming
Th Fam Af 130-1 are **alarming** and disagreeable,
Alateen
To Wives 121-18 **Alateen,** for teenaged children
Alcohol
Doc's Op xxiv-22 an allergy to **alcohol**
Doc's Op xxvi-5 action of **alcohol** on
Doc's Op xxvi-8 never safely use **alcohol**
Doc's Op xxvi-31 effect produced by **alcohol**
Doc's Op xxvii-14 control his desire for **alcohol**
Doc's Op xxviii-17 **alcohol** for a period of time
Doc's Op xxviii-22 in the effect **alcohol** has
Doc's Op xxix-10 elimination of **alcohol**
Doc's Op xxix-20 with no return to **alcohol.**
Bill's Story 1- 10 and again turned to **alcohol.**
Bill's Story 8-11 **Alcohol** was my master.
Bill's Story 13-3 was separated from **alcohol**
Th Is A Sol 22-31 once he takes any **alcohol**
Th Is a Sol 26-23 no control whatever over **alcohol**
Mo Ab Al 33-14 be immune to **alcohol**
Mo Ab Al 38-23 where **alcohol** has been involved
We Ag 48-10 **alcohol** was a great persuader.
Ho It Wo 58-25 we deal with **alcohol**- cunning, baffling
Ho It Wo 59-9 were powerless over **alcohol**-
Ho It Wo 66-18 The insanity of **alcohol** returns
Ho It Wo 66-31 any more than **alcohol.**
Into Ac 76-26 any lengths for victory over **alcohol**
Into Ac 84-31 anything or anyone- even **alcohol.**
Into Ac 85-15 for **alcohol** is a subtle foe.
Wo Wi Ot 98-3 before conquering **alcohol**

Wo Wi Ot 98-14 claiming he cannot master **alcohol**
Wo Wi Ot 101-5 or be reminded about **alcohol**
Wo Wi Ot 101-15 would escape the **alcohol** problem.
Wo Wi Ot 102-17 why **alcohol** disagrees with you.
Wo Wi Ot 103-12 be told anything about **alcohol** by
To Wives 114-2 have been so impaired by **alcohol**
To Wives 119-6 **alcohol** is no longer a problem
Th Fam Af 132-14 We have been dealing with **alcohol**
Th Fam Af 133-10 A body badly burned by **alcohol**
Th Fam Af 134-7 **Alcohol** is so sexually stimulating to
To Emp 140-18 caused by the action of **alcohol** on his brain
To Emp 140-31 abnormal action of **alcohol** on his mind.
To Emp 143-5 and body of the effects of **alcohol**
To Emp 146-9 a life which knows no **alcohol,**
A Vi Fo You 151-15 became subjects of King **Alcohol,**
A Vi Fo You 152-7 He cannot picture life without **alcohol.**
A Vi Fo You 152-8 to imagine life with **alcohol** or without it.
Dr Bob Ni 176-29 twelve ounce bottles of **alcohol**
Dr Bob Ni 176-32 My bootlegger had hidden alcohol
Alcoholic -*Noun*
Doc's Op xxiii-15 was an **alcoholic** of a type
Doc's Op xxiv-11 who have suffered **alcoholic** torture
Doc's Op xxiv-12 the body of the **alcoholic**
Doc's Op xxiv-19 picture of the **alcoholic**
Doc's Op xxiv-30 the **alcoholic** who is very
Doc's Op xxv-34 an **alcoholic** ought to be freed
Doc's Op xxx-5 advise every **alcoholic** to read
Bill's Story 2-8 Potential **alcoholic** that I was
Bill's Story 14-32 true for the **alcoholic!**
Bill's Story 14-33 if an **alcoholic** failed to
Bill's Story 15-14 work with another **alcoholic**
Bill's Story 16-4 An **alcoholic** in his cups
Th Is A Sol 18-16 **alcoholic** to discuss his
Th Is A Sol 18-22 confidence of another **alcoholic**
Th Is A Sol 20-9 are an **alcoholic** who wants
Th Is A Sol 21-8 what about the real **alcoholic?**
Th Is A Sol 22-14 true **alcoholic,** as our behavior
Th Is A Sol 22-25 **alcoholic** reacts differently from
Th Is A Sol 22-28 while the **alcoholic** keeps away

Th Is A Sol 13-1 experience of any **alcoholic**
Th Is A Sol 23-6 problem of the **alcoholic** centers
Th Is A Sol 23-16 of an **alcoholic,** he will
Th Is A Sol 23-32 if the man be a real **alcoholic**
Th Is A Sol 24-1,2 drinking of every **alcoholic**
Th Is A Sol 24-20 **alcoholic** may say to himself
Th Is a sol 27-6,7 mind of a chronic **alcoholic**
Th Is A Sol 27-26 an **alcoholic** of your description
Th Is A Sol 29-12 many **alcoholic** men and women
Mo Ab Al 30-17 **alcoholic** ever recovers control.
Mo Ab Al 31-6 out of an **alcoholic**
Mo Ab Al 32-24 practically every **alcoholic**
Mo Ab Al 33-9 Once an **alcoholic,** always an **alcoholic**
Mo Ab Al 34-6 If he is a real **alcoholic**
Mo Ab Al 34-11 yet be a potential **alcoholic**
Mo Ab Al 34-31 service to **alcoholic** sufferers
Mo Ab Al 35-4 thinking dominates an **alcoholic**
Mo Ab al 35-30 he was a real **alcoholic**
Mo ab al 35-32 knowledge about himself as an **alcoholic**
Mo Ab Al 39-7 actual or potential **alcoholic**
Mo Ab Al 39-25 admitting he was an **alcoholic**
Mo Ab al 39-32 not believe himself an **alcoholic**
Mo Ab Al 43-26 The **alcoholic** at certain times has
We Ag 44-3 distinction between the **alcoholic** and the
We Ag 44-12 an **alcoholic** of the hopeless variety
We Ag 56-12 approached by an **alcoholic** who
Ho It Wo 60-13 Our description of the **alcoholic**
Ho It Wo 62-3 the **alcoholic** who has lost all
Ho It Wo 62-15 the **alcoholic** is an extreme example
Ho It Wo 66-13 But with the **alcoholic**
Into Ac 73-11 the **alcoholic** leads a double life.
Into Ac 81-4 After a few years with an **alcoholic**
Into Ac 82-15 we hear an **alcoholic** say that
Into Ac 82-24 The **alcoholic** is like a tornado
Wo Wi Ot 91-33 describe yourself as an **alcoholic.**
Wo Wi Ot 92-9 satisfied that he is a real **alcoholic**
Wo Wi Ot 92-16 not to brand him as an **alcoholic.**
Wo Wi Ot 92-31 of the traits of the **alcoholic.**
Wo Wi Ot 95-10 Never talk down to an **alcoholic**

Wo Wi Ot 96-2 Search out another **alcoholic**

Wo Wi Ot 96-9 deny some other **alcoholic** an opportunity

Wo Wi Ot 97-27 seldom allow an **alcoholic** to live in

Wo Wi Ot 97-25 Though an **alcoholic** does not respond,

Wo Wi Ot 97-33 **alcoholic** who is able and willing

Wo Wi Ot 98-11 the **alcoholic** commences to rely upon

Wo Wi Ot 99-12 the **alcoholic** continues to demonstrate

Wo Wi Ot 99-27 **alcoholic** continue his program

Wo Wi Ot 99-30 Let no **alcoholic** say he cannot recover

Wo Wi Ot 101-7 An **alcoholic** who cannot meet them

Wo Wi Ot 101-18 If the **alcoholic** tries to shield himself

Wo Wi Ot 101-27 had experience with an **alcoholic**,

Wo Wi Ot 102-8 work with another **alcoholic** instead.

Wo Wi Ot 102-6 Every new **alcoholic** looks for this spirit

To Wives 104-16 affection to an **alcoholic**.

To Wives 108-11 the **alcoholic** only seems to be unloving

To Wives 108-16 Try not to condemn your **alcoholic**

To Wives 108-24 An **alcoholic** of this temperament

To Wives 109-8,9 insulted if he were called an **alcoholic**.

To Wives 109-29 earmarks of a real **alcoholic**.

To Wives 113-4,5 or thinks he is not an **alcoholic**,

To Wives 117-29 resentment is a deadly hazard to an **alcoholic**.

To Wives 118-30 work of another **alcoholic** has

To Wives 119-29 many times isolates the wife of an **alcoholic**.

Th Fam Af 122-8 The **alcoholic**, his wife, his children

Th Fam Af 122-22 Years of living with an **alcoholic**

Th Fam Af 123-6 family of an **alcoholic** longs for the

Th Fam Af 123-30 almost every **alcoholic** has been marked

Th Fam Af 124-27 the **alcoholic** or his wife have had love affairs

Th Fam Af 125-4 In most cases, the **alcoholic** survived this

Th Fam Af 13-32 the **alcoholic** will find he has much in

Th Fam Af 134-17 The **alcoholic** may find it hard to re-establish

To Emp 136-4 He knows the **alcoholic** as the employer sees

To Emp 137-15 I became an **alcoholic** myself!

To Emp 137-27 not always done so for the **alcoholic**

To Emp 137-28 the **alcoholic** has often seemed a fool

To Emp 139-8 as to what really ails the **alcoholic**,

To Emp 139-16 may be more annoyed with an **alcoholic**

To Emp 139-19 so far as the **alcoholic** is concerned,

To Emp 139-27 When dealing with an **alcoholic,**
To Emp 139-31 A look at the **alcoholic** in your organization
To Emp 140-22 No wonder an **alcoholic** is strangely irrational.
To Emp 140-25 the aberrations of the **alcoholic.**
To Emp 140-33 an **alcoholic,** sometimes the model of honesty
To Emp 142-24 if an **alcoholic,** he is almost certain to have.
To Emp 145-29 an **alcoholic** was sent to a hospital
To Emp 146-21 An **alcoholic** who has recovered,
To Emp 147-30 If you are an **alcoholic,** you are a mighty sick
To Emp 148-13 be fired just because he is an **alcoholic.**
To Emp 149-25 between such people and the **alcoholic.**
A Vi Fo You 157-20 deteriorates the body of an **alcoholic**
A Vi Fo You 160-18 Many an **alcoholic** who entered there
A Vi Fo You 162-20 that every **alcoholic** who journeys
Alcoholic -*Descriptive*
Doc's Op xxiii-8 **alcoholic** and drug addiction
Doc's Op xxiv-11 have suffered **alcoholic** torture
Doc's Op xxv-5 afflicted with **alcoholic** addiction.
Doc's Op xxv-31 in this **alcoholic** field
Doc's Op xxvi-15 these **alcoholic** people
Doc's Op xxvi-33 their **alcoholic** life seems
Doc's Op xxix-32 His **alcoholic** problem was so complex
Bill's Story 9-4 for **alcoholic** insanity
Bill's Story 9-21 last summer an **alcoholic** crackpot
Th Is A Sol 18-5 with the **alcoholic** illness
Th Is A Sol 24-30 individual with **alcohol** tendencies
Th Is A Sol 25-25 are as seriously **alcoholic** as
Th Is A Sol 27-3 Some of our **alcoholic** readers
Mo Ab Al 31-30 any individual as **alcoholic**
Mo Ab Al 39-11 upon our **alcoholic** readers
Mo Ab Al 39-21 Yet, he is **alcoholic.**
Mo Ab Al 41-31 remembered what my **alcoholic** friends
Mo Ab Al 41-32 if I had an **alcoholic** mind
Mo Ab Al 42-6 that I had an **alcoholic** mind
Mo Ab Al 42-13 asked me if I thought myself **alcoholic**
Mo Ab Al 42-16 an **alcoholic** mentality such as I had
Mo Ab Al 42-30 that my **alcoholic** condition was
We Ag 44-6 you are probably **alcoholic**
We Ag 44-13 To be doomed to an **alcoholic** death

We Ag 45-20 as we discuss his **alcoholic** problems
We Ag 48-7 Faced with **alcoholic** destruction
We Ag 56-32 His **alcoholic** problem was taken away.
Ho It Wo 60-16 That we were **alcoholic**
Into Ac 79-17 to save himself from the **alcoholic** pit
Wo Wi Ot 92-6 If he is **alcoholic**, he will
Wo Wi Ot 92-18 if he is not too **alcoholic.**
Wo Wi Ot 92-26 loathe to tell **alcoholic** patients
Wo Wi Ot 92-32 is willing to tell him that he is **alcoholic,**
Wo Wi Ot 101-8 still has an **alcoholic** mind;
Wo Wi Ot 102-32 they are not **alcoholic.**
Wo Wi Ot 103-16 gravity of the **alcoholic** problem,
To Wives 107-13 the nature of the **alcoholic** illness,
To Wives 108-4 who has an **alcoholic** husband.
To Wives 111-28 talk about his **alcoholic** problem.
To Wives 119-22 his enthusiasm for **alcoholic** work.
To Wives 119-24 many times isolates the wife of an **alcoholic.**
Th Fam Af 125-10 about the other's **alcoholic** troubles.
Th Fam Af 130-21 principles by which the **alcoholic** member
Th Fam Af 135-2 the **alcoholic** member has to if he would
To Emp 138-8 was undoubtedly **alcoholic** .
To Emp 138-21 with some of our **alcoholic** crowd?
To Emp 140-11 where the **alcoholic** sickness is discussed
To Emp 143-27 that his **alcoholic** derelictions
To Emp 146-20 giving you the **alcoholic** run-around
To Emp 146-27 Long experience with **alcoholic** excuses
To Emp 148-6 not show it to his **alcoholic** prospect.
To Emp 148-11 for covering up an **alcoholic** employee.
To Emp 149-1 We don't have any **alcoholic** problem.
To Emp 149-10 at least from the **alcoholic** angle,
To Emp 149-17 organization has no **alcoholic** problem,
To Emp 149-26 that an **alcoholic** employee will receive
To Emp 150-1 **alcoholic** employees, who produce as much
A Vi Fo You 155-6 nearing the nadir of **alcoholic** despair.
A Vi Fo You 155-12 what it meant to be an **alcoholic.**
A Vi For You 155-20 the familiar **alcoholic** obsession
A Vi Fo you 156-20 a first class **alcoholic** prospect
A Vi Fo You 162-2 of **alcoholic** and drug addiction

Dr. Bob Ni 172-25 I was an **alcoholic** almost from the start.
Alcoholic's
Th Is A Sol 23-11 of the havoc an **alcoholic's**
Mo Ab Al 43-15 hopelessness of the average **alcoholic's**
Th Fam Af 124-10 **alcoholic's** past thus becomes the
To Emp 145-28 about an **alcoholic's** drinking exploits.
Alcoholics
Doc's Op xxiii-20 conceptions to other **alcoholics**
Doc's Op xxv-13 urgent importance to **alcoholics**
Doc's Op xxv-33 **alcoholics** back from the gates of death.
Doc's Op xxvi-5 these chronic **alcoholics**
Doc's Op xxvi-20 **alcoholics** we appear somewhat
Doc's Op xxviii-7 classification of **alcoholics**
Doc's Op xxviii-35 chronic **alcoholics** are doomed
Bill's Story 7-9 rehabilitation of **alcoholics**
Bill's Story 7-14 to learn that in **alcoholics**
Bill's Story 14-24 thousands of hopeless **alcoholics**
Bill's Story 15-7 helping other **alcoholics** to a solution
Th Is A Sol 24-6 fact is that most **alcoholics**
Th Is A Sol 24-33 confirmed by legions of **alcoholics**
Th Is a Sol 27-14 once in a while, **alcoholics**
Mo Ab Al 30-2 we were real **alcoholics**
Mo Ab Al 30-12 that we were **alcoholics**
Mo Ab Al 30-15 **alcoholics** are men and women
Mo Ab Al 30-22 **alcoholics** of our type
Mo Ab Al 30-27 which will make **alcoholics**
Mo Ab Al 31-8 many who are real **alcoholics**
Mo Ab Al 32-8 few **alcoholics** have enough desire
Mo Ab Al 33-27 Potential female **alcoholics**
Mo Ab Al 33-20 insulted if called **alcoholics**
Mo Ab Al 33-32 numbers of potential **alcoholics**
Mo Ab Al 43-9 Most **alcoholics** have to be
We Ag 44-19 were not true **alcoholics**
We Ag 53-15 When we became **alcoholics**
Ho It Wo 60-2,3 carry this message to **alcoholics**
Ho It Wo 62-18 we **alcoholics** must be rid of
Ho It Wo 64-24 It destroys more **alcoholics**
Ho It Wo 66-22 for **alcoholics** these things are poison.
Into Ac 73-31 have a low opinion of **alcoholics**

Into Ac 74-12 people who do not understand **alcoholics.**
Into Ac 78-19 Most **alcoholics** owe money.
Into Ac 81-2 **alcoholics** are fundamentally much
Into Ac 82-22 wives have had with **alcoholics.**
Into Ac 88-9 We **alcoholics** are undisciplined.
Wo Wi Ot 89-3 work with other **alcoholics.**
Wo Wi Ot 89-5 Carry this message to other **alcoholics!**
Wo Wi Ot 89-24 uniquely useful to other **alcoholics.**
Wo Wi Ot 94-12 that he will try to help other **alcoholics**
Wo Wi Ot 95-8 will be most successful with **alcoholics** if
Wo Wi Ot 95-31 we **alcoholics** have much in common
Wo Wi Ot 100-32 things **alcoholics** are not supposed to do.
Wo Wi Ot 103-8 intolerance might repel **alcoholics**
To Wives 109-12 will become true **alcoholics**
To Wives 112-10 has several **alcoholics** among his
To Wives 112-30 Show him that as **alcoholics,** the writers
To Wives 114-13 working with **alcoholics** committed to
To Wives 114-15 released thousands of **alcoholics** from asylums
To Wives 119-11 on other people, especially **alcoholics.**
To Wives 121-16 and others close to **alcoholics.**
To Wives 121-19 teenage children of **alcoholics,**
Th Fam Af 125-27 We **alcoholics** are sensitive people.
Th Fam Af 125-30 Many **alcoholics** are enthusiasts.
Th Fam Af 129-31 in helping other **alcoholics.**
Th Fam Af 131-23 spend much time with other **alcoholics**
Th Fam Af 131-30 **Alcoholics** who have derided religious
Th Fam Af 133-33 He thought all **alcoholics** should
To Emp 141-4 This is not to say that all **alcoholics** are honest
To Emp 142-11 many **alcoholics,** being warped and drugged,
To Emp 142-33 For most **alcoholics** who are drinking,
To Emp 145-18 greatest enemies of us **alcoholics** are resentments
To Emp 145-22 we **alcoholics** have an idea that people
To Emp 146-5 As a class, **alcoholics** are energetic people.
To Emp 146-12 wish to do a lot more for other **alcoholics**
To Emp 147-17 no quarrel with the **alcoholics** of your
To Emp 149-14 many actual or potential **alcoholics.**
To Emp 149-20 this chapter refers to **alcoholics,** sick people,.
A Vi Fo You 152-27 Near you, **alcoholics** are dying helplessly
A Vi Fo You 154-30 ah- yes, those other **alcoholics?**

A Vi Fo You 158-25 there were three **alcoholics** in that town,
A Vi Fo You 159-14 knew they must help other **alcoholics**
A Vi Fo You 161-9 **Alcoholics** are being attracted from far
A Vi Fo You 163-13 contained more **alcoholics** per square mile
A Vi Fo You 163-24 certain other **alcoholics** from a clinic
Dr Bob Ni 178-31 we **alcoholics** seem to have the gift of picking
Alcoholics Anonymous
Doc's Op xxiii-1 We of **Alcoholics Anonymous** believe
Doc's Op xxiii-9 gave **Alcoholics Anonymous** this letter.
Th Is A Sol 17-1 We of **Alcoholics Anonymous** know
Mo Ab Al 42-11 Two members of **Alcoholics Anonymous**
Wo Wi Ot 90-1 a prospect for **Alcoholics Anonymous**
Wo Wi Ot 94-32 Fellowship of **Alcoholics Anonymous**
Wo Wi Ot 103-14 we hope that **Alcoholics Anonymous**
To Wives 104-13&17 wives of **Alcoholics Anonymous**
To Wives 113-30 Many of **Alcoholics Anonymous** were
To Wives 121-13 entirely separate from **alcoholics Anonymous**
Th Fam Af 125-8 families of **Alcoholics Anonymous**
Th Fam Af 135-19 member of **Alcoholics Anonymous**
A Vi Fo You 152-18 a fellowship in **Alcoholics Anonymous**
A Vi Fo You 152-30 future fellows of **alcoholics Anonymous**
A Vi Fo You 153-20, 162-21 fellowships of **Alcoholics Anonymou** A Vi
Fo You 157-4 fellow of **Alcoholics Anonymous** stared
A Vi Fo You 161-13 fellows of **Alcoholics Anonymous**
A Vi Fo You 161-16 But life among **Alcoholics Anonymous**
A Vi Fo You 163-32 become fellows of **Alcoholics Anonymous**
Alcoholism
Doc's Op xxiii-11 in the treatment of **alcoholism**
Doc's Op xxiv-2 in the annals of **alcoholism.**
Doc's Op xxvii-29 who believe that **alcoholism** is
Doc's Op xxix-4 treated for chronic **alcoholism**
Th Is A Sol 17-26 those who suffer from **alcoholism**
Th Is A Sol 28-31 **alcoholism**, as we understand it
Mo Ab Al 31-4 are familiar with **alcoholism**
Mo Ab Al 32-10 definite signs of **alcoholism**
Mo Ab Al 34-24 baffling feature of **alcoholism**
Mo Ab Al 35-21 what we knew of **alcoholism**
Mo Ab al 40-1 we knew about **alcoholism.**
Mo Ab Al 40-17 you fellows said about **alcoholism,**

Mo Ab al 42-4 I had learned of **alcoholism**
We Ag 44-2 learned something of **alcoholism**
We Ag 44-26 were sufficient to overcome **alcoholism**
We Ag 56-8 more serious **alcoholism**
Ho It Wo 60-19 could have relieved our **alcoholism.**
Into Ac 78-18 afraid of disclosing our **alcoholism**
Into Ac 85-16 We are not cured of **alcoholism.**
Wo Wi Ot 92-6 in the chapter on **alcoholism.**
Wo Wi Ot 92-21 speak of **alcoholism** as an illness,
Wo Wi Ot 92-28 the hopelessness of **alcoholism**
Wo Wi Ot 94-22 about the question of **alcoholism.**
Wo Wi Ot 101-16 any scheme of combating **alcoholism**
To Wives 107-10 out of ignorance of **alcoholism.**
To Wives 108-7 strange world of **alcoholism**
To Wives 112-1, 112-33 the chapter on **alcoholism.**
To Wives 112-9 succeed in interesting him in **alcoholism.**
To Wives 112-30 what you have found out about **alcoholism.**
To Wives 114-3 where **alcoholism** is complicated by other
To Wives 114-21 cannot or will not get over **alcoholism.**
To Wives 116-18 age-old riddle of **alcoholism,**
To Wives 118-28 not .cure our husbands of **alcoholism**
To Wives 118-30 we forget that **alcoholism** is an illness
Th Fam Af 127-24 man who is getting over **alcoholism**
Th Fam Af 131-25 who know nothing of **alcoholism**
Th Fam Af 132-20 into the mire that is **alcoholism**
To Emp 137-14 because I did not understand **alcoholism**
To Emp 138-10 I spent two hours talking about **alcoholism,**
To Emp 141-27 You now know more about **alcoholism.**
To Emp 142-7 might be well to explain **alcoholism,**
To Emp 144-8 the grim truth about **alcoholism.**
To Emp 147-30 have been learning something about **alcoholism.**
To Emp 148-21 **Alcoholism** may be causing your organization
To Emp 149-6 But **alcoholism** - well, they just don't believe
To Emp 149-12 how mush **alcoholism** is costing his
A Vi Fo You 153-16 on the world tide of **alcoholism.**
A Vi Fo You 155-19 might find out about his **alcoholism.**
A Vi Fo You 157-9 giving you a treatment for **alcoholism.**
Dr. Bob Ni 172-5 important part in bringing on my **alcoholism.**
Dr Bob Ni 180-10 anything about the subject of **alcoholism.**

Dr Bob Ni 180-16 information about the subject of **alcoholism**

Dr Bob Ni 180-20 to **alcoholism** from actual experience.

Alibis

Th Is A So 23-9 any one of a hundred **alibis.**

Alimony

Into Ac 79-2 haven't kept up the **alimony** to number one.

Into Ac 79-18 he had not paid **alimony** to his first wife.

All

Th Is A So 17-3 Nearly **all** have recovered.

Th Is A So 17-5 **All** sections of this country

Th Is A So 18-7 It engulfs **all** whose lives touch

Th Is A So 20-5 why it is that **all** of us became so

Th Is A So 21-11 he begins to lose **all** control

Mo Ab Al 31-8 Despite **all** we can say,

Mo Ab Al 36-32 Yet **all** reasons for not drinking were

Mo Ab Al 37-16 in **all** earnestness and sincerety,

Mo Ab Al 39-19 To **all** appearance he is a stable,

We Ag 46-11 Who, then, made **all** this?

We Ag 56-16 Is it possible that **all** the religious people

We Ag 56-20 It crowded out **all** else.

We Ag 57-10 restored us **all** to our right minds.

We Ag 57-12 He has come to **all** who have

Ho It Wo 59-19 to have God remove **all** these defects

Ho It Wo 59-22 Made a list of **all** persons

Ho It Wo 59-23 to make amends to them **all.**

Ho It Wo 60-3 practice these principles in **all** our affairs.

Ho It Wo 61-21 Is it not evident to **all** the rest

Ho It Wo 61-23 snatching **all** they can get out of

Ho It Wo 61-31 who are sure **all** would be Utopia

Ho It Wo 63-1 **all** sorts of remarkable things followed.

Ho It Wo 63-3 Being **all** powerful, He provided

Ho It Wo 64-24 From it stem **all** forms of spiritual disease,

Ho It Wo 67-11 We cannot be helpful to **all** people,

Ho It Wo 69-17 We got this **all** down on paper

Into Ac 76-4 let God remove from us **all** the things

Into Ac 76-5 Can He now take them **all-**

Into Ac 76-9 willing that you should have **all** of me,

Into Ac 76-17 We have a list of **all** persons we have

Into Ac 82-20 Passing **all** understanding is the patience

Into Ac 85-19 God's will into **all** of our activities.

Into Ac 85-22 will power along this line **all** we wish.

Into Ac 85-26 Him who has **all** knowledge and power.

Into Ac 86-10 Were we kind and loving toward **all**?

Wo Wi Ot 91-32 When he sees you know **all** about the drinking

Wo Wi Ot 92-31 if not **all**, of the traits of the alcoholic.

Wo Wi Ot 99-14 Of course, we **all** fall much below

Wo Wi Ot 99-25 to the best interest of **all** concerned

Th Fam Af 122-6 **All** members of the family should meet

Th Fam Af 122-23 that **all** will not be fair weather.

A Vi Fo Yo 153-11 Should you wish them above **all** else,

All Powerful Creator

A Vi Fo You 161-6 loving and **All Powerful Creator.**

Allergic

Doc's Op xxvi-8 These **allergic** types can never safely use

Allergy

Doc's Op xxiv-22 theory that we have an **allergy** to alcohol

Doc's Op xxvi-6 manifestation of an **allergy;**

Doc's Op xxviii-27 may be the manifestation of an **allergy**

Alone

Ho It Wo 63-26 Better to meet God **alone** than

Into Ac 75-15 We can be **alone** at perfect peace and ease.

To Wives 119-28 have been living too much **alone,**

A Vi Fo You 163-4 I'm jittery and **alone.**

Dr Bob Ni 181-22 strong enough to beat the game **alone,**

Always

A Vi Fo Yo 151-11 There was **always** one more attempt-

A Vi Fo You 164-8 your real reliance is **always** upon Him.

Amazed

Into Ac 83-30 we will be **amazed** before we are half way

Amazing

Th Fam Af 128-12 or exhibit **amazing** indifference to them

Amends

Bill's Story 8-7 What would I not give to make **amends.**

Ho It Wo 59-23 became willing to make **amends**

Ho It Wo 59-24 Made direct **amends** to such people

Ho It Wo 69-27 We must be willing to make **amends**

Into Ac 76-18 to whom we are willing to make **amends.**

Into Ac 84-27 make **amends** quickly if we have harmed

Americans

Th Is A So 17-5 We are average **Americans.**

Among

Th Is A So 28-33 this class are now **among** our members.

Mo Ab Al 33-32 potential alcoholics **among** young people

Ho It Wo 60-7 no one **among** us has been able

Analysis

We Ag 55-21 In the last **analysis** it is only there that He may be

Analyze

To Wives 104-19 We want to **analyze** mistakes we have made.

Analyzed

Ho It Wo 70-25 We have listed and **analyzed** our resentments.

Anew

To Wives 114-26 sometimes you must start life **anew.**

Anger

Ho It Wo 66-20 we had to be free of **anger.**

Th Fam Af 135-14 finally threw him into a fit of **anger.**

Angers

To Wives 108-19 When he **angers** you, remember that his is

Angle

To Emp 149-10 at least from the alcoholic **angle,**

Angrily

Th Fam Af 124-32 and **angrily** cast it's ashes about.

Angry

Ho It Wo 64-31 with whom we were **angry.**

Ho It Wo 64-31 why we were **angry.**

Ho It Wo 67-7 God save me from being **angry.**

To Wives 111-2 that you should never be **angry.**

To Wives 113-10 for he may be **angry.**

Annihilation

Th Is A So 18-5 there goes **annihilation** of all the things worth

Annoyed

To Emp 139-15 more **annoyed** with an alcoholic

Answer

Ho It Wo 69-31 The right **answer** will come, if we want it.

To Emp 144-31 Ask him if he thinks he has the **answer.**

A Vi Fo You 160-19 came away with an **answer.**

Dr Bob Ni 181-25 we know that we have an **answer** for you.

Answered

To Wives 108-5 We hope this book has **answered** some

Answers

Into Ac 86-33 surprised how the right **answers** come after we

A Vi Fo You 164-15 The **answers** will come,

Dr Bob Ni 180-21 He knew all the **answers,**

Anxious

Wo Wi Ot 95-5 Sometimes a new man is **anxious** to proceed

To Wives 121-7 we are **anxious** that you understand,

Anything

A Vi Fo Yo 158-11 willing to do **anything** necessary.

A Vi Fo Yo 158-33 to have **anything** to do with the church

Apologize

Ho It Wo 68-18 We never **apologize** to anyone for depending upon

Ho It Wo 68-23 We never **apologize** for God.

To Wives 115-15 or feel that you must **apologize**

Apology

Into Ac 86-7 Do we owe an **apology?**

Appreciate

To Emp 141-32 You might say you **appreciate** his abilities.

Apprehension

Th Fam Af 128-9 at their strange new dad with **apprehension,**

Approach

A Vi Fo You 162-8 suggests our **approach** to one of his

Approval

Into Ac 80-29 His action met widespread **approval,**

A Vi Fo You 151-19 companionship and **approval.**

Approve

Th Fam Af 125-20 unless we are sure he would **approve.**

Th Fam Af 130-22 can hardly fail to **approve** these simple

Arbiter

Ho It Wo 69-9 the **arbiter** of anyone's sex conduct.

Argue

Th Fam Af 126-33 It is of little use to **argue**

Th Fam Af 132-2 If he does not **argue** about religion,

Argument

Ho It Wo 67-9 We avoid retaliation or **argument.**

Wo Wi Ot 98-32 **Argument** and fault-finding are to be avoided

To Wives 115-22 not to take sides in any **argument**

Th Fam Af 127-30 without heated **argument,**

Th Fam Af 129-21 on the wrong side of every **argument,**

Arouse

Ho It Wo 69-14 Did we unjustifiably **arouse** jealousy, suspicion,

Arrange

Into Ac 88-7 trying to **arrange** life to suit ourselves.

Th Fam Aft 122-17 each trying to **arrange** the family

Arrest

Into Ac 79-20 and got an order for his **arrest.**

Assert

Th Fam Af 131-6 often begins to **assert** himself.

Asset

Th Fam Af 124-10 past then becomes the principle **asset**

Astonishing

Mo Ab Al 30-9 persistence of this illusion is **astonishing.**

Atheist

Bill's Story 10-18 I was not an **atheist.**

We Ag 44-10 To one who feels he is an **atheist**

We Ag 44-23 thought we were **atheist**s

We Ag 49-17 agnostics and **atheist**s chose to believe

We Ag 55-31 a man who thought he was an **atheist.**

Wo Wi Ot 93-5 If the man be agnostic or **atheist,**

Attempt

A Vi Fo Yo 151-11 There was always one more **attempt-**

Attention

To Wives 19-10 jealous of the **attention** he bestows

To Wives 119-20 and urge more **attention** for yourself.

Attentions

To Wives 107-18 fresh resolves and new **attentions.**

Attitude

Th Is A Sol 18-29 **attitude** of Holier than Thou

Th Is A Sol 25-18 revolutionized our whole **attitude**

We Ag 50-26 a certain **attitude** toward

We Ag 55-27 With this **attitude** you cannot fail.

Into Ac 72-3 trying to get a new **attitude**

Into Ac 77-21 have acquired a better **attitude** toward him,

Into Ac 84-6 our whole **attitude** and outlook

Into Ac 85-3 new **attitude** toward liquor has been

Into Ac 86-2 the proper **attitude** and work at it.

Wo Wi Ot 99-24 a new **attitude** and spirit all around.

Wo Wi Ot 103-5 such an **attitude** is not helpful

Wo Wi Ot 103-17 if our **attitude** is one of bitterness

To Wives 117-2,3 the radically changed **attitude** toward him

Th Fam Af 122-10 family's **attitude** towards himself or herself.

To Emp 143-20 a transformation of thought and **attitude.**

To Emp 143-26 can you adopt the **attitude** that so far

To Emp 144-21 your changed **attitude** plus the contents of

To Emp 145-17 such an **attitude** will command undying

To Emp 149-8 Perhaps this is a typical **attitude.**

To Emp 150-3 They have a new **attitude,**

Attitudes

Th Is A Sol 19-33 their opinions are **attitudes** which

Th Is A Sol 27-19 **attitudes** which were once

Th Fam Af 122-1 have suggested certain **attitudes**

Attracted

A Vi Fo You 161-10 Alcoholics are being **attracted** from far

Attractive bar

A Vi Fo Yo 154-14 a door opened into an **attractive bar.**

Authorities

A Vi Fo You 163-15 The **authorities** were much concerned.

Available

Wo Wi Ot 96-20 Let him know you are **available.**

Average

Ho It Wo 58-10 Their chances are less than **average.**

Avert

Th Fam Af 124-23 **avert** death and misery

Avoid

We Ag 44-18 some of us tried to **avoid** the issue,

Ho It Wo 67-9 We **avoid** retaliation or argument.

Ho It Wo 70-3 We **avoid** hysterical thinking

Into Ac 72-25 Trying to **avoid** this humbling experience

Wo Wi Ot 91-4 **avoid** meting a man through his family.

Wo Wi Ot 97-3 Never **avoid** these responsibilities,

Wo Wi Ot 101-2 we must **avoid** moving pictures

Wo Wi Ot 101-23 So our rule is not to **avoid** a place

To Wives 113-5 **Avoid** urging him to follow our program.

To Wives 114-33 You **avoid** the subject of drinking,

To Wives 115-29 **Avoid** answering these inquiries

To Wives 118-8 everything in his power to **avoid** disagreement

To Wives 121-8 **avoid** these unnecessary difficulties.

Th Fam Af 133-6 **Avoid** then, the deliberate manufacture

Avoided

Wo Wi Ot 98-33 Argument and fault-finding are to be **avoided**

Th Fam Af 123-5 we suggest how they may be **avoided-**

Th Fam Af 126-31 This sort of thing can be **avoided.**

Avoiding

Into Ac 85-6 neither are we **avoiding** temptation.

To Wives 117-28 carry the burden of **avoiding** them

A Vi Fo You 162-28 **avoiding** certain alluring distractions

Awaken

To Wives 119-33 Both of you will **awaken** to a new sense

Awakening

Ho It Wo 60-1 Having had a spiritual **awakening**

A Vi Fo You 151-20 and the awful **awakening** to face the

Awe

We Ag 46-11 There was a feeling of **awe** and wonder,

Awful

A Vi Fo You 151-20 the **awful** awakening to face

B

Back

Mo Ab Al 43-5 I would not go **back** to it even if I could.

Bad

To Wives 115-2 When your husband is **bad**

To Wives 120-12 it is by no means a **bad** thing

Bad intentioned

To Wives 108-22 some men are thoroughly **bad-intentioned.**

Badly

Th Fam Af 133-10 A body **badly** burned by alcohol

Baffle

Into Ac 84-10 situations which used to **baffle** us.

Baffled

Th Is A Sol 23-24 they are a **baffled** lot.

We Ag 51-1 Once confused and **baffled** by the seeming

Wo Wi Ot 92-1 Tell him how **baffled** you were,

Baffling

Th Is A Sol 26-16 More **baffling** still, he could give

Mo Ab Al 34-24 the **baffling** feature of alcoholism

Ho It Wo 58-25 alcohol- cunning, **baffling**. Powerful!

To Wives 107-23 It was so **baffling**, so heartbreaking.

Balanced

Th Fam Af 131-24 but this activity should be **balanced.**

Balked

Ho It Wo 58-19 At some of these we **balked.**

Balmy

Th Fam Af 128-28 father is a bit **balmy!**

Bank

To Emp 138-20 **bank** was doing the man an injustice.

Bar

A Vi Fo Yo 154-14 door opened into an attractive **bar.**

A Vi Fo Yo 154-27 still floated to him from the **bar.**

Barrel

To Emp 137-4 the **barrel** was in his mouth.

Barrier

Th Fam Af 126-16 with such complaints, a **barrier** arises.

Barriers

We Ag 56-26 The **barriers** he had built through the years

To Wives 115-12 **Barriers** which have sprung up

Basic

Ho It Wo 61-18 What is his **basic** trouble?

Battle grounds

To Wives 105-15 Our homes have been **battle-grounds**

Bearable

Wo Wi Ot 97-32 the family will find life more **bearable.**

Beaten up

A Vi Fo Yo 156-23 He's just **beaten up** a couple of nurses.

Beautifully

To Wives 120-7 just as things are going **beautifully**

Bed

A Vi Fo Yo 157-18 The man in the **bed** was told of the

Bedevilments

We Ag 52-21 basic solution of these **bedevilments** more

Beds

Th Is A So 19-2 take up their **beds** and walk again

Beer

Dr Bob Ni 173-11 my enormous capacity for **beer.**

Dr Bob Ni 177-28 When **beer** first came back,

Dr Bob Ni 178-3 all smelled up with **beer**

Dr Bob Ni 178-4 fortify my **beer** with straight alcohol.

Dr Bob Ni 180-1 one bottle of **beer** the next morning.

Beer experiment

Dr Bob Ni 177-27 mention the so-called **beer experiment.**

Dr Bob Ni 178-6 and that ended the **beer experiment.**

Dr Bob Ni 178-7 About the time of the **beer experiment**

Begged

To Wives 105-10 we have **begged,** we have been patient,

Beginning

Th Is A So 19-6 elimination of our drinking is but a **beginning.**

Mo Ab Al 35-22 He made a **beginning.**

Mo Ab Al 37-21 But even in this type of **beginning**

Ho It Wo 63-29 This was only a **beginning,**

Ho It Wo 71-5 you have made a good **beginning.**

To Wives 118-24 he is just **beginning** his development.

Th Fam Af 125-31 At the **beginning** of recovery a man will

Behave

Ho It Wo 62-1 if the rest of the world would only **behave;**

Behaved

To Wives 107-13 we might have **behaved** differently

Behavior

Mo Ab Al 37-28 Our **behavior** is absurd

Into Ac 83-15 Our **behavior** will convince them more than

Wo Wi Ot 90-9 Get an idea of his **behavior,**

Th Fam Af 129-14 dad's current **behavior** is but a phase

Belief

Doc's Op xxiv-19 In our **belief,** any picture of the alcoholic

Bill's Story 13-32 **Belief** in the power of God,

Mo Ab Al 32-24 fell victim to a **belief** which

We Ag 55-28 The consciousness of your **belief**
Wo Wi Ot 101-16 In our own **belief** any scheme of combating
Th Fam Af 133-4 to the **belief** that this life is a vale of tears,
A Vi Fo You 162-7 has told us of his **belief** in ours.
Beliefs
Th Is A Sol 28-22 disturbing to their **beliefs**
We Ag 49-28 dissecting spiritual **beliefs** and practices
Into Ac 75-17 may have had certain spiritual **beliefs,**
Believe
Doc's Op xxiii-1 We of AA **believe** that the reader will be
Doc's Op xxv-31 They **believe** in themselves,
Doc's Op xxvi-4 We **believe,** and so suggested
Doc's Op xxvii-29 those who **believe** that alcoholism is
Bill's Story 10-26 I simply had to **believe** in a Spirit of the
Bill's Story 12-19 being willing to **believe**
Th Is a Sol 18-1 we have come to **believe** it an illness
Th Is A Sol 25-8 we had come to **believe**
Th Is A sol 29-14 we **believe** that it is only by fully
Mo Ab Al 31-9 are not going to **believe** they are
Mo Ab Al 32-5 we **believe** that early in our drinking careers
Mo Ab Al 39-32 would not **believe** himself an alcoholic,
Mo Ab Al 40-18 frankly did not **believe** it would be possible
We Ag 45-16 a book which we **believe** to be spiritual
We Ag 46-33 It is open, we **believe,** to all men.
We Ag 47-15 Do I now **believe,** or am I even willing to **believe,**
We Ag 47-17 can say that he does **believe,** or is willing to **believe**
We Ag 47-25 which seemed difficult to **believe.**
We Ag 47-27 if I could only **believe** as he believes.
We Ag 48-14 why he should **believe** in a Power
We Ag 49-11 thinking we **believe** this universe needs no God
We Ag 49-17 we agnostics and atheists chose to **believe**
We Ag 50-25 they have come to **believe** in a power
We Ag 54-1 For did we not **believe** in our own reasoning
We Ag 57-8 Circumstances made him willing to **believe.**
Ho It Wo 70-10 we **believe** we will be forgiven
Into Ac 86-3 we **believe** we can make some definite
Wo Wi Ot 93-9 be willing to **believe** in a Power greater than
To Wives 116-26 some of us did not **believe** we needed
Th Fam Af 123-14 God, they **believe,** almost owes this

Th Fam Af 130-8 the world of spiritual make-**believe**

Th Fam Af 130-12 We have come to **believe** He would like us

To Emp 138-32 He simply could not **believe** that his

To Emp 142-8 Say that you **believe** he is a gravely ill person.

To Emp 142-18 We **believe** a man should be thoroughly

To Emp 143-11 we **believe** it should be made plain that any

To Emp 149-7 they just don't **believe** they have it.

To Emp 149-14 We **believe** that managers of large enterprises

A Vi Fo You 163-1 We **believe** and hope it contains all you

Believed

Doc's Op xxix-9 **believed** that for him there was no hope.

Bill's Story 10-16 **believed** in a Power greater than myself

Bill's Story 12-27 I saw, I felt, I **believed.**

Th Is A Sol 26-12 he **believed** he had acquired

Mo Ab Al 33-5 Most of us have **believed** that if

We Ag 54-23 But we **believed** in life-

To Wives 105-21 We have **believed** them when no one else

Believes

Doc's Op xxviii-16 always **believes** that after being entirely free

We Ag 47-28 I could only believe as he **believes.**

We Ag 48-26 **believes** in scores of assumptions

Believing

Th Fam Af 135-4 Seeing is **believing** to most families

Belittle

Th Fam Af 133-27 never **belittle** a good doctor

Belladonna

Bill's Story 7-9 the so-called **belladonna** treatment

Bender

Bill's Story 5-20 Then I went on a prodigious **bender,**

Th Is A So 23-8 why he started on that last **bender,**

To Emp 139-23 you can go on a mild **bender,**

To Emp 142-23 discharged after the next **bender**

A Vi Fo Yo 155-29 he went on a roaring **bender.**

Beneficial

Th Fam Af 134-6 have found this practice **beneficial.**

Benefit

Into Ac 84-3 our experience can **benefit** others.

Better

To Wives 120-5 to find one much **better.**

To Wives 120-10 it is infinitely **better** that he have no

To Emp 143-7 Your man will fare **better** if placed

Bewilderment

A Vi Fo Yo 151-21 **Bewilderment,** Frustration, Despair,

Beyond human aid

Th Is A Sol 24-31 placed himself **beyond human aid,**

Th Fam Af 128-22 father was **beyond human aid.**

Bidding

Into Ac 76-13 to do your **bidding.**

Binds

Th Is A So 17-19 powerful cement which **binds** us.

Binge

Wo Wi Ot 90-14 wait til he goes on a **binge.**

Bitter

Mo Ab Al 39-12 revealed to us out of **bitter** experience.

To Wives 105-1 sympathy, to **bitter** resentment.

Bitterly

We Ag 56-13 rose as he **bitterly** cried out:

A Vi Fo Yo 154-6 **Bitterly** discouraged, he found himself

Bitterly-hated

Into Ac 80-8 from a **bitterly-hated** business rival

Bitterness

Bill's Story 15-25 **bitterness** of all sorts wiped out.

Wo Wi Ot 103-17 if our attitude is one of **bitterness**

Blacker

A Vi Fo Yo 151-17 It thickened, ever becoming **blacker.**

Blame

Ho It wo 61-17 that other people are more to **blame.**

Ho It Wo 67-20 Where were we to **blame?**

To Wives 120-27 If he gets drunk, don't **blame** yourself.

Th Fam Aft 123-22 Father knows he is to **blame;**

Th Fam Af 127-12 he is mainly to **blame** for what befell

To Emp 136-24 that you were not to **blame** in any way.

Blank

Mo Ab Al 42-8 those strange mental **blank** spots.

Dr Bob Ni 174-13 three absolutely **blank** books.

Bless you

A Vi Fo You 164-27 May God **bless you** and keep you-

Blessed
Wo Wi Ot 100-23 the **blessed** fact of his sobriety.
Blessing
To Wives 116-11 Maybe it will prove a **blessing.**
To Emp 141-12 Firing such an individual may prove a **blessing**
Dr Bob Ni 180-24 It is a most wonderful **blessing** to be
Blessings
To Wives 119-5 pause and count your **blessings.**
Blight
Th Fam Af 124-26 so they become a **blight,**
Blind
To Wives 107-29 how could they be so **blind** about themselves?
Blocking
Ho It Wo 64-5 which had been **blocking** us.
Blood
To Wives 104-15 bound by ties of **blood** or affection
Body
Th Fam Af 133-10 A **body** badly burned by alcohol
Boiled
A Vi Fo Yo 158-3 I'd be **boiled** as an owl.
Bondage
Ho It Wo 63-16 Relieve me of the **bondage** of self,
Book
Wo Wi Ot 90-31 You might place this **book** where he can see it
To Wives 113-11 find him reading the **book** once more.
To Wives 113-18 practically sure to read the **book**
To Emp 144-22 the contents of this **book** will turn the trick.
To Emp 144-29 by the use of the **book** alone.
To Emp 147-16 executives might be provided with this **book.**
A Vi Fo Yo 164-6 contact with you who write this **book.**
A Vi Fo You 164-11 Our **book** is meant to suggestive only.
Bootlegger
Dr Bob Ni 175-26 knowledge of the **bootlegger** who soon
Dr Bob Ni 176-31 My **bootlegger** had hidden alcohol
Booze racket
A Vi Fo You 158-8 trying to fight this **booze racket** alone.
Boredom
A Vi Fo You 151-3 from care, **boredom,** and worry.
A Vi Fo Yo 152-16 from care, **boredom** and worry.

Boring

Th Fam Af 126-13 he may seem dull and **boring,**

A Vi Fo Yo 152-13 I shall be stupid, **boring** and glum,

Born

Ho It Wo 58-8 they seem to have been **born** that way.

Boss

To Emp 136-23 you were the best **boss** he ever had

Bottle

Th Is A So 22-1 searches madly for the **bottle** he misplaced

Bottles

Wo Wi Ot 103-20 **Bottles** were only a symbol.

Bound

A Vi Fo yo 152-32 You will be **bound** to them with new

Bout

To Emp 140-32 or getting over a **bout,**

Brain

To Emp 140-18 by the action of alcohol on his **brain?**

To Emp 140-22 spinal fluid actually ruptured the **brain.**

To Emp 140-23 with such a fevered **brain?**

Dr Bob Ni 173-24 When I got the fog out of my **brain,**

Brains

Mo Ab Al 39-6 their **brains** and bodies have not been

Into Ac 86-25 God gave us **brains** to use.

Brainstorm

Ho It Wo 66-21 The grouch and the **brainstorm** were not for us.

Brand

Th Fam Af 128-16 had better get his **brand** of spirituality

Brand new

A Vi Fo Yo 159-13 These men had found something **brand new**

Brawl

Bill's Story 4-28 as the result of a **brawl** with a taxi driver.

Breaking point

Dr Bob Ni 178-15 my health was at the **breaking point,**

Bright

Th Fam Af 132-4 family can be a **bright** spot

Brilliant

To Emp 139-32 Is he not usually **brilliant,**

Broad Highway

We Ag 55-27 you can join us on the **Broad Highway.**

Broke

Ho It Wo 64-10 no regular inventory usually goes **broke.**

Wo Wi Ot 96-23 He may be **broke** and homeless.

A Vi Fo Yo 154-7 discredited and almost **broke.**

Broken

Into Ac 82-25 Hearts are **broken.**

Brotherly

Th Is A So 17-24 in **brotherly** and harmonious action.

Build

Ho It Wo 63-15 to **build** with me and do with me as Thou wilt.

Building

Into Ac 75-28 **building** an arch through which we shall walk

Burden

To Wives 117-27 Often you must carry the **burden**

Burn

Wo Wi Ot 98-20 **Burn** the idea into the consciousness of

Burned

Ho It Wo 65-2 We were "**burned** up."

Th Fam Af 133-10 A body badly **burned** by alcohol

Burning

Th Fam Af 135-21 was wrong to make a **burning** issue out of

Bury

Th Fam Af 123-32 to **bury** these skeletons in a dark closet

Business

To Emp 141-26 only a matter of good **business.**

Business man

To Emp 140-12 as a **business man,** want to know

Bust

To Emp 138-19 would go on a bigger **bust** than ever.

By-gones

Into Ac 82-8 is to let **by-gones** be by-gones.

By-paths

Th Fam Aft 123-1 alluring shortcuts and **by-paths**

C

Calamity
Ho It Wo 68-17 enables us to match **calamity** with serenity.
To Wives 116-14 this apparent **calamity** has been a boon
Candy
Th Fam Af 134-4 which would be satisfied by **candy.**
Cannot
To Wives 114-20 Some men **cannot** or will not get over
To Emp 148-14 If he **cannot** or does not want to stop,
A Vi Fo Yo 152-6 He **cannot** picture life without alcohol.
A Vi Fo You 164-16 **cannot** transmit something you haven't got
Capacity
Ho It Wo 58-13 if they have the **capacity** to be honest.
Dr Bob Ni 173-11 my enormous **capacity** for beer,
Care
Bill's Story 13-8 unreservedly under his **Care** and direction.
To Wives 119-1 it was your devotion and **care**
Th Fam Af 128-27 that God will take **care** of them?
A Vi Fo You 151-3 It means release from **care,** boredom,
A Vi Fo You 158-9 gave his life to the **care** and direction
Carefully
Ho It wo 65-33 we considered it **carefully.**
Careless
Th Fam Af 125-26 one **careless,** inconsiderate remark
Carry
Wo Wi Ot 89-4 **Carry** this message to other alcoholics!
Carrying
To Emp 145-29 he was slyly **carrying** tales.
Case
Dr Bob Ni 177-32 drinking at least a **case** and a half a day.
Cases
To Wives 114-3 Sometimes there are **cases** where alcoholism
Cast
Into Ac 73-8 Now these are about to be **cast** out.
Categories
To Wives 108-32 usually falls within one of four **categories**

Cause

To Wives 119-30 and a great **cause** to live for

Caused

Ho It Wo 64-19 in our make-up which **caused** our failure.

Causes

Ho It Wo 64-6 we had to get down to **causes**

Centered

Dr Bob Ni 172-26 seemed to be **centered** around doing what I wanted

Cessation

Th Fam Aft 122-20 **Cessation** of drinking is

Chance

Wo Wi Ot 92-20 may be little **chance** he can recover

Wo Wi Ot 95-3 give him a **chance** to think it over.

Wo Wi Ot 96-14 have since recovered, of their **chance.**

Wo Wi Ot 97-30 there is a much better **chance** that the head

Wo Wi Ot 100-16 may spoil your **chance** of being helpful

Wo Wi Ot 101-10 His only **chance** for sobriety

To Wives 114-9 give him a **chance** to try our method,

To Wives 120-19 may lessen your husband's **chance**

Th Fam Af 136-13 he had but one more **chance.**

To Emp 138-16 this was his last **chance.**

To Emp 138-22 He might have a **chance.**

To Emp 145-33 decreased this man's **chance** of recovery.

To Emp 147-11 you may wish to give him another **chance.**

To Emp 148-14 he should be afforded a real **chance.**

To Emp 148-26 give your worthwhile man a **chance.**

Chances

To Wives 113-27 your **chances** are good at this stage.

To Wives 118-23 The **chances** are he will not for,

Change

We Ag 50-27 revolutionary **change** in their way of living and

We Ag 51-5 They show how the **change** came over them.

We Ag 52-14 readiness to **change** our point of view.

We Ag 55-32 His **change** of heart was dramatic, convincing,

Into Ac 83-15 They will **change** in time.

Into Ac 84-7 outlook upon life will **change.**

To Emp 143-19 must undergo a **change** of heart.

Changed

To Wives 117-3 as the radically **changed** attitude

To Emp 144-21 that your **changed** attitude plus
Changes
Wo Wi Ot 95-19 drop him until he **changes** his mind.
Th fam Af 13-28 will be other profound **changes**
Character
Into Ac 75-12 illuminating every twist of **character,**
Cheer
To Wives 120-16 **Cheer** him up
Into Ac 78-11 every single defect of character
Cheerfully
Ho It Wo 67-4 would **cheerfully** grant a sick friend.
To Wives 113-21 **Cheerfully** see him through more sprees.
Th Fam Af 133-8 **cheerfully** capitalize it as an opportunity
Cheerfulness
Th Fam Af 132-26 So we think **cheerfulness** and laughter
Cherished
To Wives 118-23 to that **cherished** vision.
Chief psychiatrist
A Vi Fo You 163-26 the **chief psychiatrist** of a large public
Child
Th Fam Af 130-33 treat father as a sick or wayward **child.**
Dr. Bob Ni 172-3 I was the only **child,**
Childishness
Th Fam Af 130-9 seen the **childishness** of it.
Children
Th Is A So 18-9 warped lives of blameless **children,**
To Wives 106-16 They struck the **children,**
To Wives 108-28 and the lives of your **children?**
To Wives 114-24 **children** of such men suffer horribly,
To Wives 116-8 which will befall you and the **children.**
Th Fam Af 126-11 He may take small interest in the **children**
Th Fam Af 131-17 mother and **children** demand that he stay
Th Fam Af 134-18 friendly relations with his **children.**
Th Fam Af 134-22 **children** are sometimes dominated by
Chilling
A Vi Fo Yo 151-16 the **chilling** vapor that is loneliness
Chocolate
Th Fam Af 134-1 alcoholics should constantly have **chocolate**

Choice

Th Is A So 24-7 lost the power of **choice** in drink.

Choose

Mo Ab Al 34-21 power to **choose** whether he will drink

Into Ac 74-2 before we **choose** the person or persons with whom

Chosen

Ho It Wo 70-5 Suppose we fall short of the **chosen** ideal

Christ

Bill's Story 11-1 To **Christ** I conceded

Chronic

Doc's Op xxv-32 pulls **chronic** alcoholics back from

Doc's Op xxvi-5 action of alcohol on these **chronic** alcoholics

Doc's Op xxviii-35 most **chronic** alcoholics are doomed.

Doc's Op xxix-4 brought in to be treated for **chronic** alcoholism

Th Is A So 27-6 You have the mind of a **chronic** alcoholic.

Church

Into Ac 80-26 He attended **church** for the first time

A Vi Fo You 157-33 I used to be strong for the **church,**

A Vi Fo You 158-24 is a power in the **church** from which he

A Vi Fo You 159-1 have anything to do with the **church.**

A Vi Fo Yo 157-33 I used to be strong for the **church,**

A Vi Fo Yo 158-24 and is a power in the **church**

A Vi Fo Yo 159-1 to have anything to do with the **church.**

Dr Bob Ni 172-7 more or less forced to go to **church,**

Dr Bob Ni 172-12 never again darken the doors of a **church.**

Churches

A Vi Fo Yo 154-13 glass covered directory of local **churches.**

Circumstances

We Ag 57-7 **Circumstances** made him willing to believe.

Ho It Wo 67-30 **circumstances** which brought us misfortune.

Classification

To Wives 113-28 that men in the fourth **classification**

Classroom

Dr Bob Ni 173-17 not daring to enter the **classroom**

Clean

Into Ac 83-7 So we **clean** house with the family,

Wo Wi Ot 98-22 trust in God and **clean** house.

Cleaned

Into Ac 84-20 as we **cleaned** up the past.

Cleaning

A Vi Fo Yo 161-17 **Cleaning** up old scrapes,

Clear

Th Fam Aft 123-18 It will take time to **clear** away

To Emp 143-5 to thoroughly **clear** mind and body

A Vi Fo You 164-22 **Clear** away the wreckage of your past.

Clemency

To Emp 136-20 I still expected a plea for **clemency,**

Clergyman

A Vi Fo Yo 154-32 He would phone a **clergyman,**

Cling

Into Ac 76-6 If we still **cling** to something we will not let go,

Th Fam Af 124-20 **Cling** to the thought that,

Closer

Th Fam Af 124-29 and drew **closer** together.

Close-mouthed

Into Ac 74-14 for a **close-mouthed,** understanding friend.

Club

To Wives 108-25 use this chapter as a **club** over your head

Clubs

Dr Bob Ni 176-16 hide out in one of the **clubs**

Coal bin

Dr Bob Ni 176-22 and hide it in the **coal bin,**

Cocktail

Mo Ab Al 41-12 I ordered a **cocktail** and my meal.

Cocktails

Mo Ab Al 41-11 have a couple of **cocktails** with dinner.

Cocky

Ho It Wo 68-10 When it made us **cocky,** it was worse.

Into Ac 85-10 We are neither **cocky** nor are we afraid.

Code

Into Ac 84-29 Love and tolerance of others is our **code.**

Code of morals

We Ag 44-25 If a mere **code of morals** or a better philosphy

Collapse

We Ag 56-9 mental and physical **collapse,**

Collision

Ho It wo 60-27 almost always in **collision** with something or

Colorful

A Vi Fo Yo 151-2 companionship and **colorful** imagination.

Commitment

Bill's Story 9-29 the judge to suspend his **commitment.**

Mo Ab Al 31-28 voluntary **commitment** to asylums-

Mo Ab Al 36-28 Here was the threat of **commitment**

Committed

Bill's Story 9-3 had been **committed** for alcoholic insanity.

Bill's Story 16-4 One poor chap **committed** suicide.

Mo Ab Al 35-19 that he had to be **committed.**

Into Ac 78-26 Perhaps we have **committed** a criminal offense

To Wives 110-18 advise you to have him **committed.**

To Wives 114-13 alcoholics **committed** to institutions.

To Wives 114-20 but who should be **committed.**

Common

Th Is A Sol 17-22 we have discovered a **common** solution.

Ho It Wo 64-21 we considered it's **common** manifestations.

Wo Wi Ot 95-32 we alcoholics have much in **common**

Common ground

Th Fam Af 122-6 should meet upon the **common ground** of

Common journey

A Vi Fo Yo 153-1 shoulder to shoulder your **common journey.**

Common sense

Bill's Story 13-22 **Common sense** would thus become

Th Is A So 22-21 What has become of the **common sense** and

Into Ac 77-18 our convictions with tact and **common sense**

To Wives 107-30 of their judgement, their **common sense,**

Communicative

Wo Wi Ot 91-24 If he is not **communicative,**

Th Fam Af 126-28 He becomes still less **communicative.**

Companionship

To Wives 111-16 They need your **companionship**

To Wives 119-12 have been starving for his **companionship,**

A Vi Fo You 151-2 **companionship** and colorful imagination.

A Vi Fo You 151-18 understanding **companionship** and

A Vi Fo You 154-16 would find **companionship** and release.

A Vi Fo You 160-10 loving and understanding **companionship**
Competent
To Emp 143-6 In **competent** hands, this seldom takes long
Complain
To Wives 119-32 cooperate, rather than **complain**
Th Fam Af 126-14 Mother may **complain** of inattention.
Complaints
Th Fam Af 126-16 with such **complaints,** a barrier arises.
Complete
Th Fam Af 123-21 will take years to **complete.**
Completely
Ho It Wo 58-3 cannot or will not **completely** give themselves
Complicated
To Wives 114-3 alcoholism is **complicated** by other disorders.
Complications
To Wives 114-5 whether these **complications** are serious.
Comprehend
We Ag 46-19 **comprehend** that Power, which is God.
Ho It Wo 70-26 We have begun to **comprehend** their futility
Into Ac 83-33 We will **comprehend** the word serenity
Conceal
To Emp 140-26 **conceal** a number of scrapes,
Concede
Mo Ab Al 42-14 I had to **concede** both propositions.
Th Fam Aft 122-13 that the others **concede** to him.
To Emp 140-14 If you **concede** that your employee is ill,
Concentrate
Wo Wi Ot 98-31 **concentrate** on his own spiritual demonstration
Concept
Ho It Wo 62-31 and this **concept** was the keystone
Conception
Doc's Op xxv-15 difficulties beyond our **conception.**
Bill's Story 12-14 choose your own **conception** of God?
We Ag 45-31 we rejected this particular **conception**
We Ag 46-22 consider another's **conception** of God.
We Ag 46-23 Our own **conception,** however inadequate,
We Ag 47-2 we mean your own **conception** of God.
We Ag 47-12 So we used our own **conception,**
We Ag 49-27 we used to have no reasonable **conception**

We Ag 50-11 a particular approach or **conception**
Wo Wi Ot 93-6 agree with your **conception** of God.
Wo Wi Ot 93-7 He can choose any **conception** he likes,
Conceptions
Doc's Op xxiii-20 present his **conceptions** to other alcoholics
Bill's Story 12-8 such **conceptions** as Creative Intelligence,
Th Is A Sol 27-21 a new set of **conceptions** and motives
Mo ab Al 42-27 throw several lifelong **conceptions** out
Wo Wi Ot 93-14 certain theological terms and **conceptions**
Concerned
A Vi Fo You 163-15 The authorities were much **concerned.**
Conclude
Ho It Wo 66-2 To **conclude** that others were wrong
Conclusion
Wo Wi Ot 92-16 Let him draw his own **conclusion.**
Condemn
To Wives 108-16 try not to **condemn** your alcoholic husband
Th Fam Af 129-18 should the family **condemn** and criticize.
To Emp 142-4 to lecture, moralize, or **condemn.**
Condition
Doc's Op xxix-26 and in desperate **condition,**
Bill's Story 9-2 coming to New York in that **condition.**
Into Ac 85-12 we keep in fit spiritual **condition.**
Into Ac 85-17 maintenance of our spiritual **condition.**
Wo Wi Ot 90-10 the seriousness of his **condition,**
Wo Wi Ot 90-16 in a dangerous physical **condition,**
Wo Wi Ot 92-12 the queer mental **condition** surrounding
Wo Wi Ot 93-1 admitted his **condition,**
Wo Wi Ot 98-22 the only **condition** is that he trust in God
Th Fam Aft 122-21 a highly strained, abnormal **condition.**
Th Fam Af 125-10 This is a **condition** which,
Th Fam Af 134-15 or psychologist if the **condition** persists.
To Emp 144-17 tell the patient the truth about his **condition.**
Conditions
Ho It Wo 64-7 get down to causes and **conditions.**
Wo Wi Ot 92-22 the **conditions** of body and mind
A Vi Fo You 161-30 under only slightly different **conditions,**
Conduct
Ho It Wo 69-10 the arbiter of anyone's sex **conduct.**

Ho It Wo 70-12 and our **conduct** continues to harm others,

Ho It Wo 70-31 people we have hurt by our **conduct,**

Confessing

Into Ac 77-27 **confessing** our former ill feeling

Confession

Into Ac 74-5 religious denomination which requires **confession**

Confidence

Bill's Story 14-11 There was utter **confidence.**

We Ag 54-2 Did we not have **confidence** in our ability

Into Ac 74-31 important that he be able to keep a **confidence;**

Into Ac 75-10 they will be honored by our **confidence.**

Into Ac 75-10 they will be honored by our **confidence.**

To Wives 112-6 **confidence** in his power to stop or moderate.

Th Fam Aft 123-11 Family **confidence** in dad is rising

To Emp 143-24 **confidence** in his ability to recover?

Confidential

Into Ac 74-4 this intimate and **confidential** step.

Conflict

Th Fam Af 124-3 in direct **conflict** with the new way

Confusion

Ho It wo 61-27 a producer of **confusion** rather than harmony?

Connections

Th Fam Af 131-28 family has no religious **connections,**

Conquering

Wo Wi Ot 98-3 before **conquering** alcohol,

Conscience

Wo Wi Ot 95-29 encourage him to follow his own **conscience.**

Th Fam Af 132-12 should consult his own **conscience.**

Conscientiously

To Emp 147-3 If he is **conscientiously** following the program

Conscious

We Ag 47-8 our first **conscious** relation with God as we

We Ag 56-29 **conscious** companionship with his Creator.

Ho It Wo 59-30 to improve our **conscious** contact with God

Ho It Wo 63-10 as we became **conscious** of His Presence,

Into Ac 87-4 made **conscious** contact with God,

Consciousness

We Ag 51-7 **consciousness** of the Presence of God

We Ag 55-28 the **consciousness** of your belief is sure to come

Consent

To Emp 143-29 will never be discussed without his **consent?**

Consequences

Th Is A Sol 24-13 The almost certain **consequences** that follow

Into Ac 79-10 no matter what the personal **consequences**

Considerate

Into Ac 74-22 but always **considerate** of others.

Into Ac 83-25 We should be sensible, tactful, **considerate**

Consideration

To Emp 140-4 Should he have the same **consideration**

Consigned

A Vi Fo Yo 152-12 to be **consigned** to a life

Console

To Wives 111-12 seek someone else to **console** him-

Constitutionally

How It Wo 58-5 **constitutionally** incapable of being honest

Constructive

Th Fam Af 127-29 family talks will be **constructive**

Consult

Th Fam Af 132-11 Each individual should **consult** his own

Contact

Into Ac 87-4 made conscious **contact** with God,

Wo Wi Ot 89-13 Frequent **contact** with newcomers

Th Fam Af 131-28 may wish to make **contact** with or take

To Emp 144-27 may be put in personal **contact** with some of us.

A Vi Fo Yo 164-6 not have the benefit of **contact** with you

Contention

To Wives 118-9 to avoid disagreement or **contention.**

Contentment

Doc's Op xxix-16 with self-reliance and **contentment.**

Continue

Into Ac 84-23 **continue** fot our lifetime.

Into Ac 84-23 **Continue** tom watch for selfidhness,

Contribute

Ho It Wo 63-8 what we could **contribute** to life.

Contrition

Th Fam Af 126-25 to show his **contrition** for what they

Control

Doc's Op xxiv-14 we could not **control** our drinking

Doc's Op xxvii-14 able to **control** his desire for alcohol,

Doc's Op xxviii-2 beyond their mental **control.**

Bill's Story 5-11 I still thought I could **control** the situation,

Th Is A Sol 21-11 he begins to lose **control**

Th Is A Sol 21-14 especially in his lack of **control**

Th Is A Sol 24-1 He has lost **control.**

Th Is a Sol 26-22 Yet he had no **control**

Mo Ab Al 30-7 will **control** and enjoy his drinking

Mo Ab Al 30-16 lost the ability to **control** our drinking

Mo Ab Al 30-17 no real alcoholic ever recovers **control.**

Mo Ab Al 30-18 that we were regaining **control,**

Mo Ab Al 30-20 by still less **control,**

Mo Ab Al 31-13 inability to **control** his drinking

Mo Ab Al 32-18 Once he started he had no **control** whatever.

We Ag 44-6 little **control** over the amount you take,

Wo Wi Ot 92-17 that he can still **control** his drinking,

To Wives 109-13 Your husband is showing lack of **control,**

To Wives 117-28 or keeping them under **control.**

To Emp 139-22 you want to, you **control** your drinking.

A Vi Fo yo 151-10 that some new miracle of **control**

A Vi Fo Yo 155-28 thought he was getting **control** of his

Controlled

Mo Ab Al 31-32 and try some **controlled** drinking.

Controversy

Ho It Wo 69-8 We want to stay out of this **controversy.**

A Vi Fo Yo 154-5 with much hard feeling and **controversy.**

Convalescence

Th Fam Af 129-32 during those first days of **convalescence,**

Convenient

Bill's Story 11-4 those parts which seemed **convenient**

Conversation

Wo Wi Ot 91-19 At first engage in general **conversation.**

Wo Wi Ot 95-4 let him steer the **conversation**

Convert

Th Fam Af 124-9 and **convert** them into assets.

Conviction

We Ag 56-24 overwhelmed by a **conviction** of the Presence of

Convictions

Into Ac 77-17 willing to announce our **convictions**

Wo Wi Ot 93-16 no matter what your own **convictions** are.

Wo Wi Ot 93-22 why his own **convictions** have not worked

Th Fam Af 130-20 has spiritual **convictions** or not

Convince

Into Ac 83-16 Our behavior will **convince** them

To Wives 116-11 It may **convince** your husband

Convinced

Mo Ab Al 40-12 absolutely **convinced** he had to stop drinking,

Ho It Wo 71-2 We hope you are **convinced** now that God can

Wo Wi Ot 96-7 become **convinced** that he cannot recover by

Th Fam Af 133-12 We are **convinced** that a spiritual mode

Conviviality

A Vi Fo Yo 151-1 drinking means **conviviality,**

Cooperate

To Wives 119-31 **cooperate,** rather than complain

Cooperation

To Wives 123-3 your **cooperation** will mean a great deal.

Corker

A Vi Fo Yo 156-22 Yes , we've got a **corker.**

Cornerstone

We Ag 47-20 upon this simple **cornerstone**

We Ag 56-31 our friend's **cornerstone** fixed in place.

Cost

To Emp 143-11 to advance the **cost** of treatment,

Costing

To Emp 149-12 how much alcoholism is **costing** his

Could not

Bill's Story 11-16 what he **could not** do for himself

Counsel

Ho It Wo 69-33 **Counsel** with persons is often desirable,

To Wives 119-25 They need the **counsel** and love of

Count

Th Is A So 23-26 they are down for the **count.**

To Wives 119-5 pause and **count** your blessings.

Couple

A Vi Fo You 160-7 This **couple** has since become so fascinated

Courage

We Ag 53-25 fresh **courage** to flagging spirits.

Ho It Wo 68-22 that faith means **courage.**

To Wives 115-17 Your new **courage,**

Th Fam Af 132-5 bring new hope and new **courage**

Courageous

Into Ac 81-14 married to a loyal and **courageous** girl

Course

We Ag 54-18 determine the **course** of our existence?

To Emp 142-32 a definite **course** of action.

Crankiness

Th Fam Af 127-8 his periods of **crankiness,**

Crave

A Vi Fo You 164-10 create the fellowship you **crave.**

Craved

Dr Bob Ni 176-4 morning drink which I **craved so badly,**

Craves

To Emp 143-9 and no longer **craves** liquor.

Craving

Doc's Op xxvi-1 his physical **craving** for liquor,

Doc's Op xxvi-6 the phenomenon of **craving** is limited to

Doc's Op xxvii-4 and the phenomenon of **craving** develops,

Doc' Op xxvii-34 the phenomenon of **craving** at once became

Doc's Op xxviii-2 drinking to overcome a **craving** beyond their

Doc's Op xxviii-5 the phenomenon of **craving** which cause men

Doc's Op xxviii-26 developing the phenomenon of **craving.**

Th Fam Af 134-3 in the night a vague **craving** arose

Dr Bob Ni 176-7 I would yield to the morning **craving,**

Dr Bob Ni 181-8 I did not get over my **craving** for liquor

Crawl

Into Ac 83-27 we don't **crawl** before anyone.

Crazy

Mo Ab Al 38-17 Such a man would be **crazy** wouldn't he?

Create

A Vi Fo You 164-9 how to **create** the fellowship you crave.

Creative Intelligence

Bill's Story 12-8 such conceptions as **Creative Intelligence**

Creator

Bill's Story 13-30 a new relationship with my **creator.**

Th Is A Sol 25-21 our **creator** has entered into

Th Is A Sol 28-18 **Creator** by with whom we may

We Ag 56-30 conscious companionship with his **Creator.**
Ho It Wo 68-19 for depending upon our **Creator.**
Into Ac 72-3 a new relationship with our **Creator,**
Into Ac 75-16 feel the nearness of our **Creator.**
Into Ac 76-8 "**Creator**, I am now willing
Into Ac 80-23 stand before his **Creator** guilty of
Into Ac 83-9 that our **Creator** show us the way
A Vi Fo You 158-10 care and direction of his **Creator,**
A Vi Fo You 161-7 loving and All Powerful **Creator.**

Creditors

Into Ac 78-14 We do not dodge our **creditors.**
Into Ac 78-23 We must lose our fear of **creditors**

Criminal

Into Ac 78-26 Perhaps we have committed a **criminal** offense

Critical

Wo Wi Ot 100-28 without becoming **critical** of them.
To Wives 111-29 Br sure you are not **critical**
To Wives 111-32 helpful rather than **critical**
To Wives 117-33 in a resentful or **critical** spirit.

Criticism

Wo Wi Ot 100-30 is worth any amount of **criticism.**
Th Fam Af 125-23 but **criticism** or ridicule coming from
Th Fam Af 129-23 If the family persists in **criticism,**
To Emp 146-4 needless provocation and unfair **criticism.**

Criticize

Into Ac 77-29 Under no condition do we **criticize** such a
Into Ac 83-5 being very careful not to **criticize** them.
Wo Wi Ot 89-25 cooperate; never **criticize.**
To Wives 117-23 and you will want to **criticize.**
To Wives 118-18 little need to **criticize** each other.
Th Fam Af 125-22 may **criticize** or laugh at himself
Th Fam Af 126-29 They **criticize,** pointing out how he
Th Fam Af 129-19 should the family condemn and **criticize.**

Criticized

To Wives 106-26 severely **criticized** by our husband's parents

Crooked

To Emp 140-17 a victim of **crooked** thinking,

Crowd

To Wives 113-20 you should not **crowd** him.

A Vi Fo You 160-7 of this strangely assorted **crowd.**
Cruel
To Wives 106-4 how **cruel** to be told they understood our men
To Wives 107-15 be so unthinking, so callous, so **cruel?**
Crushing
Mo Ab Al 42-10 It was a **crushing** blow.
Cunning
Ho It Wo 58-25 alcohol- **cunning,** baffling, powerful!
Curb
To Emp 146-10 You may have to **curb** his desire to work
Cure
To Emp 138-14 has taken a **cure,** looks fine, and to clinch
To Wives 118-27 and loyalty could not **cure** our husbands
Cured
Into Ac 85-15 We are not **cured** of alcoholism.
Th Fam Af 135-23 ailments were being rapidly **cured.**
Dr Bob Ni 180-13 had been **cured** by the very means I had
Curious
Wo Wi Ot 93-22 But he will be **curious** to learn
Curse
Dr Bob Ni 180-25 relieved of the terrible **curse**
Customers
To Emp 145-7 to take your best **customers** away from you.
Cynicism
Th Fam Af 132-18 We try not to indulge in **cynicism**
Th Fam Af 134-23 pathetic hardness and **cynicism.**

D

Daily reprieve
Into Ac 85-16 What we really have is a **daily reprieve**
Damage
Into Ac 76-21 and repair the **damage** done in the past.
Wo Wi Ot 99-16 repair the **damage** immediately
Th Fam Af 127-6 his drinking wrought all kinds of **damage**

Damaged

Ho It Wo 64-13 to disclose **damaged** or unsalable goods

Th Fam Aft 123-18 are now ruined or **damaged.**

Danger

To Wives 109-28 We think this person is in **danger.**

Th Fam Af 127-13 the **danger** of over-concentration

Dangerous

Mo Ab Al 34-5 he has entered this **dangerous** area

Wo Wi Ot 90-16 in a **dangerous** physical condition,

To Wives 114-11 too abnormal or **dangerous.**

To Wives 114-21 When they become too **dangerous,**

To Wives 117-26 family dissensions are very **dangerous,**

Th Fam Af 126-5 We think it **dangerous** if he rushes

A Vi Fo Yo 154-9 his predicament was **dangerous.**

Daring

A Vi Fo Yo 158-12 scarcely **daring** to be hopeful,

Dark

Into Ac 75-12 every **dark** cranny of the past.

Th Fam Af 124-21 the **dark** past is the greatest possession

Dazed

A Vi Fo You 160-16 **dazed** from his hospital experience

Dead

Bill's Story 11-20 in effect, had been raised from the **dead,**

Bill's Story 14-31 Faith without works was **dead,**

Bill's Story 15-5 Then faith would be **dead** indeed.

Into Ac 76-16, 88-12 Faith without works is **dead.**

Into Ac 82-23 no home today, would perhaps be **dead.**

Into Ac 82-26 Sweet relationships are **dead.**

Mo Ab Al 33-3 and was **dead** within four years.

Dead-wrong

Th Fam Af 135-16 our friend was wrong- **dead wrong.**

Deadly

Bill's Story 16-12 just underneath there is **deadly** earnestness.

To Wives 117-29 resentment is a **deadly** hazard

Death

Doc's Op xxv-33 back from the gates of **death.**

Mo Ab Al 30-10 into the gates of insanity or **death.**

We Ag 44-13 To be doomed to an alcoholic **death**

Th Fam Af 124-23 you can avert **death** and misery

To Emp 150-3 they have been saved from a living **death.**
Debauch
Bill's Story 8-20 the beginning of my last **debauch.**
To Wives 104-8 in fear of the next **debauch;**
Deceiving
To Emp 142-20 he is not **deceiving** himself or you.
Decide
Into Ac 75-3 When we **decide** who is to hear our story,
Into Ac 82-6 It may be that both will **decide**
Into Ac 82-12 may **decide** that the problem be attacked
Wo Wi Ot 90-33 The family must **decide** these things.
Wo Wi Ot 95-23 he must **decide** for himself whether he
Wo Wi Ot 103-2 ought to **decide** for themselves.
To Wives 113-21 Let him **decide** for himself.
To Emp 144-20 The man must **decide** for himself.
To Emp 147-7 will have to **decide** whether to let him go.
Decided
Mo Ab Al 38-7 **decided** to stop jay-walking
Mo Ab Al 41-13 After dinner I **decided** to take a walk.
Ho It Wo 60-22 we **decided** to turn our will and our life
Into Ac 79-7 we have **decided** to go to any lengths
Decides
Th Is a sol 28-27 with which one **decides** for himself
Deciding
Doc's Op xxix-23 and **deciding** his situation hopeless,
Decision
Doc's Op xxviii-12 many resolutions, but never a **decision.**
Th Is A Sol 21-23 some important **decision** must be
Ho It Wo 59-13 Made a **decision** to turn our will
Ho It Wo 64-2 our **decision** was a vital and crucial step,
Ho It Wo 71-4 If you have already made a **decision,**
Into Ac 86-31 an intuitive thought or **decision.**
Wo Wi Ot 96-20 are available if he wishes to make a **decision**
To Emp 140-5 If your **decision** is yes, whether
Decisions
Ho It Wo 62-12 made **decisions** based on self
Into Ac 88-4 worry, self-pity, or foolish **decisions.**
Declining
Bill's Story 7-24 **declining** moral and bodily health

Decreased

To Emp 145-33 **decreased** the man's chance of recovery.

Dedicated

A Vi Fo You 160-8 they have **dedicated** their home to the work.

Defeat

Bill's Story 11-18 he had admitted complete **defeat.**

Defeated

Mo Ab Al 42-10 problem had them hopelessly **defeated.**

Ho It Wo 64-21 was what had **defeated** us,

A Vi Fo yo 153-16 **defeated** drinkers will seize upon it,

Defect

Into Ac 76-11 every single **defect** of character

Defectives

Doc's Op xxiv-16 were outright mental **defectives.**

Defects

We Ag 50-1 looked at the human **defects**

Ho It Wo 59-20 remove all these **defects** of character.

Into Ac 72-5 We ahve admitted certain **defects;**

Into Ac 72-11 the exact nature of our **defects.**

Into Ac 72-15 discussing our **defects** with another person

Into Ac 83-6 Their **defects** may be glaring,

Wo Wi Ot 99-6 family may see their own **defects** and admit

Wo Wi Ot 100-20 point out that his **defects** of character are

To Wives 118-17 willingness to remedy your own **defects,**

Defend

To Emp 146-3 can always **defend** a man from

Defense

Th Is A Sol 24-12 are without **defense** against the

Th Is A Sol 24-18 failure of the kind of **defense**

Mo Ab Al 43-27 no effective mental **defense** against

Mo Ab Al 43-29 can provide such a **defense.**

Mo Ab Al 43-29 His **defense** must come from a higher

Deficiency

To Wives 120-15 remind him of his spiritual **deficiency-**

Define

We Ag 46-19 impossible for any of us to fully **define**

Deflation

Th Fam Aft 122-8 a process of **deflation.**

Delay

Into Ac 83-24 we don't **delay** if it can be avoided.

Deliberately

Mo Ab Al 37-18 gone out **deliberately** to get drunk

Mo Ab Al 37-24 when we began to drink **deliberately,**

Delinquencies

Th Fam Af 126-12 when reproved for his **delinquencies.**

Delirium

To Wives 107-7 there were screaming **delirium** and insanity.

Delirium tremens

Bill's Story 7-29 with heart failure during **delirium tremens**

Bill's Story 13-5 for I showed signs of **delirium tremens.**

To Wives 110-16 Perhaps he has had **delirium tremens.**

Delusion

Mo Ab Al 30-13 The **delusion** that we are like other people,

Ho It Wo 61-20 Is he not a victim of the **delusion** that he can

Demand

Th Fam Aft 123-13 they **demand** that dad bring them

Th Fam Af 128-11 may **demand** that the family find God

Th Fam Af 131-17 mother and children **demand** that he stay

Demanding

Ho It Wo 61-14 next occasion, still more **demanding**

Demands

Th Fam Aft 122-13 one member of the family **demands** that

To Emp 145-9 **demands** rigorous honesty.

Democracy

A Vi Fo You 160-31 the genuine **democracy,**

Demonstrate

We Ag 48-28 **demonstrate** that visual proof is the weakest

Ho It Wo 68-24 let Him **demonstrate,** through us, what He can

Wo Wi Ot 99-12 the alcoholic continues to **demonstrate**

Th Fam Af 133-9 to **demonstrate** His omnipotence.

Demonstrated

Mo Ab Al 33-9 We have seen the truth **demonstrated**

Demonstrating

We Ag 49-29 and creeds were **demonstrating** a degree of

Demonstration

Bill's Story 19-6 important **demonstration** of our principles

Into Ac 77-13 in a **demonstration** of good will

Into Ac 78-13 We have made our **demonstration,**
Demonstrations
We Ag 55-14 miraculous **demonstrations** of that power in
Demoralization
Mo Ab Al 30-21 pitiful and incomprehensible **demoralization**
Denied
Into Ac 80-9 **denied** having received the money
Denizens
A Vi Fo Yo 151-15 shivering **denizens** of his mad realm,
Deny
Wo Wi Ot 96-9 to **deny** some other alcoholic an opportunity
Dependence
Wo Wi Ot 98-17 **dependence** upon other people
Wo Wi Ot 98-18 **dependence** on God.
Dependent
Wo Wi Ot 99-33 his recovery is not **dependent** upon people.
Wo Wi Ot 100-1 **dependent** upon his relationship with God.
Depressed
Mo Ab Al For a few days he was **depressed** about his condition.
We Ag 56-7 embittered and **depressed** him.
Wo Wi Ot 91-16 He may be more receptive when **depressed.**
To Emp 144-14 while acutely **depressed,**
Depression
Doc's Op xxix-32 and his **depression** so great,
Mo Ab Al 37-20 anger, worry, **depression**
To Wives 106-32 remorse, **depression** and inferiority
Th Fam Af 127-8 crankiness, **depression,** or apathy,
Th Fam Af 133-12 nor do twisted thinking and **depression**
Deprive
Wo Wi Ot 96-25 you should not **deprive** your family
Deranged
To Emp 149-21 sick people, **deranged** men.
Derelictions
To Emp 142-28 that his alcoholic **derelictions.**
Derided
Th Fam Af 131-30 Alcoholics who have **derided** religious
Describe
Wo Wi Ot 91-33 **describe** yourself as an alcoholic.

Deserve

Into Ac 73-15 knows in his heart he doesn't **deserve** it.

Design for living

Bill's Story 15-17 It is a **design for living** that works

Into Ac 81-32 Our **design for living** is not a one-way street.

Desirability

To Wives 116-24 we began to see the **desirability** of

Desirable

Ho It Wo 63-23 We found it very **desirable**

Ho It Wo 70-1 Counsel with persons is often **desirable,**

To Emp 143-2 amount of physical treatment is **desirable,**

Desire

Doc's Op xvii-3 succumbed to the **desire** again,

Doc's Op xxvii-14 control his **desire** for alcohol,

Bill's Story 7-18 a desperate **desire** to stop

Th Is A Sol 18-30 the sincere **desire** to be helpful;

Th Is A Sol 24-3 the most powerful **desire** to stop drinking

Mo Ab al 32-8 few alcoholics have enough **desire** to stop

Mo Ab Al 32-12 an overpowering **desire** to do so

Ho It Wo 70-9 have the honest **desire** to let God

Into Ac 83-12 Unless one's family expresses a **desire**

Wo Wi Ot 95-26 the **desire** must come from within.

To Wives 105-5 Our loyalty and the **desire** that our husbands

To Wives 115-31 Your **desire** to protect him

To Emp 139-11 If you **desire** to help it might be well to

To Emp 146-10 curb his **desire** to work sixteen hours a day.

A Vi Fo You 155-8 He had a desperate **desire** to stop,

Desires

Mo Ab Al 34-18 that the reader **desires** to stop.

Despair

Bill's Story 8-8 tell of the loneliness and **despair**

Bill's Story 15-16 gone to my old hospital in **despair.**

We Ag 50-29 In the face of collapse and **despair**

To Wives 110-13 husband of whom you completely **despair.**

A Vi Fo You 151-22 Terror, Bewilderment, Frustration, **Despair**

A Vi Fo You 155-6 the nadir of alcoholic **despair.**

Despaired

Doc's Op xxvii-13 so many problems he **despaired**

Despairing

Doc's Op xxvi-22 **despairing** wives, little children;

Doc's Op xxvii-17 in sincere and **despairing** appeal:

Doc's Op xxix-15 From a trembling, **despairing,** nervous wreck

Bill's Story 7-27 My weary and **despairing** wife

Desperate

Doc's Op xxix-26 and in **desperate** condition,

Bill's Story 7-18 in the face of a **desperate** desire to stop

Mo Ab Al 35-5 **desperate** experiment of the first drink?

Wo Wi Ot 96-3 You are sure to find someone **desparate** enough

A Vi Fo Yo 155-8 He had a **desperate** desire to stop,

Desperately

Th Is A So 29-13 men and women, **desperately** in need,

To Wives 110-8 he **desperately** wants to stop but cannot.

Desperation

Th Is A So 28-6 the **desperation** of drowning men.

To Wives 106-20 In **desperation,** we ahve even got tight ourselves

Destroy

Ho It Wo 67-10 we **destroy** our chance of being helpful.

Into Ac 80-16 would **destroy** the reputation of his partner,

Destroying

Into Ac 80-11 **destroying** the reputation of another

Destroys

Ho It Wo 64-23 It **destroys** more alcoholics than anything

Destruction

We Ag 48-7 Faced with alcoholic **destruction,**

Wo Wi Ot 97-1 You may be aiding in his **destruction**

Destructiveness

Ho It Wo 70-27 commenced to see their terrible **destructiveness**

Deteriorates

A Vi Fo You 157-19 how it **deteriorates** the body of an

Determine

Into Ac 86-29 able to **determine** which course to take.

A Vi Fo You 164-7 God will **determine** that,

Determination

Bill's Story 4-19 the old fierce **determination** to win came

Development

To Wives 118-24 he is just beginning his **development.**

Th Fam Af 129-14 is but a phase of his **development,**

Devil

Bill's Story 11-12 If there was a **devil**

Th Fam Af 125-27 been known to raise the very **devil.**

To Emp 149-31 He will work like the **devil**

A Vi Fo You 158-30 to be a **devil**-may-care young fellow

A Vi Fo You 159-12 the lawyer and the **devil**-may-care chap.

Devoted

A Vi Fo Yo 159-18 **devoted** their spare hours to fellow-sufferers.

Devotion

To Wives 119-1 it was your **devotion** and care

Th Fam Af 128-23 love and **devotion** did not straighten him

Diagnose

Mo Ab Al 31-31 you can quickly **diagnose** yourself.

Die

Th Is A So 21-1 to **die** a few years before his time.

Th Is A So 24-32 may **die** or go permanently insane.

Ho It Wo 66-19 And with us, to drink is to **die.**

A Vi Fo You 154-29 the men who would **die** because they

Difference

Wo Wi Ot 98-9 **difference** between failure and success.

To Wives 117-31 an honest **difference** of opinion.

Differences

A Vi Fo You 161-18 helping to settle family **differences,**

Different

Mo Ab Al 30-3 bodily and mentally **different** from

A Vi Fo You 158-13 saw something **different** about her husband.

Difficult

To Wives 110-23 he is often **difficult** to deal with.

Difficulties

Ho It Wo 63-17 Take away my **difficulties,**

To Wives 121-8 avoid these unnecessary **difficulties.**

A Vi Fo You 156-17 **difficulties** presented themselves.

Difficulty

To Wives 119-9 Still another **difficulty** is that

Dig up

Th Fam Af 124-25 It is possible to **dig up** past misdeeds

Dilemma

Th Is A So 28-1 Here was the terrible **dilemma**

We Ag 45-9 Lack of power, that was our **dilemma.**

Diligently

We Ag 55-25 search **diligently** within yourself,

Direction

Bill's Story 10-31 love, superhuman strength, and **direction,**

Bill's Story 13-8 unreservedly under His care and **direction.**

Bill's Story 13-24 asking only for **direction** and strength

We Ag 49-25 faiths have given purpose and **direction** to millions.

We Ag 50-31 sense of **direction** flowed into them.

A Vi Fo Yo 158-10 the care and **direction** of his Creator,

Directions

Th Is A So 29-3 **directions** are given showing how we recovered

Into Ac 85-27 If we have carefully followed **directions**

Th Fam Af 131-3 made all the plans and gave the **directions.**

Director

Ho It Wo 62-29 God was going to be our **Director.**

Disagree

To Wives 117-32 be careful not to **disagree** in a resentful

Disagreeable

Th Fam Af 130-1 are alarming and **disagreeable,**

Disagreement

To Wives 118-9 to avoid **disagreement** or contention.

Disagrees

Wo Wi Ot 102-17 why alcohol **disagrees** with you.

Disappointed

Th Fam Af 126-15 They are all **disappointed,**

Disaster

Th Is A So 17-16 our joy in escape from **disaster**

Th Is A So 27-1 other free men may go without **disaster,**

We Ag 44-12 to continue as he is means **disaster,**

A Vi Fo Yo 152-33 you will escape **disaster** together

Discard

To Emp 140-8 Can you **discard** the feeling that you

Discharge

To Emp 137-10 I had been obliged to **discharge** him for

To Emp 139-4 Following his **discharge,**

To Emp 147-9 no doubt you should **discharge** him.

Discharged

To Emp 137-5 I had **discharged** him for drinking

To Emp 141-10 he may as well be **discharged,**

To Emp 142-23 he might as well be **discharged** after

To Emp 148-15 not want to stop, he should be **discharged.**

Discipline

Into Ac 88-10 we let God **discipline** us in the simple way

Disclose

Ho It Wo 64-13 **disclose** damaged or unsalable goods,

Into Ac 74-17 we cannot **disclose** anything to our wives

A Vi Fo You 164-12 God will constantly **disclose** more

Disclosed

We Ag 57-14 He **disclosed** himself to us.

Disclosing

Into Ac 78-18 Nor are we afraid of **disclosing** our alcoholism

Discord

Th Fam Aft 122-14 This makes for **discord**

Discouraged

Ho It Wo 60-6 Do not be **discouraged.** No one among us

Wo Wi Ot 96-1 Do not be **discouraged** if your prospect

A Vi Fo You 154-6 Bitterly **discouraged,** he found himself in

Discouragement

To Emp 138-30 throw up my hands in **discouragement**

Discover

Ho It Wo 64-12 an effort to **discover** the truth

Wo Wi Ot 99-4 people **discover** they have a basis

Discovered

We Ag 46-21 we **discovered** we did not need to consider

Ho It Wo 63-9 as we **discovered** we could face life

A Vi Fo You 164-1 have **discovered** the joy of helping others

Discovery

To Wives 116-15 led to the **discovery** of God.

A Vi Fo You 159-31 present their **discovery** to some newcomer.

Discredited

A Vi Fo You 154-7 **discredited** and almost broke.

A Vi Fo You 161-22 No one is too **discredited**

Discuss

Into Ac 84-26 We **discuss** them with someone immediately

Wo Wi Ot 92-15 unless he has seen it and wishes to **discuss** it.

To Emp 144-32 feels free to **discuss** his problems with you,

Discussed

Into Ac 86-8 should be **discussed** with another person

Discussing

Into Ac 74-24 great necessity for **discussing** ourselves

Into Ac 87-26 principles we have been **discussing.**

Disgrace

Into Ac 80-17 **disgrace** his family and take away his means

To Wives 116-7 the **disgrace** and hard times

Disgusting

To Emp 140-28 They may be **disgusting.**

Dishonest

Th Is A Sol 21-27 **dishonest** and selfish.

Ho It Wo 61-8 egotistical, selfish and **dishonest**

Ho It Wo 67-16 selfish, **dishonest**, self-seeking

Ho It Wo 69-13 Where we had been selfish, **dishonest,**

Into Ac 86-6 Were we resentful, selfish, **dishonest**

Into Ac 86-23 **dishonest** or self-seeking motives.

Dishonesty

into Ac 84-24 selfishness, **dishonesty,** resentment and fear.

To Wives 116-22 not above selfishness or **dishonesty.**

Disinherited

A Vi Fo You 161-19 explaining the **disinherited** son to his

Desire

To Emp 146-10 **desire** to work sixteen hours a day.

Disgrace

Into Ac 80-17 **disgrace** his family and take away his means

Disinherited

A Vi Fo Yo 161-19 explaining the **disinherited** son to his irate

Dislike

Into Ac 77-23 with a person we **dislike,** we take

Dismal

A Vi Fo Yo 154-11 One **dismal** afternoon he paced a hotel

Dismays

To Wives 120-8 **dismays** you by coming home drunk.

Disorders

To Wives 114-4 alcoholism is complicated by other **disorders.**

Dispose

To Wives 118-1 you can **dispose** of serious problems

Dispute

To Wives 117-25 great thunderclouds of **dispute**

Disregard

Ho It Wo 67-19 we tried to **disregard** the other person entirely.

Th Fam Af 133-19 does not mean that we **disregard** human

Dissensions

To Wives 117-26 family **dissensions** are very dangerous

Dissipation

Th Fan Af 133-18 shows any mark of **dissipation.**

Distortion

Th Fam Af 129-9 suffering from a **distortion** of values.

Distracted

A Vi Fo You 160-9 Many a **distracted** wife

Distractions

A Vi Fo You 162-28 avoiding certain alluring **distractions**

Disturbed

To Wives 118-6 I'm sorry I got **disturbed.**

Disturbing

Th Is A So 28-21 will find here nothing **disturbing**

Divine

Mo Ab Al 43-19 100% hopeless apart from **divine** help.

Divorce

Wo Wi Ot 98-23 There may be **divorce,** separation,

To Wives 106-24 Perhaps at this point we got a **divorce**

Divorced

Into Ac 79-1 Maybe we are **divorced** and have remarried

Doctor

A Vi Fo Yo 162-6 We are greatly indebted to the **doctor**

A Vi Fo Yo 163-18 The **doctor** proved to be able

A Vi Fo Yo 163-23 the **doctor** agreed to a test among his patients

Doctor's

Th Fam Af 133-33 depending upon a **doctor's** advice.

Dodge

Into Ac 78-14 We do not **dodge** our creditors.

Domestic

Into Ac 80-32 chances are that we have **domestic** troubles.

To Wives 117-24 on the **domestic** horizon,

Dominated

Ho It Wo 66-27 and it's people really **dominated** us.

Th Fam Af 134-22 sometimes **dominated** by a pathetic hardness
Done
To Emp 138-13 I'm sure this man is **done** drinking.
To Emp 142-4 that if this was **done** formerly,
Doomed
We Ag 44-13 **doomed** to an alcoholic death
Wo Wi Ot 92-25 many are **doomed** who never realize
Wo Wi Ot 101-18 from temptation is **doomed** to failure.
Double life
Into Ac 73-11 the alcoholic leads a **double life.**
Doubt
We Ag 53-14 we threw up our hands in **doubt**
Into Ac 72-17 There is **doubt** about that.
Into Ac 81-1 We **doubt** if, in this respect,
Th Fam Aft 135-4 beyond the shadow of a **doubt.**
To Emp 147-8 there is no **doubt** you should discharge him.
Doubtful
Into Ac 87-32 when agitated or **doubtful,** and ask for the right
Doubting
We Ag 52-26 we had to stop **doubting** the power of God.
Down
Th Is A So 23-26 they are **down** for the count.
Drag
To Wives 117-18 they will not **drag** you down.
Drank
Bill's Story 4-19 As I **drank,** the old fierce determination
Bill's Story 7-24 day came when I **drank** once more
Bill's Story 15-4 if he **drank** he would surely die.
Th Is A Sol 20-22 if he ever **drank** again it would kill him,
Mo Ab Al 32-17 would get nowhere if he **drank** at all.
Th Fam Af 126-25 used to have before he **drank** so much,
A Vi Fo You 158-21 He never **drank** again.
Dr Bob Ni 173-3 I **drank** as much as my purse permitted,
Dr Bob Ni 175-27 I **drank** with moderation at first,
Dr Bob Ni I drank all the scotch they had on the train
Dr Bob Ni 179-23 I **drank** all I dared in the bar,
Drastic
Mo Ab Al 42-26 though entirely sensible, was pretty **drastic.**
Into Ac 76-20 to a **drastic** self-appraisal.

Into Ac 80-1 Before taking **drastic** action which might

Into Ac 80-4 and the **drastic** step is indicated

Dream world

Th Fam Af 130-9 This **dream world** has been replaced

Drew

We Ag 57-14 When we **drew** near to Him He disclosed Himself

Drink

Doc's Op xxvi-30 Men and women **drink** essentially because

Doc's Op xxvi-6 firm resolution not to **drink** again.

Doc's Op xxvii-33 They took a **drink** a day

Doc's Op xxviii-17 can take a **drink** without danger

Doc's Op xxix-8 living, one might say, to **drink.**

Doc's Op xxix-31 to resist the impulse to **drink.**

Doc's Op xxx-2 He has not had a **drink** for a great many years.

Bill's Story 2-19 Out of this alloy of **drink**

Bill's Story 3-17 **Drink** was taking an important and

Bill's Story 5-23 I could not take so much as one **drink.**

Bill's Story 5-30 Someone had pushed a **drink** my way,

Bill's Story 8-15 insidious insanity of that first **drink,**

Bill's Story 9-6 then I could **drink** openly with him.

Bill's Story 9-15 I pushed a **drink** across the table.

Bill's Story 13-13 I have not had a **drink** since.

Bill's Story 15-3 he would surely **drink** again,

Bill's Story 15-13 nearly drove me back to **drink,**

Th Is A Sol 17-4 They have solved the **drink** problem.

Th Is a Sol 20-17 Why don't you **drink** like a gentleman

Th Is a Sol 21-12 once he starts to **drink.**

Th Is A Sol 21-20 Yet let him **drink** for a day.

Th Is A Sol 22-17 one **drink** means another debacle

Th Is A Sol 22-19 why is it he takes that one **drink?**

Th Is A sol 22-29 while the alcoholic keeps away from **drink,**

Th Is A Sol 23-4 never took the first **drink,**

Th Is A Sol 23-20 why he took that first **drink**

Th Is A sol 24-7 lost the power of choice in **drink.**

Th Is A Sol 24-12 without defense against the first **drink.**

Th Is A sol 24-23 How often have some of us begun to **drink**

Th Is A Sol 24-27 "Well, I'll stop with the sixth **drink."**

Mo Ab Al 30-6 prove we could **drink** like other people

Mo Ab Al 31-14 and **drink** like a gentleman,

Mo Ab Al 31-16 to **drink** like other people!
Mo Ab Al 31-33 Try to **drink** and stop abruptly.
Mo Ab Al 32-26 had qualified him to **drink** as other men.
Mo Ab Al 33-6 we could therefore **drink** normally.
Mo Ab Al 33-10 Commencing to **drink** after a period
Mo Ab Al 33-25 have to **drink** a long time
Mo Ab Al 34-16 who are unable to **drink** moderately
Mo Ab Al 34-21 choose whether he will **drink** or not
Mo Ab Al 35-6 Desperate experiment of the first **drink?**
Mo Ab Al 37-14 excuse for taking that first **drink.**
Mo Ab Al 37-24 when we began to **drink** deliberately
Mo Ab Al 37-29 with respect to the first **drink**
Mo Ab Al 40-19 possible for me to **drink** again.
Mo Ab Al 40-20 insanity which precedes the first **drink,**
Mo Ab Al 41-28 no fight whatever against the first **drink.**
Mo Ab Al 41-29 commenced to **drink** as carelessly
Mo Ab Al 41-33 I would **drink** again.
Mo Ab Al 42-3 some trivial reason for having a **drink.**
Mo Ab Al 43-27 defense against the first **drink.**
We Ag 51-3 Leaving aside the **drink** question
We Ag 57-2 the thought of **drink** has never returned;
We Ag 57-4 he could not **drink** if he would.
Ho It Wo 66-19 and we **drink** again.
Ho It Wo 66-19 And with us, to **drink** is to die.
Ho It Wo 70-13 we are quite sure to **drink.**
Into Ac 75-19 The feeling that the **drink** problem has
Into Ac 78-24 we are liable to **drink** if we are afraid to
Wo Wi Ot 92-4 leads to the first **drink** of a spree.
Wo Wi Ot 92-12 condition surrounding that first **drink**
Wo Wi Ot 93-31 not have applied it or he would not **drink.**
Wo Wi Ot 97-31 even though he continues to **drink,**
Wo Wi Ot 101-2 we must shun friends who **drink;**
Wo Wi Ot 102-19 few people will ask you to **drink.**
Wo Wi Ot 102-22 just because your friends **drink** liquor.
To Wives 104-4 in behalf of women who **drink**
To Wives 104-14 the wives of men who **drink** too much.
To Wives 107-22 why they commenced to **drink** again,
To Wives 107-31 that **drink** meant ruin to them?
To Wives 109-21 that he cannot **drink** like other people.

To Wives 109-27 how he can **drink** moderately next time.

To Wives 110-5 He admits he cannot **drink** like other people,

To Wives 111-10 use that as an excuse to **drink** more.

To Wives 111-18 though your husband continues to **drink.**

To Wives 117-7 the pressing problem of **drink**

To Wives 120-21 insanely trivial excuses to **drink.**

Th Fam Af 130-5 He will be less likely to **drink** again.

To Emp 138-6 knows I no longer **drink.**

To Emp 138-23 had nothing to **drink** whatever for three years,

To Emp 138-25 nine out of ten men **drink** their heads off.

To Emp 139-15 Those who **drink** moderately may be

To Emp 140-2 these qualities and did not **drink**

To Emp 142-1 but cannot if he continues to **drink.**

To Emp 142-23 still thinks he can ever **drink** again,

To Emp 147-2 shielded from temptation to **drink.**

A Vi Fo You 154-19 Of course he couldn't **drink,**

A Vi Fo You 154-24 old, insidious insanity- that first **drink.**

A Vi Fo You 156-12 He has not had a **drink** since.

A Vi Fo you 157-17 That's me. I **drink** like that.

A Vi Fo you 157-21 mental state preceding the first **drink.**

Dr Bob Ni 175-2 because if I did not **drink**

Dr Bob Ni 176-4 I did not take the morning **drink**

Dr Bob Ni 177-23 I would **drink** no more- promises

Dr Bob Ni 177-29 I could **drink** all I wanted of that.

Dr Bob Ni 180-3 June 10, 1935, and that was my last **drink.**

Dr Bob Ni 181-28 you were getting another **drink.**

Drinker

Doc's Op xxvi-8 in the average temperate **drinker.**

Th Is A Sol 18-20 But the ex-problem **drinker** who has

Th Is A Sol 20-32 a certain type of hard **drinker**

Th Is A Sol 21-9 start off with a moderate **drinker**

Th Is A Sol 21-10 become a continuous hard **drinker;**

Mo Ab Al 31-5 making a normal **drinker** out of

Wo Wi Ot 103-11 not one **drinker** in a thousand likes to be

To Wives 108-33 husband may be only a heavy **drinker.**

To Wives 112-20 help the wife of another serious **drinker.**

To Wives 114-29 If your husband is a **drinker,**

To Wives 115-26 home of every problem **drinker**

Th Fam Af 135-5 who have lived with a **drinker.**

To Emp 139-13 a hard **drinker,** a moderate **drinker,** or a
To Emp 130-20 As a moderate **drinker,** you can
To Emp 149-23 the habitual or whoopee **drinker.**
A Vi Fo You 151-24 Now and then a serious **drinker,**
Drinkers
Doc's Op xxiv-25 as ex-problem **drinkers,**
Bill's Story 9-11 **Drinkers** are like that.
Th Is a Sol 20-1 Our very lives, as ex-problem **drinkers,**
Th Is a Sol 20-24 observations on **drinkers** which we
Th Is A Sol 20-29 Moderate **drinkers** have little trouble
Th Is A Sol 23-21 Some **drinkers** have excuses with
Th Is A Sol 23-28 and friends sense that these **drinkers**
Mo Ab Al 33-29 Certain **drinkers,** who would be
Mo Ab Al 34-9 becoming serious **drinkers**
Wo Wi Ot 89-15 with any **drinkers** who want to recover
Wo Wi Ot 103-17 **Drinkers** will not stand for it.
To Wives 112-12 **Drinkers** like to help other **drinkers.**
To Emp 140-24 Normal **drinkers** are not so affected,
To Emp 147-23 trying to help serious **drinkers** who should
A Vi Fo You 151-22 Unhappy **drinkers** who read this page
A Vi Fo You 151-26 As ex-problem **drinkers,**
A Vi Fo You 153-17 defeated **drinkers** will seize upon it,
Drinking
Doc's Op xxiv-14 could not control our **drinking**
Doc's Op xxviii-2 these men were not **drinking** to escape; they were **drinking** to overcome a craving
Doc's Op xxviii-14 He plans various ways of **drinking.**
Doc's Op xxviii-25 cannot start **drinking** without
Bill's Story 2-10 Though my **drinking** was not yet continuous,
Bill's Story 3-22 My **drinking** assumed more serious
Bill's Story 3-33 Golf permitted **drinking** every day and
Bill's Story 4-21 But **drinking** caught up with me again
Bill's Story 7-1 Next day found me **drinking**
Bill's Story 7-4 I could eat little or nothing when **drinking,**
Bill's Story 8-25 I sat **drinking** in my kitchen.
Th Is A Sol 19-5 elimination of our **drinking** is but a beginning
Th Is a Sol 19-24 concerned with a **drinking** problem..
Th Is a sol 20-5 so very ill from **drinking.**
Th Is A Sol 21-11 at some stage of his **drinking** career

Th Is A Sol 21-15 tragic things while **drinking.**
Th Is A Sol 21-18 His disposition while **drinking** resembles
Th Is A Sol 23-12 an alcoholic's **drinking** bout
Th Is A Sol 24-1 At a certain point in the **drinking** of
Th Is A Sol 24-3 powerful desire to stop **drinking**
Mo Ab Al 30-4 our **drinking** careers have been
Mo Ab Al 30-7 will control and enjoy his **drinking**
Mo Ab Al 30-16 lost the ability to control our **drinking.**
Mo ab al 31-13 inability to control his **drinking**
Mo Ab Al 31-17 **Drinking** beer only,
Mo Ab Al 31-19 never **drinking** alone,
Mo Ab Al 31-19 never **drinking** in the morning,
Mo Ab Al 31-19 **drinking** only at home,
Mo Ab Al 31-21 never **drinking** during business hours,
Mo Ab Al 31-21 **drinking** only at parties,
Mo Ab Al 31-22 **drinking** only natural wines,
Mo Ab Al 31-33 and try some controlled **drinking.**
Mo Ab Al 32-6 we believe that early in our **drinking** careers
Mo Ab Al 32-7 could have stopped **drinking.**
Mo Ab Al 32-14 a great deal of spree **drinking.**
Mo Ab Al 32-29 He tried to regulate his **drinking**
Mo Ab Al 33-12 planning to stop **drinking**
Mo Ab Al 33-21 had been **drinking** only a few years,
Mo Ab Al 33-23 as those who had been **drinking** twenty
Mo Ab Al 34-2 we had gone on **drinking** many years
Mo Ab Al 34-8 In the early days of our **drinking**
Mo Ab Al 35-2 precede a relapse into **drinking,**
Mo Ab al 35-17 no **drinking** until he was thirty-five.
Mo Ab Al 35-24 business he had lsor through **drinking.**
Mo Ab Al 36-9 I had no intention of **drinking.**
Mo Ab Al 36-15 Still no thought of **drinking.**
Mo Ab al 36-30 suffering which **drinking** always caused him.
Mo Ab Al 36-32 all reasons for not **drinking** were
Mo Ab al 38-32 everything in life through **drinking**
Mo Ab Al 39-4 though **drinking** foolishly and heavily
Mo Ab Al 39-9 unable to stop **drinking** on the basis
Mo Ab al 39-29 made up his mind to quit **drinking**
Mo Ab Al 40-13 convinced he had to stop **drinking,**
Mo Ab Al 40-13 who had no excuse for **drinking,**

We Ag 44-5 or if when **drinking,**
Ho It Wo 65-24 Threatens to fire me for **drinking**
Into Ac 72-23 we may not overcome **drinking.**
Into Ac 73-23 that makes for more **drinking.**
Into Ac 77-31 will never get over **drinking** until we
Into Ac 78-16 make no bones about our **drinking;**
Into Ac 78-22 Our **drinking** has made us slow to pay.
Into Ac 79-18 because of resentment and **drinking,**
Into Ac 80-7 While **drinking,** he accepted a sum of money
Into Ac 80-25 or he would soon start **drinking** again,
Into Ac 81-3 But **drinking** does complicate
Wo Wi Ot 89-2 insure immunity from **drinking** as intensive
Wo Wi Ot 89-23 because of your own **drinking** experience
Wo Wi Ot 90-3 If he does not want to stop **drinking,**
Wo Wi Ot 90-31 the end of his next **drinking** bout.
Wo Wi Ot 91-20 turn the talk to some phase of **drinking.**
Wo Wi Ot 91-21 Tell him enough about your **drinking** habits,
Wo Wi Ot 91-25 a sketch of your **drinking** career
Wo Wi Ot 91-32 you know all about the **drinking** game,
Wo wi Ot 92-17 that he can still control his **drinking,**
Wo Wi Ot 98-17 we simply do not stop **drinking** so long as we
Wo Wi Ot 101-3 which show **drinking** scenes;
Wo Wi Ot 101-24 not to avoid a place where there is **drinking**
Wo Wi Ot 102-10 in places where there is **drinking**
Wo Wi Ot 102-19 While you were **drinking,** you were
Wo Wi Ot 103-4 or hatred of **drinking** as an institution.
Wo Wi Ot 103-11 the cause of temperate **drinking** any good,
To Wives 105-20 that they were through **drinking** forever.
To Wives 107-25 When **drinking,** they were strangers.
To Wives 108-30 before him a way to stop his **drinking**
To Wives 109-1 His **drinking** may be constant or it
To Wives 109-7 that **drinking** is necessary to his business.
To Wives 109-16 gets entirely out of hand when **drinking.**
To Wives 109-24 He is remorseful after serious **drinking** bouts
To Wives 110-24 He enjoys **drinking.**
To Wives 110-25 Perhaps you enjoy **drinking** with him
To Wives 110-28 chatting and **drinking** before your fire.
To Wives 111-7 what he must do about his **drinking.**
To Wives 111-14 Be determined that your husband's **drinking**

To Wives 112-26 like to get over **drinking** for good.
To Wives 113-9 of this after he has been **drinking,**
To Wives 114-33 You avoid the subject of **drinking,**
To Wives 115-23 argument he has with them while **drinking.**
To Wives 116-12 he wants to stop **drinking** forever.
To Wives 116-29 nicer if our husbands stopped **drinking.**
To Wives 119-28 for **drinking** many times isolates the wife
To Wives 120-9 he really wants to get over **drinking,**
Th Fam Af 122-20 Cessation of **drinking** is but the first step
Th Fam Af 123-29 the **drinking** career of almost every
Th Fam Af 127-5 Let them remember that his **drinking**
Th Fam Af 129-20 his **drinking** has placed him on the wrong
Th Fam Af 131-1 for his **drinking** placed him constantly
Th Fam Af 131-10 **Drinking** isolates most homes from
Th Fam Af 133-15 who have recovered from serious **drinking,**
Th Fam Af 134-10 when **drinking** is stopped the man tends
Th Fam Af 134-19 were impressionable while he was **drinking.**
To Emp 137-3 After two weeks of **drinking,** he had placed
To Emp 137-5 had discharged him for **drinking** six weeks
To Emp 137-11 obliged to discharge him for **drinking,**
To Emp 138-13 I'm sure this man is done **drinking.**
To Emp 139-12 well to disregard your own **drinking,**
To Emp 139-17 **Drinking** occasionally, and understanding
To Emp 139-22 you control your **drinking.**
To Emp 140-32 When **drinking,** or getting over a bout
To Emp 141-5 honest and upright when not **drinking.**
To Emp 141-25 He wants to quit **drinking**
To Emp 141-31 State that you know about his **drinking,**
To Emp 142-13 to stop **drinking** forever?
To Emp 142-33 For most alcoholics who are **drinking,**
To Emp 143-19 To get over **drinking** will require a
To Emp 145-24 sometimes our **drinking** will be used politically
To Emp 145-28 jokes about an alcoholic's **drinking** exploits.
To Emp 146-17 has gone along without **drinking** for a few
To Emp 147-27 Do you want to stop **drinking** or not?
To Emp 148-3 cannot or will not stop **drinking,**
To Emp 148-29 glad you fellows got over your **drinking.**
A Vi Fo You 151-1 For most normal folks, **drinking** means
A Vi Fo You 151-6 in those last days of heavy **drinking.**

A Vi Fo You 155-15 could stop his **drinking** for long.
A Vi Fo You 155-20 obsession that few knew of his **drinking.**
A Vi Fo You 156-6 learned that many knew of his **drinking.**
A Vi Fo You 156-14 liabilities of thirty years of hard **drinking**
A Vi Fo You 156-24 his head completely when he's **drinking.**
A Vi Fo You 157-16 told him about their **drinking** experiences
A Vi Fo You 158-31 whether he wanted to stop **drinking** or not.
Dr Bob Ni 172-16 where **drinking** seemed to be a major
Dr Bob Ni 173-9 I took up the business of **drinking**
Dr Bob Ni 173-12 membership in one of the **drinking** societies
Dr Bob Ni 173-20 after a prolong period of **drinking**
Dr Bob Ni 174-3 my **drinking** became so much worse
Dr Bob Ni 174-7 for I kept on **drinking**
Dr Bob Ni 175-23 even if I should do some **drinking.**
Dr Bob Ni 176-14 go to the hospital if I had been **drinking,**
Dr Bob Ni 177-32 I was **drinking** at least a case and a half a day.
Dr Bob Ni 180-11 many years of frightful **drinking,**
Dr Bob Ni 181-23 to quit **drinking** liquor for good and all,
Drinks
Doc's Op xxvii-2 at once by taking a few **drinks**
Mo Ab Al 31-18 limiting the number of **drinks,**
Mo Ab Al 40-31 I had no trouble refusing **drinks,**
To Wives 104-7 But for every man who **drinks**
To Wives 105-28 husbands sneaked so many **drinks** that they
To Wives 109-22 He sometimes **drinks** in the morning
To Wives 110-15 Sometimes he **drinks** on the way home
To Wives 112-5 the risk he takes if he **drinks** too much.
Th Fam Af 128-19 While grateful that he **drinks** no more,
To Emp 142-17 to get away with a few **drinks**
To Emp 148-31 If a man **drinks** so much that
A Vi Fo You 152-4 take a half dozen **drinks** and get away with
A Vi For You 154-17 Unless he took some **drinks,** he might not
A Vi Fo You 154-22 Perhaps he could handle, say, three **drinks**
Dr Bob Ni 174-27 a couple of **drinks** would alleviate my gastric
Dr Bob Ni 180-1 gave me a few **drinks** that night,
Drug
Doc's Op xxiii-8 specializing in alcoholic and **drug** addiction,
Doc's Op xxv-9 treating alcoholic and **drug** addiction.

Drugged

To Emp 142-11 many alcoholics, being warped and **drugged,**

Drunk

Bill's Story 2-9 I was too **drunk** to think or write.

Bill's Story 2-13 conceived their best projects when **drunk;**

Bill's story 4-32 coming home exhausted to find me **drunk.**

Bill's Story 5-27 Shortly afterward i came home **drunk.**

Bill's Story 6-7 I might as well get good and **drunk** then.

Th Is A Sol 21-17 always more or less insanely **drunk.**

Th Is A Sol 22-9 and gets **drunk** all over again.

Th Is A sol 26-15 he was **drunk** in a short time

Mo Ab Al 31-23 to resign if ever **drunk** on the job,

Mo Ab Al 34-13 Some will be **drunk** the day after

Mo Ab al 35-27 found himself **drunk** half a dozen times

Mo Ab Al 36-1 Yet he got **drunk** again.

Mo Ab Al 37-19 gone out deliberately to get **drunk,**

Ho It Wo 70-6 Does this mean we are going to get **drunk?**

Into Ac 73-1 Almost invariably they got **drunk.**

Wo Wi Ot 90-17 Don't deal with him when he is very **drunk,**

Wo Wi Ot 97-15 A **drunk** may smash the furniture

To Wives 106-21 the **drunk** to end all drunks.

To Wives 108-1 then got **drunk** again immediately?

To Wives 110-15 appears definitely insane when **drunk.**

To Wives 120-8 dismays you by coming home **drunk.**

To Wives 120-27 If he gets **drunk,** don't blame yourself.

Th Fam Af 135-15 He got **drunk.**

To Emp 136-15 so **drunk** he could hardly speak.

To Emp 146-29 might jump to the conclusion he is **drunk.**

To Emp 147-28 on the spot every time you get **drunk.**

A Vi Fo You 157-12 I got **drunk** on the way home from here.

Dr Bob Ni 177-13 that I get **drunk** every night,

Dr Bob Ni 177-19 smuggling it home, getting **drunk,**

Dr Bob Ni 178-4 nobody could tell who had been **drunk,**

Drunkard's

Dr Bob Ni 180-12 all the **drunkard's** experiences known to man,

Drunkenness

Bill's Story 3-28 helped at times be extreme **drunkenness**

Into Ac 83-17 ten or twenty years of **drunkenness** would

Dry

To Wives 109-19 various means of moderating or staying **dry.**

A Vi Fo Yo 151-24 serious drinker, being **dry** at the moment

Dr Bob Ni 174-16 and remain absolutely **dry,**

Dry spell

Dr Bob Ni 179-16 This **dry spell** lasted for about three weeks;

Dull

To Wives 110-29 parties which would be **dull** without liquor.

Th Fam Af 126-13 he may seem **dull** and boring,

Duty

Dr Bob Ni 181-1 1. Sense of **duty.**

Dying

A Vi Fo Yo 152-27 alcoholics are **dying** helplessly

E

Eagerness

Wo Wi Ot 96-4 to accept with **eagerness** what you offer.

Earmarks

To Wives 109-28 These are the **earmarks** of a real alcoholic.

Earnest

To Wives 117-18 if you are in **earnest** they will not

Earnestly

We Ag 46-32 to those who **earnestly** seek.

Ho It Wo 70-15 We **earnestly** pray for the right ideal,

A Vi Fo You 155-9 had **earnestly** tried many avenues of escape.

Earnestness

Bill's Story 16-12 underneath there is a deadly **earnestness.**

Mo Ab Al 37-16 in all **earnestness** and sincerity

Ho It Wo 58-21 with all the **earnestness** at our command,

Dr Bob Ni 173-10 with much greater **earnestness** than I

Earth

Th Fam Af 130-14 to be firmly planted on **earth.**

Ease

Into Ac 75-15 at perfect peace and **ease.**

Easier

Ho It Wo 58-20 could find an **easier,** softer way.

Into Ac 72-26 they have turned to **easier** methods.

Easy

Th Fam Af 135-28 **Easy** does it.

Economic

Into Ac 84-8 **economic** insecurity will leave us.

Education

To Wives 117-16 regarded as part of your **education,**

Effective

Mo Ab Al 43-27 no **effective** mental defense against the first

We Ag 47-20 a wonderfully **effective** spiritual structure can

Effectiveness

Into Ac 84-22 grow in understanding and **effectiveness.**

Effort

Ho It wo 63-4 by a strenuous **effort** to face and to be

Ho It Wo 64-12 it is an **effort** to discover the truth

Egoism

Into Ac 73-6 only thought they had lost their **egoism**

Eighteenth Amendment

Dr Bob Ni 175-18 With the passing of the **eighteenth Amendment**

Elation

Th Fam Af 128-30 have experienced dad's **elation.**

Embarrass

To Wives 115-9 not to **embarrass** or harm your husband.

Embarrassment

To Wives 109-5 Sometimes he is a source of **embarrassment**

To Wives 115-5 most of this **embarrassment** is unnecessary

Embittered

We Ag 56-6 **embittered** and depressed him.

Emotion

Into Ac 82-11 most terrible human **emotion**- jealousy.

Emotional

Doc's Op xxvi-14 Frothy **emotional** appeal seldom suffices.

We Ag 52-16 couldn't control our **emotional** natures,

Ho It Wo 58-11 suffer from grave **emotional** and mental

Th Fam Af 134-11 there may be an **emotional** upset.

Emotionally

Doc's Op xxviii-9 who are **emotionally** unstable

Employee

To Emp 140-14 If you concede that your **employee** is ill,

To Emp 145-16 With this kind of **employee**

To Emp 148-11 for covering up an alcoholic **employee.**

To Emp 149-26 an alcoholic **employee** will receive

Employees

To Emp 139-10 in salvaging their sick **employees.**

To Emp 144-26 we hope your **employees** may be put

To Emp 144-30 On your **employee's** return, talk with him.

To Emp 146-19 **employees** who are giving you the alcoholic

To Emp 149-6 in the well-being of **employees.**

Employer

To Emp 136-4 knows the alcoholic as the **employer** sees him.

To Emp 137-24 every modern **employer** feels a moral

To Emp 146-2 The **employer** cannot play favorites,

Employers

To Emp 136-1 Among many **employers** nowadays,

To Emp 137-32 Some **employers** have tried every known

Enables

A Vi Fo You 162-27 **enables** us to lend a hand,

Encourage

To Emp 146-11 need to **encourage** him to play once in a while.

End

We Ag 49-17 the beginning and **end** of all.

Into Ac 77-2 But this is not an **end** in itself.

A Vi Fo You 152-10 He will wish for the **end.**

Enemies

Into Ac 78-9 former **enemies** sometimes praise what we

To Emp 145-18 greatest **enemies** of us alcoholics are

Enemy

Into Ac 77-24 harder to go to an **enemy** than to a friend,

Energetic

To Emp 146-5 alcoholics are **energetic** people.

Energy

Th Fam Af 134-2 chocolate available for its quick **energy**

Engulfs

Th Is A So 18-6 It **engulfs** all whose lives

Enjoying

Th Fam Af 132-17 We absolutely insist on **enjoying** life.

Enlarge

Mo Ab Al 35-25 failed to **enlarge** his spiritual life

Enthusiasm

To Wives 113-17 He may not share your **enthusiasm,**

To Wives 114-7 His reaction may be one of **enthusiasm.**

To Wives 119-21 mistake to dampen his **enthusiasm**

To Wives 119-32 his excess **enthusiasm** will tone down

Enthusiast

Th Fam Af 128-6 He becomes a religious **enthusiast.**

Enthusiastically

Wo Wi Ot 102-13 attend to your business **enthusiastically**

Entirely

Into Ac 73-33 We must be **entirely** honest with somebody

Envy

To Emp 145-19 resentment, jealousy, **envy,** frustration

Episodes

Into Ac 73-18 he is revolted at certain **episodes** he

Errors

Th Fam Af 124-9 willingness to face and rectify **errors**

Escapades

Th Fam Af 123-30 has been marked by **escapades,**

Escape

A Vi Fo You 152-33 you will **escape** disaster together

A Vi Fo You 155-10 tried many avenues of **escape.**

Evaded

We Ag 45-24 thought he had neatly **evaded**

Events

A Vi Fo You 164-18 great **events** will come to pass for you

Everyone

A Vi Fo Yo 164-3 **everyone** in that town has had his

Evidence

We Ag 53-5 to examine the **evidence** of our senses,

Evil

Ho It Wo 67-28 It was an **evil** and corroding thread;

Examine

We Ag 53-5 **examine** the evidence of our senses,

Example

Bill's Story 12-3 Despite the living **example** of my friend

Mo Ab Al 35-11 Our first **example** is a friend we shall call

Ho It Wo 62-16 extreme **example** of self-will run riot.

Ex-problem

Doc's Op xxiv-24 But as **ex-problem** drinkers,

Th Is A Sol 18-20 But the **ex-problem** drinker

Th Is a Sol 20-1 as **ex-problem** drinkers, depend upon our

Exceptional

To Emp 137-13 Here were three **exceptional** men lost

Exceptions

Into Ac 81-29 though there may be justifiable **exceptions,**

Excessive

Dr Bob Ni 174-30 my former **excessive** indulgence.

Exchange

Mo Ab Al 43-4 I would not **exchange** it's best moments

Excuse

Mo Ab Al 37-13 some insanely trivial **excuse** for taking

Mo Ab Al 40-13 who had no **excuse** for drinking,

Into Ac 75-2 not use this as a mere **excuse** to postpone.

Into Ac 77-15 We don't use this as an **excuse**

To Wives 107-22 reply with some silly **excuse,**

To Wives 111-10 use that as an **excuse** to drink more.

Excuses

Th Is A Sol 23-21 Some drinkers have **excuses** with which they

To Wives 120-21 insanely trivial **excuses** to drink.

To Emp 146-27 Long experience with alcoholic **excuses**

Exert

Ho It Wo 61-13 He decides to **exert** himself more

Exhausted

A Vi Fo Yo 156-11 At midnight he came home **exhausted,**

Exhaustion

To Wives 107-3 falling back on **exhaustion**

Exist

Into Ac 85-9 It does not **exist** for us.

Existence

Bill's Story 8-22 call the fourth dimension of **existence.**

Th Is A Sol 25-15 dimension of **existence** of which we had

Ho It Wo 67-29 the fabric if our **existence**

Th Fam Af 132-16 could see no joy or fun in our **existence,**
A Vi Fo You 152-22 years of your **existence** lie ahead
Exists
Th Is A So 17-9 But there **exists** among us a fellowship,
Expense
Into Ac 74-19 to save our own skin at another person's **expense.**
Experience
Doc's Op xxiii-5 **experience** with the sufferings of our members
Doc's Op xxv-7 I say this after many years' **experience**
Doc's Op xxvi-26 We feel, after many years of **experience**
Doc's Op xxvi-35 unless they can gain **experience**
Doc's Op xxvii-8 **experience** an entire psychic change
Doc's Op xxix-3 one year prior to this **experience**
Bill's Story 9-33 had come to pass his **experience** along to me
Bill's Story 12-29 The real significance of my **experience**
Th Is a Sol 19-22 our combined **experience** and knowledge
Th Is A Sol 26-9 **experience** had made him skeptical
Th Is A Sol 27-32 the necessary vital spiritual **experience.**
Th Is A Sol 28-2 he had the extraordinary **experience.**
Th Is A Sol 28-11 "Varieties of Religious **Experience**"
Th Is A Sol 29-2 no great obstacle to a spiritual **experience.**
Mo Ab Al 33-16 encouraged by this man's **experience**
Mo Ab Al 39-12 to us out of bitter **experience.**
Mo Ab Al 39-23 It was his first **experience** of this kind,
Mo Ab Al 40-5 that this humiliating **experience**
Mo Ab Al 42-18 cases out of their own **experience**
We Ag 44-8 only a spiritual **experience** will
We Ag 44-11 such an **experience** seems impossible
We Ag 44-23 Our **experience** shows that
We Ag 50-12 **Experience** has taught us that
We Ag 55-30 **experience** of a man who thought he was an
We Ag 56-13 who had known a spiritual **experience.**
Ho It Wo 66-15 growth of a spiritual **experience,**
Ho It Wo 70-14 These are facts out of our **experience.**
Into Ac 72-25 Trying to avoid this humbling **experience,**
Into Ac 75-18 we begin to have a spiritual **experience.**
Into Ac 79-8 any lengths to find a spiritual **experience,**
Into Ac 84-3 will see how our **experience** can benefit
Into Ac 85-11 That is our **experience.**

Wo Wi Ot 89-1 Practical **experience** shows that nothing will
Wo Wi Ot 89-11 this is an **experience** you must not miss.
Wo Wi Ot 89-23 because of your own drinking **experience**
Wo Wi Ot 92-11 Show him from your own **experience,**
Wo Wi Ot 92-24 mainly on your personal **experience.**
Wo Wi Ot 96-18 Having had the **experience** yourself,
Wo Wi Ot 101-6 Our **experience** shows that this is not
Wo Wi Ot 101-27 who has had **experience** with an alcoholic,
Wo Wi Ot 103-4 **Experience** shows that such an attitude
To Wives 116-8 This **experience** may come to you.
To Wives 119-3 where he could have a spiritual **experience.**
To Wives 121-5 have related is based upon **experience,**
Th Fam Af 124-6 **experience** is the thing of supreme value
Th Fam Af 124-28 first flush of spiritual **experience**
Th Fam Af 126-3 With these we have had **experience** galore.
Th Fam Af 128-4 a stirring spiritual **experience.**
Th Fam Af 130-18 a powerful spiritual **experience** and a life
Th Fam Af 131-32 Being possessed of a spiritual **experience**
Th Fam Af 132-28 tragic **experience** out of the past.
Th Fam Af 134-12 Some of us have had this **experience,**
To Emp 137-6 Still another **experience:**
To Emp 146-26 Long **experience** with alcoholic excuses
A Vi Fo You 153-12 willing to make use of your **experience.**
A Vi Fo You 155-13 When our friend related his **experience,**
A Vi Fo You 155-15 A spiritual **experience,** he conceded,
A Vi Fo you 157-30 friends spoke of their spiritual **experience**
A Vi Fo you 158-14 had begun to have a spiritual **experience.**
Dr Bob Ni 180-20 to alcoholism from actual **experience.**
Experienced
Doc's Op xxix-12 I **experienced** a very strange sensation.
Dr Bob Ni 180-11 a man who had **experienced** many years of
Experiences
Doc's Op xxix-2 by relating one of my **experiences.**
Bill's Story 14-22 men who have had such **experiences.**
Th Is A Sol 22-17 hundreds of **experiences** have shown
Th Is A Sol 25-17 deep and effective spiritual **experiences**
Th Is A Sol 27-15 called vital spiritual **experiences.**
Th Is A sol 29-5 forty-three personal **experiences.**
We Ag 46-14 had these thoughts and **experiences.**

Wo Wi Ot 91-21 drinking habits, symptoms, and **experiences**
Th Fam Af 125-19 we do not relate intimate **experiences**
A Vi Fo You 157-16 told him about their drinking **experiences.**
Dr Bob Ni 180-12 all the drunkard's **experiences** known to man,
Experiment
Mo Ab Al 34-29 The **experiment** of quitting
Mo Ab Al 35-5 desperate **experiment** of the first drink?
Mo Ab Al 36-23 The **experiment** went so well
Experimentation
Mo Ab Al 31-10 form of self-deception and **experimentation,**
Explodes
Th Fam Af 126-28 Sometimes he **explodes** over a trifle.
Expression
A Vi Fo You 160-25 The **expression** on the faces of the women,
Extreme
Doc's Op xxiii-27 of **extreme** medical importance;
Bill's Story 3-28 helped at times by **extreme** drunkenness.
Ho It Wo 62-16 **extreme** example of self-will run riot,
Wo Wi Ot 90-21 would go to any **extreme** to do so.
To Wives 105-2 Some of us veered from **extreme** to **extreme,**
To Emp 142-31 he will go to any **extreme** to do so,
Extremes
Ho It Wo 68-31 we find human opinions running to **extremes.**
Wo Wi Ot 98-4 we do go to great **extremes**
Th Fam Af 125-30 They run to **extremes.**
Eyes
A Vi Fo You 160-26 in the **eyes** of the men.

F

Face
A Vi Fo You 164-2 helping others to **face** life again,
Faces
A Vi Fo You 160-25 on the **faces** of the women,

Fact

Th is A So 25-16 The great **fact** is just this,

Th Is A So 25-20 The central **fact** of our lives today is

We Ag 51-8 the most important **fact** of their lives

We Ag 55-19 He was as much a **fact** as we were.

Wo Wi Ot 100-23 the blessed **fact** of his sobriety.

Facts

Th Is A Sol 18-21 properly armed with **facts** about himself,

Th Is A So 24-33 These stark and ugly **facts** have been

We Ag 48-18 a stickler for **facts** and results.

We Ag 55-15 **facts** as old as man himself.

Ho It Wo 70-14 These are **facts** out of our experience.

Into Ac 72-24 to keep certain **facts** about their lives.

Fail

We Ag 55-28 With this attitude you cannot **fail.**

How It Wo 58-1 Rarely have we seen a person **fail**

Into Ac 78-8 Rarely do we **fail** to make satisfactory progress.

Wo Wi Ot 89-4 It works when other activities **fail.**

Wo Wi Ot 89-7 secure their confidence when others **fail.**

Th Fam Af 130-22 They can hardly **fail** to approve

Failed

Doc's Op xxiii-26 other methods had **failed** completely

Bill's Story 1-20 Ominous warning- which I **failed** to heed.

Bill's Story 2-8 I nearly **failed** my law course.

Bill's Story 11-16 His human will had **failed.**

Bill's Story 14-33 For if an alcoholic **failed** to perfect

Bill's Story 15-14 when all other measures **failed,**

Mo Ab Al 33-2 Every attempt **failed.**

Mo Ab Al 35-25 he **failed** to enlarge his spiritual life.

Mo Ab Al 37-14 Our sound reasoning **failed**

Mo Ab Al 40-25 successful where you men **failed.**

We Ag 45-7 they **failed** utterly.

Ho It Wo 68-6 Wasn't it because self-reliance **failed** us?

Wo Wi Ot 96-11 One of our Fellowship **failed** entirely

Wo Wi Ot 101-22 to do the impossible have always **failed.**

Th Fam Af 128-21 accomplished the miracle where they **failed.**

To Emp 138-31 I saw that I had **failed** to help

Fails

Th Fam Af 130-23 the head of the house still **fails** somewhat

Dr Bob Ni 181-26 It never **fails,** if you go about

Failure

Bill's Story 7-25 that it would all end with heart **failure**

Th Is A sol 24-18 a complete **failure** of the kind of defense

We Ag 50-29 in the face of the total **failure**

We Ag 56-5 Business **failure,** insanity, fatal illness

Ho It Wo 64-19 which caused our **failure.**

Wo Wi Ot 98-10 makes the difference between **failure** and

Wo Wi Ot 101-18 from temptation is doomed to **failure.**

A Vi Fo You 151-12 -and one more **failure.**

Failures

A Vi Fo You 158-27 After several **failures** to find others,

A Vi Fo You 159-22 experienced a few distressing **failures,**

Fair

To Wives 120-6 husband will make a **fair** start

To Emp 147-28 It isn't **fair** to me or the firm.

To Emp 148-9 which is eminently **fair** and square.

Fair weather

Th Fam Aft 122-25 all will not be **fair weather.**

Faith

Bill's Story 10-19 **faith** in the strange proposition

Bill's Story 14-31, Into Ac 76-16 **Faith** without works was dead,

Into Ac 88-12 **Faith** without works is dead.

Bill's Story 15-4 Then **faith** would be dead indeed.

Bill's Story 16-12 **Faith** has to work twenty-four

Th Is A Sol 28-14 way by which **faith** can be

We Ag 46-1 with the thought that **faith** and

We Ag 47-24 accepted many things on **faith**

We Ag 47-29 the many articles of **faith** which are

We Ag 47-32 inability to accept much on **faith.**

We Ag 49-25 People of **faith** have a logical idea

We Ag 51-9 reason why one should have **faith**

We Ag 52-28 almost childish **faith**

We Ag 53-10 why we think our present **faith**

We Ag 53-21 with the question of **faith.**

We Ag 53-23 toward the desired shore of **faith.**

We Ag 53-33 stood by a certain kind of **faith?**

We Ag 54-3 that but a sort of **faith?**

We Ag 54-5 we discovered that **faith** had been

We Ag 54-19 had no capacity for **faith**

We Ag 54-20 we had been living by **faith**

We Ag 54-22 Imagine life without **faith!**

We Ag 55-13 **faith** in a Power greater than ourselves,

We Ag 55-16 **faith** in some kind of God

Ho It Wo 68-21 is that **faith** means courage.

Ho It Wo 68-22 All men of **faith** have courage.

Ho It Wo 70-33 **faith** did for us what we could not do

Wo Wi Ot 93-24 that **faith** alone is insufficient.

Wo Wi Ot 93-25 **faith** must be accompanied by self-sacrifice

Wo Wi Ot 93-30 however deep his **faith** and knowledge,

Wo Wi Ot 94-1 particular **faith** or denomination.

To Wives 117-14 The **faith** and sincerity of both you and

Faithful

We Ag 54-3 Yes, we had been **faithful**

We Ag 54-4 abjectly **faithful** to the God of reason.

Faiths

We Ag 49-24 various **faiths** may be, those **faiths** have

Fallacious reasoning

Th Is A So 23-15 draw this **fallacious reasoning** to the attention of

Fallacy

Th Fam Af 129-23 This **fallacy** may take a still greater hold

Family

Mo Ab Al 35-12 had a charming wife and **family.**

Mo Ab Al 35-23 His **family** was re-assembled,

Mo Ab Al 35-32 Moreover, he would lose his **family**

Mo Ab al 36-29 the loss of **family** and position

Into Ac 83-4 ought to sit down with the **family**

Into Ac 83-8 So we clean house with the **family,**

Into Ac 83-12 Unless one's **family** expresses a desire

Wo Wi Ot 90-5 This advice is given for his **family** also.

Wo Wi Ot 90-15 The **family** may object to this,

Wo Wi Ot 90-18 and the **family** needs your help.

Wo Wi Ot 90-20 let his **family** or a friend ask him

Wo Wi Ot 90-28 Neither should the **family** hysterically

Wo Wi Ot 90-33 The **family** must decide these things.

Wo Wi Ot 91-3 the **family** should not try to tell your story.

Wo Wi Ot 91-5 avoid meeting a man through his **family.**

Wo Wi Ot 91-12 Though you have talked with the **family,**

Wo Wi Ot 91-15 without being nagged by his **family.**
Wo Wi Ot 96-26 should not deprive your **family** or creditors
Wo Wi Ot 96-29 he will be welcomed by your **family,**
Wo Wi Ot 97-24 creates serious complications in a **family.**
Wo Wi Ot 97-26 why you should neglect his **family.**
Wo Wi Ot 97-27 The **family** should be offered
Wo Wi Ot 97-30 that the head of the **family** will recover.
Wo Wi Ot 97-31 the **family** will find life more bearable.
Wo Wi Ot 98-25 such reparation as he can to his **family,**
Wo Wi Ot 98-31 Though his **family** be at fault in many respects,
Wo Wi Ot 99-3 the effect on a man's **family**
Wo Wi Ot 99-5 Little by little the **family** may see their own
Wo Wi Ot 99-9 the **family** will perhaps want to go along.
Wo Wi Ot 99-31 recover unless he has his **family** back.
Wo Wi Ot 100-4 slip when the **family** came back too soon.
Wo Wi Ot 100-14 working with a man and his **family,**
Wo Wi Ot 100-17 But urge upon a man's **family** that he
Wo Wi Ot 100-26 tell the newcomer's **family** how that was
Wo Wi Ot 103-1 We feel that each **family,** in the light
To Wives 113-24 let someone outside the **family** present the
To Wives 119-5 After all, your **family** is reunited,
Th Fam Af 122-6 All members of the **family** should meet upon
Th Fam Af 122-10 fixed ideas about the **family**'s attitude
Th Fam Af 122-13 more one member of the **family** demands
Th Fam Af 122-17 trying to arrange the **family** show
Th Fam Af 122-19 what he can take from the **family** life
Th Fam Af 122-23 The entire **family** is, to some extent, ill.
Th Fam Af 123-3 some of the obstacles a **family** will meet;
Th Fam Af 123-6 **family** of an alcoholic longs for
Th Fam Af 123-10 the **family** may be unhappy.
Th Fam Af 123-11 **Family** confidence in dad is rising high.
Th Fam Af 123-25 But the wise **family** will admire him
Th Fam Af 123-28 the **family** will be plagued by specters
Th Fam Af 123-33 The **family** may be possessed by the idea
Th Fam Af 124-11 principal asset of the **family**
Th Fam Af 124-14 each **family** which has been relieved
Th Fam Af 125-25 Members of a **family** should watch
Th Fam Af 126-2 certain **family** problems will arise.
Th Fam Af 126-6 The **family** will be affected also,

Th Fam Af 126-13 and affectionate as the **family** would like

Th Fam Af 126-29 The **family** is mystified.

Th Fam Af 126-32 father and the **family** are mistaken,

Th Fam Af 127-1 The **family** must realize that dad,

Th Fam Af 127-26 As each member of a resentful **family**

Th Fam Af 127-28 These **family** talks will be constructive

Th Fam Af 128-8 the **family** may look at their strange new dad

Th Fam Af 128-11 may demand that the **family** find God

Th Fam Af 126-17 the **family** may react unfavorably.

Th Fam Af 128-26 for everyone in the world but his **family?**

Th Fam Af 129-12 does not include his **family** obligations

Th Fam Af 129-13 If the **family** will appreciate that dad's

Th Fam Af 129-16 understanding and sympathetic **family,**

Th Fam Af 129-18 happen should the **family** condemn and

Th Fam Af 129-22 If the **family** persists in criticism,

Th Fam Af 129-24 Instead of treating the **family** as he should,

Th Fam Af 129-27 Though the **family** does not fully agree

Th Fam Af 129-30 irresponsibility towards the **family,**

Th Fam Af 130-19 Whether the **family** has spiritual convictions

Th Fam Af 131-5 accustomed to wearing the **family** trousers.

Th Fam Af 131-7 unless the **family** watches for these

Th Fam Af 131-14 The **family** may feel they hold

Th Fam Af 131-21 if the **family** is going to play an effective

Th Fam Af 131-27 Though the **family** has no religious

Th Fam Af 132-4 He and his **family** can be a bright spot

Th Fam Af 133-1 So let each **family** play together

Th Fam Af 135-1 Whether the **family** goes on a spiritual basis

A Vi Fo You 154-28 his **family** and the men who would die

A Vi Fo You 155-23 bring still more suffering to his **family**

A Vi Fo You 159-24 bring the man's **family** into a spiritual way

A Vi Fo You 161-3 stricken acquaintance and his **family.**

A Vi Fo You 161-18 helping to settle **family** differences,

Families

Bill's Story 15-23 seen hundreds of **families** set their feet

Bill's Story 15-27 vital place in the lives of their **families**

Bill's Story 15-32 one thousand of us and our **families.**

Wo Wi Ot 100-3 whose **families** have not returned at all.

To Wives 106-29 as destitution faced us and our **families.**

To Wives 107-28 even if they did not love their **families,**

To Wives 119-13 helping other men and their **families.**
Th Fam Af 122-24 Let **families** realize, as they start
Th Fam Af 124-13 value to other **families** still struggling
Th Fam Af 125-8 We **families** of Alcoholics Anonymous
Th Fam Af 127-23 there are difficult wives and **families,**
Th Fam Af 135-4 Seeing is believing to most **families**
A Vi Fo You 153-25 that through you several **families** have
A Vi Fo You 161-11 **families** drive long distances to be present.
Fanatical
Ho It Wo 70-2 some people are as **fanatical** about sex as others
Fanatics
Into Ac 77-9 open to being branded **fanatics** or
Fare
To Emp 143-7 Your man will **fare** better if placed in such
Fared
Bill's Story 7-19 I **fared** forth to high hope.
Farm
Dr Bob Ni 173-23 spend a month on a large **farm**
Fascinated
A Vi Fo You 160-8 This couple has since become so **fascinated**
Fast-thinking
To Emp 139-32 Is he not usually brilliant, **fast-thinking,**
Fatal
We Ag 56-5 insanity, **fatal** illness, suicide-
Ho It wo 66-16 We found that it is **fatal.**
Wo Wi Ot 92-21 alcoholism as an illness, a **fatal** malady.
Fatality
Ho It Wo 70-26 comprehend their futility and their **fatality.**
Father *(God)*
Bill's Story 14-5 to the **Father** of Light who
Ho It Wo 62-30 He is the **Father**, and we are his children.
Father
To Wives 106-14 the love of our children for their **father.**
To Wives 106-14 told small tots that **father** was sick,
To Wives 106-25 children home to **father** and mother.
To Wives 115-22 need protection from their **father,**
Th Fam Af 123-7 They remember when **father** was romantic
Th Fam Af 123-22 **Father** knows he is to blame;
Th Fam Af 126-22 they think **father** owes them more

Th Fam Af 126-31 Both **father** and the family are mistaken,

Th Fam Af 127-32 and **father** will see he gives too little.

Th Fam Af 128-3 Assume on the other hand that **father** has,

Th Fam Af 128-17 When **father** takes this tack,

Th Fam Af 128-22 **father** was beyond human aid.

Th Fam Af 128-28 They suspect **father** is a bit balmy!

Th Fam Af 129-1 **Father** feels he has struck something

Th Fam Af 129-24 take **a** still greater hold on **father.**

Th Fam Af 130-29 Liquor incapacitated **father** for so many

Th Fam Af 130-32 obliged to treat **father** as a sick or

Th Fam Af 131-3 When sober, **father** usually obeyed.

Th Fam Af 131-5 **Father,** coming suddenly to life again,

Th Fam Af 131-11 **Father** may have laid aside for years

Th Fam Af 131-22 **Father** will necessarily spend much time

Th Fam Af 126-22 they think **father** owes them more

Th Fam Af 128-22 **father** was beyond human aid.

Th Fam Af 128-28 suspect **father** is a bit balmy!

Th Fam Af 130-29 Liquor incapacitated **father** for so many

Th Fam Af 130-32 to treat **father** as a sick or wayward child.

Th Fam Af 131-3 When sober, **father** usually obeyed.

Th Fam Af 131-5 **Father,** coming suddenly to life again,

Fathers

To Wives 108-15 better husbands and **fathers** than ever before.

Fatigue

Th Fam Aft 134-2 quick energy value at times of **fatigue.**

Fault

Ho It Wo 58-7 They are not at **fault;**

Into Ac 78-6 admits his own **fault,**

Into Ac 81-22 we should admit our **fault.**

Ho It Wo 61-16 Admitting he may be somewhat at **fault,**

Ho It Wo 69-16 Where were we at **fault,**

Into Ac 81-22 Undoubtedly we should admit our **fault.**

Fault-finding

Wo Wi Ot 98-32 Argument and **fault-finding** are to be avoided

Faults

Ho It Wo 67-21 When we saw our **faults** we listed them.

Into Ac 77-23 not too keen about admitting our **faults.**

Into Ac 78-2 His **faults** are not discussed.

Into Ac 79-28 write his first wife admitting his **faults**

A Vi Fo You 164-22 Admit your **faults** to Him and to
Favor
To Emp 141-11 You are not doing him a **favor** by keeping him on.
Favorite
To Emp 149-28 He should not be made a **favorite.**
Favorites
To Emp 146-2 The employer cannot play **favorites.**
Fear
Ho It Wo 62-8 **fear**, self-delusion, self-seeking
Ho It Wo 63-11 we began to lose our **fear** of today,
Ho It Wo 67-25 Notice that the word "**fear**" is
How It Wo 68-1 we think **fear** ought to be classed
Ho It Wo 68-9 didn't fully solve the **fear** problem,
Ho It Wo 68-25 ask him to remove our **fear**
Ho It Wo 68-26,27 we commence to outgrow **fear.**
Into Ac 73-6 thought they had lost their egoism and **fear;**
Into Ac 73-23 constant **fear** and tension-
Into Ac 78-23 We must lose our **fear** of creditors
Into Ac 84-7 **Fear** of people
Into Ac 84-24 dishonesty, resentment and **fear.**
Into Ac 88-3 less danger of excitement, **fear**, anger
To Wives 104 8 the wife who trembles in **fear**
To Wives 104-24 self-pity, misunderstanding and **fear.**
To Wives 116-5 There is another paralyzing **fear.**
To Wives 116-33 the ensuing lack of **fear,**
To Wives 120-18 slightest sign of **fear** or intolerance
To Emp 145-19 Jealousy, envy, frustration, and **fear.**
A Vi Fo You 154-22 **Fear** gripped him.
Dr Bob Ni 175-32 One was the **fear** of not sleeping,
Dr Bob Ni 175-33 the **fear** of running out of liquor.
Feared
A Vi Fo You 156-4 set out to tell those he **feared**
Fearless
Ho It Wo 58-22 be **fearless** and thorough from the
Ho It Wo 59-15 Made a searching and **fearless** moral
Fearlessly
We Ag 55-18 Sometimes we had to search **fearlessly,**
Fearlessness
Into Ac 73-8 humility, **fearlessness** and honesty,

Fears

Wo Wi Ot 68-3 We reviewed our **fears** thoroughly.

Into Ac 75-15 Our **fears** fall from us.

Feel

Wo Wi Ot 103-1 We **feel** that each family,

Th Fam Af 126-7 as they **feel** their money troubles

Th Fam Af 126-16 and often let him **feel** it.

Th Fam Af 129-25 and **feel** he has spiritual justification

Th Fam Af 131-14 The family may **feel** they hold a

To Emp 139-30 you may **feel** this feeling rising.

To Emp 143-13 better for him to **feel** fully responsible.

To Emp 148-19 you will **feel** no reluctance to rid yourself

A Vi Fo You 151-25 **Feel** better. Work better.

Feeling

Into Ac 84-3 That **feeling** of uselessness

To Wives 104-20 We want to leave you with the **feeling** that

To Wives 118-26 Another **feeling** we are very likely

Th Fam Af 131-13 a **feeling** of jealousy may arise.

To Emp 139-30 you may feel this **feeling** rising.

To Emp 140-8 the **feeling** that you are dealing only with

To Emp 142-6 express a lack of hard **feeling** toward him.

A Vi Fo You 151-4 and a **feeling** that life is good.

A Vi Fo You 154-5 with much hard **feeling** and controversy.

Feelings

We Ag 54-17 Did not these **feelings,** after all, determine the

Ho It Wo 66-17 For when harboring such **feelings**

To Wives 117-22 hurt **feelings** and resentments.

Feels

Th Fam Af 129-19 and **feels** he is doing very well.

Th Fam Af 129-1 Father **feels** he has struck something

Th Fam Af 135-12 who really **feels** there is something rather

To Emp 144-31 If he **feels** free to discuss his problems

Fees

Th Is a So 18-31 that there are no **fees** to pay,

Feet

Th Fam Af 130-13 but that our **feet** ought to be firmly

Fellow-sufferers

A Vi Fo you 159-19 their spare hours to **fellow-sufferers.**

Fellow worker

A Vi Fo you 163-29 our **fellow worker** will soon have friends

Fellowship

Doc's Op xxiii-22 a rapidly growing **fellowship**

Bill's Story 15-19 a **fellowship** gas grown up among us

Th Is A Sol 17-9 exists among us a **fellowship**

Bill's Story 15-33 newcomers may find the **fellowship**

Th Is A Sol 17-9 there exists among us a **fellowship,**

We Ag 45-21 and explain our **fellowship.**

Wo Wi Ot 89-10 to see a **fellowship** grow up about you.

Wo Wi Ot 90-24 described to him as one of a **fellowship**

Wo Wi Ot 94-32 about the **Fellowship** of Alcoholics

Wo Wi Ot 95-13 Offer him friendship and **fellowship.**

Wo Wi Ot 96-10 One of our **Fellowship** failed entirely

To Wives 121-11 The **fellowship** of Al-Anon Family Groups

A Vi Fo Yo 152-18 a **fellowship** in Alcoholics Anonymous

A Vi Fo You 152-22 Thus we find the **fellowship,**

A Vi Fo You 161-14 **Fellowship** will number many hundreds.

A Vi Fo You 162-21 find a **Fellowship** of Alcoholics Anonymo

A Vi Fo You 164-9 how to create the **fellowship** you crave.

A Vi Fo You 164-25 in the **Fellowship** of the Spirit,

Felt

Ho It Wo 63-8 as we **felt** new power flow in,

Fences

Th Fam Af 135-18 and mend his spiritual **fences.**

Fevered

To Emp 140-23 with such a **fevered** brain?

Fictitious name

Dr Bob Ni 176-17 at a hotel under a **fictitious name.**

Fifteen

A Vi Fo Yo 161-12 has **fifteen** fellows of Alcoholics Anonymous.

Fifth step

Into Ac 72-12 This brings us to the **fifth step**

Fight

Mo Ab Al 41-27 I had made no **fight** whatever against the first

Wo Wi Ot 97-16 You may have to **fight** with him if

A Vi Fo Yo 158-8 trying to **fight** this booze racket.

Fighting

Into Ac 84-30 we have ceased **fighting** anything or anyone-

Wo Wi Ot 103-21 we have stopped **fighting** anything or

Finally

To Emp 136-16 he was through- **finally** and forever.

Financial

Wo Wi Ot 96-25 or give him a little **financial** assistance.

Find

Ho It Wo 59-3 May you **find** Him now!

Fire

To Emp 148-32 so much that his job suffers, we **fire** him.

Fired

To Emp 139-3 the man did slip and was **fired.**

To Emp 141-17 Had they **fired** me first,

To Emp 147-23 who should have been **fired** long ago,

To Emp 148-12 No man should be **fired** just because he is

A Vi Fo Yo 152-20 Your imagination will be **fired.**

Firing

To Emp 141-11 **Firing** such an individual may prove a blessing

Firing line

Doc's Op xxvi-21 stand with us while on the **firing line,**

Wo Wi Ot 102-27 Keep on the **firing line** of life

Firmly

Th Fam Af 130-14 to be **firmly** planted on earth.

First

Th Fam Af 135-26 **First** things **first**

First class

A Vi Fo Yo 156-20 if she had a **first class** alcoholic prospect.

First drink

Bill's story 8-15 insidious insanity of that **first drink,**

Wo Wi Ot 92-4 leads to the **first drink** of a spree.

Wo Wi Ot 92-12 surrounding that **first drink**

A Vi Fo Yo 154-24 insidious insanity- that **first drink.**

A Vi Fo Yo 157-21 the mental state preceding the **first drink.**

First step

Mo Ab Al 30-13 This the **first step** in recovery.

Ho It Wo 63-33 the **first step** of which is a personal

Th Fam Aft 122-20 the **first step** away from a highly strained

Fit

Th Fam Af 135-14 finally threw him into a **fit** of anger.

Fix

A Vi Fo Yo 157-11 Nothing would **fix** me.

Flavor

Ho It Wo 69-6 would allow man no **flavor** for his fare

Flaws

Ho It Wo 64-18 we searched out the **flaws** in our make-up

Foe

Into Ac 85-15 alcohol is a subtle **foe.**

Fog

Dr Bob Ni 173-24 When I got the **fog** out of my brain,

Fool

Ho It Wo 64-16 he cannot **fool** himself about values.

To Emp 137-28 alcoholic has often seemed a **fool**

Fooling

We Ag 55-9 Actually we were **fooling** ourselves,

To Emp 142-16 does he think he is **fooling** you,

Foolish

Mo Ab Al 37-1 the **foolish** idea that he could take whiskey

Mo Ab Al 37-33 label him as a **foolish** chap

Into Ac 79-15 be the hasty and **foolish** martyr

Dr Bob Ni 173-25 quitting school was very **foolish**

Foolishly

Mo Ab Al 39-4 drinking **foolishly** and heavily

Into Ac 88-6 we are not burning up energy **foolishly**

A Vi Fo Yo 155-23 by **foolishly** admitting his plight

Fools

A Vi Fo Yo 152-3 He **fools** himself.

Footsore

Th Fam Aft 122-26 may be **footsore** and may straggle.

Footsteps

To Emp 137-17 I might have followed in their **footsteps**

Forbiding

We Ag 46-32 never exclusive or **forbidding** to those who

Force

Wo Wi Ot 90-27 never **force** yourself upon him.

Forcibly

Wo Wi Ot 91-7 not **forcibly** unless he is violent.

Foregoing

Th Fam Af 132-7 We intend the **foregoing** as a helpful

Forever

To Wives 116-12 he wants to stop drinking **forever.**

To Emp 136-16 through- finally and **forever.**

To Emp 142-13 to stop drinking **forever?**

Forgave

Th Fam Af 124-29 they **forgave** each other and drew

Forget

To Wives 106-12 we would forgive and try to **forget.**

Th Fam Af 134-24 cannot seem to forgive and **forget.**

Forgetfulness

Th Fam Af 124-1 **forgetfulness** of the past

Forgive

To Wives 106-11 we would **forgive** and try to forget.

Th Fam Af 134-23 cannot seem to **forgive** and forget.

Forgiven

Ho It Wo 70-11 we believe we will be **forgiven**

To Emp 140-15 can he be **forgiven** for what he has done

Forgiveness

Into Ac 79-28 admitting his faults and asking **forgiveness.**

Into Ac 86-17 we ask God's **forgiveness** and inquire

Forgiving

Into Ac 77-26 go to him in a helpful and **forgiving** spirit,

Forgotten

To Emp 140-16 Can his past absurdities be **forgotten?**

To Emp 147-33 your past will be **forgotten**

Former patients

A Vi Fo You 162-12 Many of us, **former patients,** go there to

Fortify

Dr Bob Ni 178-4 so I began to **fortify** my beer with

Fortune

Th Fam Af 126-18 He is striving to recover **fortune**

Found

A Vi Fo You 158-20 But he had **found** God-

A Vi Fo You 158-20 finding God he had **found** himself.

Foundation

Bill's Story 12-22 upon a **foundation** of complete willingness

Wo Wi Ot 97-5 Helping others is the **foundation** stone

Th Fam Af 13-2 dad will be on a firmer **foundation**

Four

To Wives 110-12 **Four:** You may have a husband of whom

Four Horsemen

A Vi Fo Yo 151-21 face the hideous **Four Horsemen-**

Four ounce bottles

Dr Bob Ni 177-2 put it up in **four ounce bottles**

Four reasons

Dr Bob Ni 180-32 I do it for **four reasons:**

Four years

Dr Bob Ni 180-4 As I write nearly **four years** have passed.

Fourth

To Wives 113-28 that men in the **fourth** classification

A Vi Fo Yo 158-28 a **fourth** turned up.

Frankly

To Emp 145-15 Can he talk **frankly** with you

Frankness

Into Ac 82-5 the utmost **frankness** is demanded.

Frantic

Th Fam Af 125-33 plunge into a **frantic** attempt

Fraternity

Dr Bob Ni 173-15 walk back to the **fraternity** house

Dr Bob Ni 174-4 the boys in the **fraternity** house where

Free

Doc's Op xxviii-16 after being entirely **free** from alcohol

Th Is A Sol 26-32 where other **free** men may go

Ho It Wo 66-20 we had to be **free** of anger.

To Wives 120-26 absolutely **free** to come and go as he likes.

Th Fam Af 133-3 to be happy, joyous, and **free.**

Free man

Th Is A Sol 26-30 And is a **free man**

Th Is A Sol 28-4 made him a **free man.**

Into Ac 75-29 we shall walk a **free man** at last.

A Vi Fo Yo 158-16 and walked from the hospital a **free man.**

Freedom

Ho It Wo 62-33 through which we passed to **freedom.**

Into Ac 83-31 We are going to know a new **freedom**
Into Ac 87-14 for **freedom** from self-will,
A Vi Fo You 160-18 threshold of that home into **freedom.**
Dr Bob Ni 178-10 with great **freedom** from embarrassment,
Freely
Bill's Story 14-25 what had been so **freely** given me.
Th Is A Sol 19-19 that which has been so **freely** given us?
Th Fam Af 126-26 But dad doesn't give **freely** of himself.
Th Fam Af 133-24 Most of them give **freely** of themselves,
A Vi Fo You 164-23 Give **freely** of what you find
Friction
Th Is A So 28-22 There is no **friction** among us over
Friend
Bill's Story 4-25 my generous **friend** had to let me go.
Bill's Story 11-32 I saw that my **friend** was much more than
Bill's Story 12-3 the living example of my **friend**
Bill's Story 12-23 I might build what I saw in my **friend.**
Bill's Story 13-11 have my new-found **Friend** take them away,
Bill's Story 13-29 My **friend** promised me when these things
Bill's Story 14-28 **friend** had emphasized the absolute necessity
Th Is A So 23-4 if our **friend** never took the first drink,
Th Is A So 27-9 Our **friend** felt as though the gates of hell
Into Ac 74-15 for a close-mouthed, understanding **friend.**
Into Ac 77-25 harder to go to an enemy than to a **friend,**
Wo Wi Ot 94-20 you have perhaps made a **friend.**
Th Fam Af 135-16 of course our **friend** was wrong-
A Vi Fo Yo 155-26 he invited our **friend** to his home.
A Vi Fo You 163-22 Our **friend** proceeded to tell him.
Friendliness
Th Is A So 17-10 among us a fellowship, a **friendliness,** and
Wo Wi Ot 99-8 atmosphere of helpfulness and **friendliness.**
Friendly
Doc's Op xviii-23 often able, intelligent, **friendly** people
We Ag 53-26 **Friendly** hands had stretched out in welcome.
Wo Wi Ot 97-27 You should continue to be **friendly** to them.
Friends
Bill's Story 3-1 Our **friends** thought a lunacy commission
Bill's Story 3-21 I made a host of fair-weather **friends.**
Bill's Story 15-19 commenced to make many fast **friends**

Th Is A So 18-17 intimate **friends** usually find us even more
Mo Ab Al 35-6 **Friends** who have reasoned with him
Into Ac 76-29 and **friends** we have hurt
Wo Wi Ot 102-22 just because your **friends** drink liquor.
To Wives 105-24 We seldom had **friends** at our homes,
To Wives 109-19 beginning to lose his **friends.**
To Wives 115-13 sprung up between you and your **friends**
To Wives 119-25 wives of his new alcoholic **friends.**
To Wives 120-21 dislike of his high-stepping **friends**
Th Fam Af 132-2 he will make new **friends**
A Vi Fo You 152-31 you will make lifelong **friends.**
A Vi Fo You 156-16 life was not easy for the two **friends.**
A Vi Fo You 163-29 fellow worker will soon have **friends**
Dr Bob Ni 175-6 I would get my **friends** to smuggle me a quart,
Dr Bob Ni 177-10 ostracized by our **friends.**
Dr Bob Ni 181-11 upset when I saw my **friends** drink and knew
Friendship
Wo Wi Ot 95-13 Offer him **friendship** and fellowship.
Friendships
A Vi Fo You 162-15 There are the same fast **friendships,**
Frightful
Dr Bob Ni 180-11 many years of **frightful** drinking
Frustration
We Ag 56-4 dogged by trouble and **frustration.**
Th Fam Af 129-1 from a life time of **frustration**
To Emp 145-19 envy, **frustration,** and fear.
Fuller
To Wives 120-4 your lives will be **fuller**
Fun
Bill's Story 16-9 a vast amount of **fun** about it all.
Mo Ab Al 38-1 having queer ideas of **fun.**
Th Fam Af 132-16 If newcomers could see no joy or **fun**
Fundamental
We Ag 55-10 the **fundamental** idea of God.
Fur lined
Dr Bob Ni 176-29 bottles of alcohol in a **fur lined** glove
Fuss
Th Fam Af 126-23 They want him to make a **fuss** over them.
To Wives 107-3 after each **futile** effort to reach solid ground.

Futility
We Ag 51-1 the seeming **futility** of existence,
Ho It Wo 66-11 leads only to **futility** and unhappiness.
Ho It Wo 70-26 We have begun to comprehend their futility
Future
A Vi Fo Yo 153-28 a glimpse of your **future** will be

G

Galileo
We Ag 51-21 came near putting **Galileo** to death
Gallantly
Th Fam Af 130-31 She met these responsibilities **gallantly.**
Game
A Vi Fo You 152-5 try the old **game** again,
Gates of hell
Th Is A So 27-9 as though the **gates of hell** had closed on him
Gathering
A Vi Fo You 159-29 little **gathering** of men and women,
Gatherings
A Vi Fo You 161-17 is more than attending **gatherings**
Genius
Th Is A So 21-22 He has a positive **genius** for getting tight
Genuine
A Vi Fo You 160-31 the **genuine** democracy,
Get-together
A Vi Fo You 159-32 In addition to these casual **get-together,**
Gifts
Th Is A Sol 21-29 He uses his **gifts** to build up a bright outlook
Ginger ale
A Vi Fo You 154-20 a bottle of **ginger ale** before him?
Girl
Into Ac 81-10 "The **girl** who understands"
Give
Wo Wi Ot 98-9 when and how to **give.**

Th Fam Aft 122-19 rather than **give?**

TH Fam Af 133-23 **give** freely of themselves.

A Vi Fo You 153-2 what it means to **give** of yourself

A Vi Fo You 158-26 had to **give** to others what they had

A Vi Fo You 164-23 **Give** freely of what you find

Giving

Th Fam Af 129-6 insist on **giving** away the entire product.

A Vi Fo Yo 159-17 in **giving** themselves for others.

Gladly

A Vi Fo Yo 159-18 and **gladly** devoted their spare hours

Glum

Th Fam Af 132-15 But we aren't a **glum** lot.

A Vi Fo Yo 152-13 be stupid, boring and **glum,**

Go back

Mo Ab Al 43-5 I would not **go back** to it even if I could.

God

Bill's Story 10-30 talked of a **God** personal to me

Bill's Story 11-11 of **God** in human affairs

Bill's Story 11-15 **God** had done for him

Bill's Story 12-5 word **God** still aroused a certain

Bill's Story 12-6 might be a **God** personal

Bill's Story 12-14,15 your own conception of **God**

Bill's Story 12-25 convinced that **God** is concerned

Bill's Story 12-31 and wanted **God**

Bill's Story 13-6 offered myself to **God**

Bill's Story 13-32,33 Belief in the power of **God.**

Bill's Story 14-13 **God** comes to most men gradually

Th Is A Sol 25-1 But for the grace of **God,**

Th Is A Sol 25-19 and toward **God**'s universe

Th Is A Sol 28-8 hand of **God.**

Th Is A Sol 28-12 men have discovered **God.**

Th Is A Sol 29-8 his relationship with **God.**

We Ag 45-18 we are going to talk about **God.**

We Ag 45-23 when we mention **God,**

We Ag 45-28 To others, the word "**God**" brought up

We Ag 45-33 had abandoned the **God** idea entirely.

We Ag 46-20 that Power, which is **God**

We Ag 46-22 to consider another's conception of **God.**

We Ag 46-29 We found that **God** does not make

We Ag 47-1 we speak to you of **God**
We Ag 47-2 your own conception of **God.**
We Ag 47-8 our first conscious relation with **God**
We Ag 49-12 nerds no **God** to explain it.
We Ag 49-16 spearheads of **God**'s ever advancing
We Ag 51-7 consciousness of the Presence of **God**
We Ag 51-33 people said **God** had reserved
We Ag 52-26 stop doubting the power of **God.**
We Ag 52-27 But the **God** idea did.
We Ag 53-17 **God** is everything or else he is nothing.
We Ag 53-18 **God** either is, or He isn't.
We Ag 54-4 faithful to the **God** of reason.
We Ag 55-5 **God** made these things possible
We Ag 55-10,11 the fundamental idea of **God**
We Ag 55-16 faith in some kind of **God**
We Ag 56-14 If there is a **God,**
We Ag 55-21 Who are you to say there is no **God?**
We Ag 55-24 conviction of the presence of **God.**
We Ag 57-4 **God** had restored his sanity.
We Ag 57-10 **God** restored us all to our right minds.
Ho It Wo 59-2 that one is **God.**
Ho It wo 59-14 over to the care of **God** as we
Ho It Wo 59-17 Admitted to **God,** to ourselves,
Ho It Wo 59-19 entirely ready to have **God** remove all
Ho It Wo 59-30 conscious contact with **God** as we
Ho It Wo 60-20 That **God** could and would
Ho It Wo 60-23 to **God** as we understood him
Ho It Wo 62-19 **God** makes that possible.
Ho It Wo 62-25 We had to have **God**'s help.
Ho It Wo 62-27 quit playing **God.**
Ho It Wo 62-28 **God** was going to be our Director.
Ho It Wo 63-14 **God,** I offer myself to Thee-
Ho It Wo 63-25 But it is better to meet **God** alone
Ho It Wo 67-3 We asked **God** to help us show them
Ho It Wo 67-7 **God** save me from being angry.
Ho It Wo 67-12 **God** will show us how to take a kindly
Ho It Wo 68-13 relying upon **God.**
Ho It Wo 68-13 We trust infinite **God** rather than
Ho It Wo 68-22,23 They trust their **God.**

Ho It Wo 68-23 We never apologize for **God.**
Ho It Wo 69-20 We asked **God** to mold our ideals
Ho It Wo 69-22 our sex powers were **God** given
Ho It Wo 69-30 In meditation, we ask **God**
Ho It Wo 69-33 **God** alone can judge our
Ho It Wo 70-1 we let **God** be the final judge.
Ho It Wo 70-9,10 honest desire to let **God** take us
Ho It Wo 71-2 **God** can remove whatever self-will
Into Ac 72-10 admitted to **God**, to ourselves, and
Into Ac 75-24 We thank **God** from the bottom
Into Ac 76-3 ready to let **God** remove from us all the
Into Ac 76-7 ask **God** to help us be willing.
Into Ac 77-3,4 be of maximum service to **God**
Into Ac 77-16 the subject of **God**
Into Ac 80-4 asked **God** to help and the drastic step
Into Ac 80-24,25 place the outcome in **God** 's hands
Into Ac 81-26 **God** willing, it shall not be repeated.
Into Ac 83-27 As **God**'s people we stand on our feet;
Into Ac 84-10 realize that **God** is doing for us
Into Ac 84-25 we ask **God** at once to remove them.
Into Ac 85-18,19 carry the vision of **God**'s will into
Into Ac 86-16 we ask **God**'s forgiveness
Into Ac 86-21 we ask **God** to direct our thinking,
Into Ac 86-25 **God** gave us brains to use.
Into Ac 86-30 Here we ask **God** for inspiration,
Into Ac 87-4 conscious contact with **God,**
Into Ac 88-9 we let **God** discipline us
Wo Wi Ot 93-6,7 with your conception of **God.**
Wo Wi Ot 95-25 If he is to find **God,**
Wo Wo Ot 95-29,30 We have no monopoly on **God;**
Wo Wi Ot 98-12 our assistance rather than upon **God.**
Wo Wi Ot 98-18,19 dependence on **God.**
Wo Wi Ot 98-22 trust in **God** and clean house.
Wo Wi Ot 100-1,2 upon his relationship with **God.**
Wo Wi Ot 100-9 put ourselves in **God**'s hands
Wo Wi Ot 102-28 **God** will keep you unharmed.
To Wives 114-17 The power of **God** goes deep.
To Wives 116-15 led to the discovery of **God.**
To Wives 116-17 If **God** can solve the age old riddle

To Wives 116-29,30 were too good to need **God.**

To Wives 117-3 **God** will show you how to have.

To Wives 120-28 **God** has either removed your husband's

To Wives 120-32,33 with everything else, in **God**'s hands.

To Wives 121-10 "Good luck and **God** bless you."

Th Fam Af 123-14 **God,** they believe, almost owes this

Th Fam Af 124-21 in **God**'s hands, the dark past is the greatest

Th Fam Af 128-11 demand that the family find **God**

Th Fam Af 128-18 They may be jealous of a **God** who has

Th Fam Af 128-20 the idea that **God** has accomplished

Th Fam Af 128-26,27 What about his talk that **God** will

Th Fam Af 129-22 superior person with **God** on his side.

Th Fam Af 130-11 the power of **God** in our lives.

Th Fam Af 133-2 We are sure **God** wants us to be happy

Th Fam Af 133-6 **God** didn't do it.

Th Fam Af 133-20 **God** has abundantly supplied

Th Fam Af 133-26 **God** has wrought miracles among us

A Vi Fo You 154-32 His sanity returned and he thanked **God.**

A Vi Fo You 156-1 that **God** might give him mastery.

A Vi Fo You 158-1 I've prayed to **God** on hangover mornings

A Vi Fo You 158-6 **God** ought to be able to do anything.

A Vi Fo you 158-20 But he had found **God**-

A Vi Fo You 158-20 in finding **God** he had found himself.

A Vi Fo You 161-26 united under one **God,**

A Vi Fo You 162-4 the Presence and Power of **God**

A Vi Fo You 164-7 **God** will determine that

A Vi Fo You 164-12 **God** will constantly disclose more to you

A Vi Fo You 164-21 Abandon yourself to **God** as you understand **God.**

God bless you

To Wives 121-10 "Good luck and **God bless you!"**

God-conscious

Into Ac 85-28.29 we have become **God-conscious.**

God-consciousness

Bill's Story 13-21 new **God-consciousness** within.

God-sufficiency

We Ag 52-23 others showed us that **God-sufficiency**

Godly

We Ag 46-6 individuals who claimed to be **godly**

Gone

A Vi Fo Yo 151-6 The old pleasures were **gone.**

Goner

A Vi Fo Yo 157-12 I'm a **goner.**

Good

To Wives 116-29 that we were too **good** to need God.

Good luck

To Wives 121-10 we say, "**Good luck** and God bless you!"

Good nature

To Wives 115-17 **good nature** and lack of

Good news

A Vi Fo You 158-29 who had heard the **good news.**

Good old days

Th Fam Aft 123-11 The **good old days** will soon be back,

Good Samaritan

Wo Wi Ot 97-7 act the **Good Samaritan** every day,

Good will

Into Ac 77-13 interested in a demonstration of **good will**

Gossip

Ho It Wo 65-20 She's a **gossip.**

Th Fam Af 125-12 there might be scandalous **gossip,**

Grant

Into Ac 76-12 **Grant** me strength,

Grasping

Ho It Wo 58-8 incapable of **grasping** and developing

Grave

Ho It Wo 58-11 who suffer from **grave** emotional and mental

Great Fact

A Vi Fo You 164-19 This is the **Great Fact** for us.

Great Reality

We Ag 55-20 We found the **Great Reality** deep down within us.

A Vi Fo You 161-6 They had visioned the **Great Reality-**

Greater

A Vi fo You 163-6 power much **greater** than yourself.

Grew

A Vi Fo You 159-21 They **grew** in numbers.

Grief

Th Fam Af 125-11 would produce untold **grief;**

Grievous

Th Fam af 124-17 no matter how **grievous,**

Grim

To Emp 144-8 will learn the **grim** truth about alcoholism.

Grouch

Ho It Wo 66-21 The **grouch** and the brainstorm were not for us.

Group

Doc's Op xxiv-1 rapid growth inherent in this **group**

Grow

We Ag 47-11 but if we wished to **grow** we had to begin

We Ag 57-12 Some of us **grow** into it more slowly.

Ho It Wo 60-9 we are willing to **grow** along spiritual lines.

Ho It Wo 69-26 willing to **grow** toward it.

Into Ac 84-21 to **grow** in understanding

Th Fam Af 124-8 We **grow** by our willingness to face

A Vi Fo You 162-31 Thus we **grow,**

Growing

Th Fam Af 130-10 by a **growing** consciousness of the power

Growing pains

Th Fam Af 124-33 a few of us have had these **growing pains**

Growth

Bill's Story 12-21 I saw that **growth** could start from that

We Ag 47-7 all we needed to commence spiritual **growth,**

We Ag 47-11 That was **growth,**

Ho It Wo 66-14 and **growth** of a spiritual experience,

Wo Wi Ot 100-22 he has entered upon a period of **growth.**

To Wives 115-13 will disappear with the **growth**

To Wives 117-10 **growth** has only begun.

Th Fam Af 129-10 that his spiritual **growth** is lopsided

Grudge

Ho It Wo 65-3 On our **grudge** list we set opposite

Guidance

Ho It Wo 70-16 for **guidance** in each questionable situation,

Guide

To Wives 120-24 to **guide** his appointments

Guides

Ho It Wo 60-10 set down are **guides** to progress.

Guilty

Into Ac 80-23 stand before his Creator **guilty** of such ruinous

Guts

To Emp 138-29 If he has your will power and **guts**

H

Habit
To Emp 140-9 that you are dealing only with **habit,**
Habits
Into Ac 82-27 Selfish and inconsiderate **habits**
Wo Wi Ot 91-21 about your drinking **habits,**
Wo Wi Ot 102-15 they are not to change their **habits** on
To Wives 118-13 are the **habits** of years.
Habitual
To Emp 149-22 the **habitual** whoopee drinker.
Half
We Ag 44-22 **half** of us thought we were atheists or agnostics
Ho It Wo 70-7 But this only a **half**-truth.
Into Ac 83-30 amazed before we are **half** way through
A Vi Fo You 163-31 more than **half** of those approached
Half measures
Ho It Wo 59-4 **Half measures** availed us nothing.
Half-truth
Ho It Works 70-7 But this is only a **half-truth.**
Hammer
Th Is A So 23-14 beats himself on the head with a **hammer**
Hand of God
Th Is A So 28-8 the loving and powerful **hand of God.**
Handicap
Th Fam Af 125-29 to outgrow that serious **handicap.**
Handicaps
Ho It Wo 71-5 an inventory of your grosser **handicaps,**
Handle
To Wives 109-6 He is positive he can **handle** his liquor
Hands
Wo Wi Ot 100-9 put ourselves in God's **hands**
Th Fam Af 124-21 in God's **hands,** the dark past is

To Emp 138-30 throw up my **hands** in discouragement,

To Emp 143-6 In competent **hands,** this seldom takes long

Hanged

To Emp 137-9 he had **hanged** himself in his woodshed.

Hangover

Wo Wi Ot 102-30 green recruits through a severe **hangover.**

A Vi Fo Yo 158-1 I've prayed to God on **hangover** mornings

Happened

Wo Wi Ot 93-3 Tell him exactly what **happened** to you.

Happens

Into Ac 78-5 out of ten the unexpected **happens.**

Happily

Into Ac 74-1 expect to live long or **happily** in this world.

Happiness

Bill's Story 8-6 There had been much **happiness** after all.

Bill's Story 8-22 I was to know **happiness**

We Ag 49-32 stability, **happiness,** and usefulness

We Ag 50-31 a new power, peace, **happiness**

Ho It Wo 61-21 wrest satisfaction and **happiness** out of

Into Ac 82-9 having the other one's **happiness** uppermost

Into Ac 83-32 a new freedom and a new **happiness.**

To Wives 117-11 In spite of your new-found **happiness,**

Th Fam Af 123-6 longs for the return of **happiness**

Th Fam Af 124-1 that future **happiness** can be based only

Th Fam Af 124-22 the key to life and **happiness**

A Vi Fo You 159-16 by the **happiness** they found in giving

Happy

Th Is A Sol 23-33 the **happy** day may not arrive

Mo Ab Al 32-23 a successful and **happy** business career.

Wo Wi Ot 96-10 an opportunity to live and be **happy.**

Wo Wi Ot 102-11 If it is a **happy** occasion, try to

To Wives 104-12 who have not yet found a **happy** solution.

To Wives 110-27 You have passed **happy** evenings together

To Wives 111-19 even **happy** under these conditions.

To Wives 117-8 you are, of course, going to be very **happy.**

Th Fam Af 130-18 and a life of sane and **happy** usefulness.

Th Fam Af 133-3 to be **happy,** joyous, and free.

A Vi Fo You 152-6 he isn't **happy** about his sobriety.

A Vi Fo You 153-7 **happy,** respected and useful once more.

A Vi Fo You 156-12 came home exhausted but very **happy.**

A Vi Fo You 159-29 **happy** in their release, and constantly

A Vi Fo You 164-26 as you trudge the Road of **Happy** Destiny.

Dr Bob Ni 178-13 they seemed to be **happy.**

Harboring

Ho It Wo 66-17 For when **harboring** such feelings

Hard

Into Ac 74-22 we must be **hard** on ourself.

To Wives 121-6 learn these things the **hard** way.

Th Fam Af 123-23 many seasons of **hard** work

To Emp 142-6 a lack of **hard** feeling toward him.

To Emp 146-6 They work **hard** and play **hard.**

Hard drinker

To Emp 139-13 Whether you are a **hard drinker,**

Hard feeling

A Vi Fo Yo 154-5 with much **hard feeling** and controversy.

Harder

Into Ac 77-24 It is **harder** to go to an enemy

Hardness

Th Fam Af 134-22 pathetic **hardness** and cynicism.

Harm

Ho It Wo 69-27 make amends where we have done **harm,**

Ho It Wo 70-12 and our conduct continues to **harm** others,

Into Ac 77-20 has done us more **harm** than we have done

Into Ac 78-19 it may cause financial **harm.**

To Wives 115-9 not to embarrass or **harm** your husband.

Harmed

Ho It wo 59-22 Made a list of all persons we had **harmed,**

Into Ac 76-18 a list of all persons we had **harmed**

Into Ac 84-27 amends quickly if we have **harmed** anyone.

Harmonious

Th Is A So 17-24 in brotherly and **harmonious** action.

Hate

To Wives 114-30 and you **hate** to meet your friends.

Th Fam Af 134-20 cordially **hate** him for what he has done

Hated

Into Ac 77-19 to approach the man we **hated**

Hatred
Wo Wi Ot 103-3 never to show intolerance or **hatred** of drinking
Haven
A Vi Fo You 160-28 that here was **haven** at last.
Havens
A Vi Fo You 153-21 **havens** for those who must find a way out.
Hazard
To Wives 117-29 resentment is a deadly **hazard** to an alcoholic
Head of the house
Th Fam Af 130-23 the **head of the house** still fails somewhat
Th Fam Af 130-30 that mother became **head of the house.**
Healing
We Ag 57-6 What is this but a miracle of **healing?**
Health
Doc's Op xxiii-6 have witnessed our return to **health.**
To Wives 104-5 women regain their **health** as readily as men
To Wives 112-8 want him to take care of his **health.**
Th Fam Af 133-14 a most powerful **health** restorative.
Th Fam Af 133-15 are miracles of mental **health.**
Th Fam Af 133-20 disregard human **health** measures.
Th Fam Af 133-23 take your **health** problems to such persons.
A Vi Fo You 153-24 and aid others to **health.**
Heart
Bill's Story 9-24 But bless his **heart,** let him rant!
Bill's Story 11-27 something at work in a human **heart**
Into Ac 73-15 knows his **heart** doesn't deserve it.
Into Ac 75-24 thank God from the bottom of our **heart**
To Wives 111-20 Do not set your **heart** on reforming
To Emp 143-19 must undergo a change of **heart.**
Hearts
Th Is A So 25-21 that our Creator has entered into our **hearts.**
Into Ac 82-25 **Hearts** are broken.
A Vi Fo You 161-26 **hearts** and minds attuned to
Heartache
Ho It Wo 70-22 when to yield would mean **heartache.**
Heartbreak
To Wives 111-24 you will save many a **heartbreak**
Heartbreaking
Mo Ab Al 43-22 People like you are too **heartbreaking.**

To Wives 106-3 How **heartbreaking** was this discovery;

To Wives 107-23 It was so baffling, so **heartbreaking.**

A Vi Fo Yo 151-9 a **heartbreaking** obsession

Heartlessness

To Wives 107-17 being convinced of their **heartlessness,**

Heated

To Wives 118-3 have a **heated** discussion,

Th Fam Af 127-30 without **heated** argument,

Heaven

Th Is A So 25-13 We have found much of **heaven**

Heavenly Father

Dr Bob Ni 181-29 Your **Heavenly Father** will never let you down!

Heavy

To Wives 108-33 Your husband may be only a **heavy** drinker.

A Vi Fo Yo 151-5 those last days of **heavy** drinking.

Hell

Th Is A Sol 27-9,10 gates of **hell** had closed on him

We Ag 56-19 he felt as though he lived in **hell.**

Into Ac 81-15 who has literally gone through **hell** for him.

Hellish

Bill's Story 6-30 and mental torture was so **hellish**

Help

Doc's Op xxvii-19 but I cannot! You must **help** me!

Th Is A So 20-3 how we may **help** meet their needs.

Th Is A So 25-32 to accept spiritual **help.**

Th Is A So 27-4 may think they can do without spiritual **help.**

We Ag 52-20 couldn't seem to be of real **help** to other people-

Ho It Wo 59-1 Without **help** it is too much for us.

Ho It Wo 62-25 We had to have God's **help.**

Ho It Wo 63-19 bear witness to those I would **help**

Into Ac 80-4 asked God to **help**

Into Ac 84-28 turn our thoughts to someone we can **help.**

Wo Wi Ot 89-5 You can **help** when no one else can.

Wo Wi Ot 89-9 to see them **help** others.

Wo Wi Ot 90-25 try to **help** others

Wo Wi Ot 95-15 you will do anything to **help.**

Wo Wi Ot 96-24 try to **help** him about getting a job,

To Wives 111-17 your companionship and your **help.**

To Wives 112-12 Drinkers like to **help** other drinkers.

To Wives 116-27 dis not believe we needed this **help.**

Th Fam Af 124-19 how we were given **help**

Th Fam Af 132-31 been given the power to **help** others.

To Emp 141-7 Seeing your attempt to understand and **help,**

To Emp 147-22 trying to **help** serious drinkers

To Emp 147-32 The firm wants to **help** you get over it.

A Vi Fo Yo 159-14 they knew they must **help** other alcoholics

Dr Bob Ni 181-25 that you must have some **help,**

Helped

Wo Wi Ot 94-18 **helped** you more than you have **helped** him.

Th Fam Af 131-31 people will be **helped** by such contacts

To Emp 137-22 **helped** by better understanding

A Vi Fo Yo 158-23 He has **helped** other men recover,

Helpful

Th Is a So 18-30 the sincere desire to be **helpful;**

Mo Ab Al 34-30 quitting for a period of time will be **helpful.**

Ho It Wo 67-6 How can I be **helpful** to him?

Ho It Wo 67-11 we destroy our chance of being **helpful.**

Ho It Wo 67-11 We cannot be **helpful** to all people.

Into Ac 77-26 go to him in a **helpful** and forgiving spirit,

Wo Wi Ot 89-25 To be **helpful** is our only aim.

Wo Wi Ot 94-6 endeavoring to be **helpful** to him.

Wo Wi Ot 102-25 go anywhere if you can be **helpful.**

To Wives 111-32 be **helpful** rather than critical.

To Wives 117-2 nothing will be so **helpful**

To Wives 120-17 how you can be still more **helpful.**

Th Fam Af 133-32 the use of sweets was often **helpful,**

To Emp 138-9 an opportunity to be **helpful,**

To Emp 145-14 make **helpful** suggestions.

A Vi Fo You 162-19 great increase in this **helpful** interchange.

Helpfulness

Wo Wi Ot 99-7 an atmosphere of **helpfulness** and friendliness.

Wo Wi Ot 102-24 be of maximum **helpfulness** to others,

A Vi Fo You 162-16 there is the same **helpfulness**

Helping

Bill's Story 15-7 **helping** other alcoholics to a solution

Wo Wi Ot 94-9 **helping** you more than you are **helping** him.

Wo Wi Ot 97-4 **Helping** others is the foundation stone of

To Wives 119-12 spends long hours **helping** other men

Th Fam Af 129-31 he likes in **helping** other alcoholics.

A Vi Fo You 161-18 **helping** to settle family differences,

A Vi Fo You 164-1 the joy of **helping** others to face life again,

Helpless

Mo Ab Al 33-22 found themselves as **helpless** as those who

Helplessly

A Vi Fo You 152-27 alcoholics are dying **helplessly**

Helps

We Ag 55-24 **helps** sweep away prejudice,

Hide

Dr Bob Ni 176-22 and **hide** it in the coal bin,

Hide out

Dr Bob Ni 176-15 I would sometimes **hide out** in one of the clubs

Highball

Mo Ab Al 41-15 a **highball** would be fine before going to bed,

High-stepping

To Wives 120-20 dislike of his **high-stepping** friends

Himself

Bill's Story 11-16 what he could not do for **himself.**

Th Is A So 21-30 outlook for his family and **himself,**

Th Is A So 24-31 placed **himself** beyond human aid.

Th Is A So 26-7 placing **himself** in the care of a celebrated

Th Is A So 28-2 found **himself** when he had the

Mo Ab Al 32-15 and quieted **himself** with more liquor.

We Ag 48-15 a Power greater than **himself.**

We Ag 50-10 Power which is greater than **himself.**

We Ag 50-15 each individual to settle for **himself.**

Ho It Wo 61-13 He decides to exert **himself** more.

Into Ac 73-21 pushes these memories far inside **himself.**

Into Ac 79-16 sacrifice others to save **himself**

Into Ac 81-7 to feel lonely, sorry for **himself.**

Wo Wi Ot 92-20 little chance he can recover by **himself.**

Th Fam Af 125-22 may criticize or laugh at **himself**

Th Fam Af 129-3 hug the new treasure to **himself.**

Th Fam Af 129-25 he may retreat further into **himself**

To Emp 142-20 not deceiving **himself**

To Emp 144-20 The man must decide for **himself.**

A Vi Fo Yo 152-3 He fools **himself.**

A Vi Fo Yo 158-20 in finding God he had found **himself.**

Holier Than Thou
Th Is A So 18-29 attitude of **Holier Than Thou,**
Home
Into Ac 82-27 have kept the **home** in turmoil.
Wo Wi Ot 97-10 sharing your money and your **home,**
Wo Wi Ot 98-29 lucky enough to have a **home.**
To Wives 115-25 terrible tension which grips the **home**
To Wives 120-8 dismays you by coming **home** drunk.
Th Fam Af 127-19 **home** has suffered more than anything else
A Vi Fo Yo 160-6 placed their large **home** at the disposal
A Vi Fo You 160-9 they have dedicated their **home** to the work.
Home life
Dr Bob Ni 180-27 My **home life** is ideal and my business is
Homeless
Wo Wi Ot 96-23 He may be broke and **homeless.**
Homes
To Wives 105-15 Our **homes** have been battle-grounds
A Vi Fo Yo 159-18 They shared their **homes,**
Honest
Bill's Story 3-6 the last **honest** manual labor on my part
Th Is A Sol 28-20 willing and **honest** enough to try
Mo Ab Al 32-2 if you are **honest** with yourself
We Ag 45-26 shared his **honest** doubt and prejudice.
Ho It Wo 58-5,6 incapable of being **honest** with themselves.
Ho It Wo 58-13 if they have the capacity to be **honest.**
Ho It Wo 70-9 and have the **honest** desire to let God
Into Ac 73-29 Unwilling to be **honest** with these
Into Ac 73-30 were **honest** with no one else.
Into Ac 73-33 We must be entirely **honest** with somebody
Into Ac 83-22 we send them an **honest** letter.
To Wives 117-31 an **honest** difference of opinion.
To Emp 141-4 This is not to say that all alcoholics are **honest**
To Emp 146-32 he knows he must be **honest**
Honestly
Th Is A Sol 26-1 because we **honestly** wanted to
We Ag 44-4 If, when you **honestly** want to
We Ag 47-5 from **honestly** asking yourself
We Ag 55-25 enables you to think **honestly,**
We Ag 57-13 all who have **honestly** sought him.

Ho It Wo 63-29 though if **honestly** and humbly made
Ho It wo 64-18 took stock **honestly.**
Ho It Wo 67-23 admitted our wrongs **honestly**
Into Ac 83-20 if we can **honestly** say to ourselves
Honesty
Bill's Story 13-33 willingness, **honesty** and humility
Ho It Wo 58-9, which demands rigorous **honesty**
Ho It Wo 65-32 thoroughness and **honesty**
Into Ac 73-8, humility, fearlessness and **honesty,**
To Emp 140-33 an alcoholic, sometimes the model of **honesty**
To Emp 145-9 demands rigorous **honesty.**
Honored
Into Ac 75-9 they will be **honored** by our confidence
Hope
Doc's Op xxvii-8 is very little **hope** of
Doc's Op xxix-9 believed that for him there was no **hope.**
Doc's Op xxix-33 felt his only **hope**
Bill's Story 5-13 renewed my wife's **hope**
Th Is A Sol 27-29 This **hope,** however, was destroyed
Th Is A Sol 29-11 We **hope** no one will
Th Is A Sol 29-12 **hope** is that many alcoholic
We Ag 44-2 We **hope** we have made clear
We Ag 44-18 hoping against **hope** we were not
We Ag 45-20 and watch his **hope** rise
We Ag 48-12 we **hope** no one else will be prejudiced
Ho It Wo 71-1 We **hope** you are convinced now that God
Wo Wi Ot 94-11 that you **hope** only that he
Wo Wi Ot 103-14 we **hope** that Alcoholics Anonymous
To Wives 108-5 We **hope** this book has answered
A Vi Fo You 153-15 Our **hope** is that when this chip of a book
A Vi Fo You 162-20 we **hope** that every alcoholic
A Vi Fo You 163-2 We believe and **hope** it contains all you will
Dr Bob Ni 174-32 and, in **hope** of relief,
Hopeful
A Vi Fo You 158-12 scarcely daring to be **hopeful,**
Hopefully
A Vi Fo You 154-19 but why not sit **hopefully** at a table

Hopeless

Doc's Op xxiii-16 as **hopeless.**

Doc's Op xxix-24 deciding his situation **hopeless**

Bill's Story 10-2 for I was **hopeless.**

Bill's Story 14-24 thousands of **hopeless** alcoholics

Th Is A Sol 17-3 just as **hopeless** as Bill

Th Is A Sol 20-8 from a **hopeless** condition of

Th Is A Sol 26-26 he was utterly **hopeless**

Mo Ab Al 42-17 was a **hopeless** condition

Mo Ab Al 43-19 that you were 100% **hopeless**

We Ag 44-12,13 an alcoholic of the **hopeless** variety

Wo Wi Ot 92-10 dwell on the **hopeless** feature of

Wo Wi Ot 94-22 The more **hopeless** he feels, the better.

To Wives 113-29 would be quite **hopeless,**

Hopelessly

Mo Ab Al 42-9 a problem had them **hopelessly** defeated

Hopelessness

Bill's Story 6-8 remorse, horror and **hopelessness**

Th Is A Sol 25-9 **hopelessness** and futility

Mo Ab al 43-15 **hopelessness** of the average alcoholic's

Wo Wi Ot 92-28 the **hopelessness** of alcoholism

A Vi Fo You 153-8 bad repute and **hopelessness?**

A Vi Fo You 157-10 **Hopelessness** was written large on

Hoping

We Ag 44-18 **hoping** against hope we were not true

To Wives 105-3 **hoping** that one day our loved ones

To Wives 105-18,19 only to be back in a little while **hoping,** 3 so **hoping.**

To Emp 147-21 **hoping** matters will take a turn for the better

A Vi Fo You 151-18 **hoping** to find understanding

Horizon

To Wives 117-24 a speck on the domestic **horizon,**

Horrible

Dr Bob Ni 177-17 It was a really **horrible** nightmare,

Horribly

To Wives 114-24 children of such men suffer **horribly,**

A Vi Fo You 159-1 He suffered **horribly** from his sprees,

Horror

Bill's Story 6-8 The remorse, **horror** and hopelessness

Horrors

Th Fam Af 132-23 relive the **horrors** of our past.

Hospital

To Emp 145-20 was sent to a **hospital** for treatment.

A Vi Fo You 160-16 dazed from his **hospital** experience,

Hospitals

A Vi Fo You 161-17 and visiting **hospitals.**

Hospitalized

A Vi Fo You 160-14 wayward mate might be **hospitalized**

Hostility

Wo Wi Ot 103-17 attitude is one of bitterness or **hostility.**

To Wives 113-26 urge action without arousing **hostility.**

Hot stove

Th Is A So 24-19 keeps one from putting his hand on a **hot stove.**

House

A Vi Fo You 161-8 this **house** will hardly accommodate

A Vi Fo You 164-15 if your own **house** is in order.

Housecleaning

Ho It Wo 63-33 is a personal **housecleaning,**

Into Ac 73-4 they never completed their **housecleaning.**

Wo Wi Ot 94-27 a drastic **housecleaning** which requires

Human

Doc's Op xxvii-23 something more than **human** power is

Bill's Story 11-16 His **human** will had failed.

Bill's Story 11-27 something at work in a **human** heart

Th Is A So 18-3 in a way no other **human** sickness can.

Th Is A So 24-31 placed himself beyond **human** aid,

Th Is A So 25-29 no return through **human** aid,

Mo Ab Al 43-29 nor any other **human** being can provide such a

We Ag 45-6 Our **human** resources, as marshalled by the will

We Ag 49-17 that our **human** intelligence was the last word,

We Ag 50-1 we looked st the **human** defects of these people,

We Ag 52-14 apply to our **human** problems this same

We Ag 55-15 demonstrations of that power in **human** lives.

Ho It Wo 59-18 to another **human** being the exact nature of

Ho It Wo 60-18 no **human** power could have relieved our

Ho It Wo 68-31 we find **human** opinions running ro extremes-

Ho It Wo 69-11 We'd hardly be **human** if we didn't.

Into Ac 82-11 that most terrible **human** emotion- jealousy.

Wo Wi Ot 94-19 quiet and full of **human** understanding,

Th Fam Af 128-22 father was beyond **human** aid.

Th Fam Af 133-19 disregard **human** health measures.

Dr Bob Ni 180-18 the first living **human** with whom I had ever

Humanitarian

To Emp 140-6 the reason be **humanitarian** or business

Humanly

We Ag 50-20 the miraculous, the **humanly** impossible.

Humans

Bill's Story 12-26 God is concerned with us **humans**

Humble

Bill's Story 12-31 had been a **humble** willingness

Into Ac 83-26 **humble** without being servile

Humbled

Into Ac 73-7 thought they had **humbled** themselves.

Humbling

Into Ac 72-25 Trying to avoid this **humbling** experience

Humbly

Bill's Story 13-6 There I **humbly** offered myself

We Ag 57-8 He **humbly** offered himself

Ho It Wo 59-29 **Humbly** asked Him to remove our

Ho It Wo 63-29 if honestly and **humbly** made

Ho It Wo 68-16 and **humbly** rely on Him,

Into Ac 88-1 **humbly** saying to ourselves

Humiliated

Mo Ab Al 32-28 puzzled and **humiliated**

Humiliating

Mo Ab Al 40-5 **humiliating** experience, plus the

Th Fam Af 123-30 funny, **humiliating,** shameful or tragic.

Humiliation

Th Is A Sol 22-18,19 attendant suffering and **humiliation**

Th Is A Sol 24-11 suffering and **humiliation** of even

Humility

Bill's Story 13-33 willingness, honesty and **humility**

Into Ac 73-8 had not learned enough of **humility,**

Hundred

Mo Ab Al 42-22 a **hundred** of them had followed successfully.

Hundreds

Th Fam Af 136-3 hired and fired **hundreds** of men.

A Vi Fo You 161-15 Fellowship will number many **hundreds.**

Hurry

To Wives 113-13 the more you **hurry** him the longer

Th Fam Af 128-11 that the family find God in a **hurry,**

Hurt

Bill's Story 13-16 made a list of people I had **hurt**

Th Is A So 18-4 and no one is angry or **hurt.**

Ho It Wo 62-10 Sometimes they **hurt** us,

Ho It Wo 62-13 later placed us in a position to be **hurt.**

Ho It Wo 70-31 listed the people we have **hurt** by our conduct

Into Ac 74-18 which will **hurt** them and make them unhappy.

Into Ac 76-30 and friends we have **hurt**

To Wives 104-23 with **hurt** pride, frustration, self pity,

To Wives 116-33 worry and **hurt** feelings is

To Wives 117-22 **hurt** feelings and resentments.

A Vi Fo Yo 156-8 made the rounds of people he had **hurt.**

Husband

To Wives 108-6 **husband** has been living in that strange world

To Wives 108-33 Your **husband** may be only a heavy drinker.

To Wives 109-13 Your **husband** is showing lack of control,

To Wives 109-32 This **husband** has gone much further

To Wives 110-22 back to **husband** number one.

To Wives 111-2 your **husband** becomes unbearable

To Wives 112-22 **husband** fits the description of number two.

To Wives 113-14 If you have a number three **husband**

To Wives 114-19 have a **husband** who is at large,

To Wives 114-29 If your **husband** is a drinker,

To Wives 115-9 not to embarrass or harm your **husband.**

To Wives 115-16 as though your **husband** were a weak

To Wives 116-6 afraid your **husband** will lose his position.

To Wives 116-11 It may convince your **husband**

To Wives 117-4 Go along with your **husband**

To Wives 117-22 **husband** will sometimes be unreasonable

To Wives 119-7 you and your **husband** are working together

To Wives 119-27 that you and your **husband** have been

To Wives 120-6 Perhaps your **husband** will make

A Vi Fo Yo 158-13 saw something different about her **husband**

Husbands

To Wives 105-5 that our **husbands** hold up their heads
To Wives 105-9 and our **husband's** reputations.
To Wives 105-28 our **husbands** sneaked so many drinks
To Wives 108-14 most of our men are better **husbands**
To Wives 110-20 many of our **husbands** were just as far gone.
To Wives 111-14 that your **husband's** drinking is not
To Wives 116-23 **husbands** began to apply spiritual
To Wives 116-28 if our **husbands** stopped drinking.
To Wives 118-28 could not cure our **husbands**
To Wives 120-19 **husband's** chance of recovery
A Vi Fo You 160-12 to hear from the lips of their **husbands**

Hysterical

Ho It Wo 70-3 We avoid **hysterical** thinking or advice.
To Wives 105-12 We have been **hysterical,**

I

Idea

Bill's Story 15-7 the **idea** of helping other alcoholics to a
Th Is A So 23-20 no more **idea** why he took that first drink
Th Is A So 24-16 old threadbare **idea** that this time we
Th Is A So 29-10 **idea** of what has actually happened
Mo Ab Al 30-6 The **idea** that somehow, someday he will control
Mo Ab Al 37-15 The insane **idea** won out.
We Ag 45-33 we had abandoned the God **idea** entirely.
We Ag 49-26 have a logical **idea** of what life is all about.
We Ag 52-27 But the God **idea** did.
We Ag 52-32 sticking to the **idea** that self-sufficiency would
We Ag 55-11 the fundamental **idea** of God.
Wo Wi Ot 98-20 Burn the **idea** into the consciousness of every
To Wives 116-29 But it was a silly **idea**
Th Fam Af 123-33 family may be possessed by the **idea**
Th Fam Af 128-20 the **idea** that God has accomplished the

Ideal

Ho It Wo 69-18 tried to shape a sane and sound **ideal** for

Ho It Wo 70-5 Suppose we fall short of the chosen **ideal**

Ho It Wo 70-16 We earnestly pray for the right **ideal,**

To Wives 118-19 a picture of the **ideal** man.

Ideals

Ho It Wo 69-21 We asked God to mold our **ideals**

Ideas

Doc's Op xxiii-18 he acquired certain **ideas** concerning a

Doc's Op xxv-22 while here he acquired some **ideas** which

Doc's Op xxx-1 become "sold" on the **ideas** contained

Bill's Story 11-28 My **ideas** about miracles were drastically

Th Is A So 27-18 **Ideas,** emotions and attitudes

Mo Ab Al 38-1 having queer **ideas** of fun.

We Ag 52-26 Our **ideas** did not work.

Ho It Wo 58-23 have tried to hold on to our old **ideas**

Ho It Wo 62-31 Most good **ideas** are simple,

Ho It Wo 60-15 make clear three pertinent **ideas:**

Ho It Wo 62-31 Most good **ideas** are simple.

Into Ac 87-7 absurd actions and **ideas.**

Th Fam Aft 122-10 likely to have fixed **ideas**

Ignorance

Bill's Story 2-29 lost money in stocks through **ignorance**

Th Is A So 20-26 a world of **ignorance** and misunderstanding.

To Wives 107-10 rose out of **ignorance** of alcoholism.

Ill

Th Is A Sol 20-5 became so very **ill** from drinking.

Ho It Wo 64-26 mentally and physically **ill,**

Into Ac 77-27 confessing our former **ill** feeling

Wo Wi Ot 89-7 Remember they are very **ill.**

To Wives 108-20 remember that he is very **ill.**

Th Fam Af 122-24 The entire family is, to some extent, **ill.**

To Emp 140-14 concede that your employee is **ill,**

To Emp 142-8 you believe he is a gravely **ill** person,

To Emp 142-9 being perhaps fatally **ill,**

A Vi Fo You 155-7 home in jeopardy, wife **ill,**

Illness

Th Is A Sol 18-1 An **illness** of this sort- and we have come to believe it an **illness-**

Th Is A Sol 18-5 not so with the alcoholic **illness,**

Mo Ab Al 30-23 the grip of a progressive **illness.**

We Ag 44-8 suffering from an **illness**

Wo Wi Ot 92-21 Continue to speak of alcoholism as an **illness,**

To Wives 115-8 know the nature of his **illness.**

To Wives 118-30 we forget that alcoholism is an **illness**

To Emp 139-1 suffered from a serious **illness.**

To Emp 142-8 to explain alcoholism, the **illness.**

Illuminating

Into Ac 75-11 **illuminating** every twist of character,

Illusion

Mo Ab Al 30-9 The persistence of this **illusion** is astonishing.

Illustration

Mo Ab Al 38-22 **illustration** would fit us exactly.

Imagination

A Vi Fo Yo 151-2 and colorful **imagination.**

A Vi Fo Yo 152-20 Your **imagination** will be fired.

Imaginative

To Emp 139-33 fast-thinking, **imaginative** and likeable?

Imagine

A Vi Fo yo 152-7 will be unable to **imagine** life

Immune

Mo Ab Al 33-14 that someday we will be **immune** to alcohol.

Immunity

Wo Wi Ot 89-2 insure **immunity** from drinking

Impaired

To Wives 114-1 Some men have been so **impaired** by alcohol

Impatient

Wo Wi Ot 100-23 remember, when they are **impatient,**

Important

Th Is A So 21-23 when some **important** decision must

We Ag 51-8 God is today the most **important** fact of their lives,

Impose

To Emp 141-6 such people often may **impose** on you.

To Emp 149-30 He will not **impose.**

Impossible

Bill's Story 11-27 which had done the **impossible.**

Bill's Story 15-24 most **impossible** domestic situations righted;

Th Is A So 18-15 **impossible** to persuade an alcoholic to
Th Is A So 22-33 virtually **impossible** for him to stop.
Th Is A So 25-27 where life was becoming **impossible,**
We Ag 44-11 such an experience seems **impossible,**
We Ag 50-20 the humanly **impossible.**
We Ag 54-18 It was **impossible** to say we had no
We Ag 46-18 It was **impossible** for any of us to fully define
We Ag 50-20 the miraculous, the humanly **impossible.**
We Ag 54-18 **impossible** to say we had no capacity for faith,
Wo Wi Ot 101-21 These attempts to do the **impossible**
Impotent
Th Fam Af 134-10 the man tends to be **impotent.**
Impressionable
Th Fam Af 134-19 their young minds were **impressionable**
Improve
Ho It Wo 59-30 **improve** our conscious contact with God
Improved
Th Fam Af 127-2 dad, though marvelously **improved**
Inability
Mo Ab Al 31-13 showing **inability** to control his drinking
Mo Ab Al 33-30 astonished at their **inability** to stop.
Mo Ab Al 34-25 this utter **inability** to leave it alone,
We Ag 47-32 **inability** to accept much on faith,
Inattention
Th Fam Af 126-14 Mother may complain of **inattention.**
Incapable
Ho It Wo 58-5 who are constitutionally **incapable** of being
Ho It Wo 58-8 are naturally **incapable** of grasping
Incapacitated
Th Fam Af 130-29 Liquor **incapacitated** father
Include
Th Fam Af 129-12 does not **include** his family obligations
Incompatibility
To Wives 108-10 is such a thing as **incompatibility.**
Incompatible
Th Fam Af 130-17 We have found nothing **incompatible**
Inconsiderate
Into Ac 82-27 Selfish and **inconsiderate** habits
To Wives 108-11 seems to be unloving and **inconsiderate;**

Th Fam Af 125-26 one careless, **inconsiderate** remark
Inconsistencies
Wo Wi Ot 92-7 your mental **inconsistencies**
Inconsistency
Into Ac 73-16 The **inconsistency** is made worse by
Increase
A Vi Fo You 162-19 we foresee a great **increase**
Incredible
To Emp 141-1 will do **incredible** things.
Incurable
Bill's Story 11-17 Doctors had pronounced him **incurable.**
Indebted
A Vi Fo Yo 162-5 We are greatly **indebted** to the doctor
Indecision
Into Ac 86-28 we may face **indecision.**
Indefinable
A Vi Fo You 160-26 that **indefinable** something in the eyes
Indifference
Th Fam Af 128-12 or exhibit amazing **indifference** to them
Individual
Th Fam Af 132-11 Each **individual** should consult his own
Indulge
Th Fam Af 132-18 We try not to **indulge** in cynicism
Indulgence
Dr Bob Ni 174-30 return to my former excessive **indulgence.**
Indulged
Th Fam Af 128-30 have **indulged** in spiritual intoxication.
Inexperienced
Into Ac 87-3 Being still **inexperienced** and having
Informal meetings
A Vi Fo You 162-13 there are **informal meetings** such as
Informality
A Vi Fo You 160-30 the **informality,**
Information
Th Fam Af 125-14 take advantage of intimate **information.**
Injure
Ho It Wo 59-25 to do so would **injure** them or others.
Injustice
Into Ac 77-6 smarts from our **injustice** to him,

Irrational

To Emp 140-22 an alcoholic is strangely **irrational.**

Insane

Th Is A Sol 24-32 die or go permanently **insane**

Mo Ab Al 37-15 The **insane** idea won out

Mo Ab Al 38-24 we have been strangely **insane.**

To Wives 110-14 appears definitely **insane** when drunk.

Insanely

Th Is A Sol 21-17 more or less **insanely** drunk.

Mo Ab Al 37-13 some **insanely** trivial excuse

Mo Ab Al 37-22 justification for a spree was **insanely**

To Wives 120-21 **insanely** trivial excuses to drink.

Insanity

Bill's Story 8-15 **insanity** of that first drink,

Bill's Story 9-4 for alcoholic **insanity**

Mo Ab Al 30-10 gates of **insanity** or death.

Mo Ab Al 37-4 we call this plain **insanity**

Mo Ab Al 40-20 the subtle **insanity** which precedes

We Ag 56-5 Business failure, **insanity,** fatal illness,

Ho It Wo 66-18 The **insanity** of alcohol returns

To Wives 107-7 screaming delirium and **insanity.**

A Vi Fo You 154-24 the old, insidious **insanity**- that first drink.

Insecurity

Th Is A so 18-8 financial **insecurity,** disgusted friends

Into Ac 84-8 of economic **insecurity** will leave us.

Insidious

A Vi Fo You 154-24 old, **insidious** insanity- that first drink.

Insincere

Wo Wi Ot 96-32 making it possible for him to be **insincere.**

Insist

Into Ac 81-22 She may **insist** on knowing all the particulars.

Th Fam Af 132-17 We absolutely **insist** on enjoying life.

Inspiration

Into Ac 85-25 receiving strength, **inspiration,**

Into Ac 86-30 we ask God for **inspiration,**

Institution

To Wives 110-13 placed on one **institution** after another.

A Vi Fo You 163-28 which flows through that **institution.**

Insufficient

Into Ac 72-18 find a solitary self-appraisal **insufficient.**

Wo Wi Ot 93-25 faith alone is **insufficient.**
Insulted
To Wives 109-8 **insulted** if he were called an alcoholic.
Insurance
To Emp 137-8 husband's company **insurance** was still in
Intelligent
Mo Ab Al 38-22 However **intelligent** we may have been
Intense
Mo Ab Al 36-29 **intense** mental and physical suffering
Intensive
Wo Wi Ot 89-2 **intensive** work with other alcoholics.
Interchange
A Vi Fo Yo 162-19 great increase in this helpful **interchange.**
Interest
Into Ac 84-5 We will lose **interest** in selfish things
Into Ac 84-5 and gain **interest** in our fellows.
Th Fam Af 126-10 small **interest** in the children
Th Fam Af 131-13 When he renews **interest** in such things,
Interested
Wo Wi Ot 95-21 if he is sincerely **interested** and wants
To Emp 136-12 I told her to say that I was not **interested.**
Internship
Dr Bob Ni 174-20 to secure a much coveted **internship**
Intervention
To Emp 137-16 **intervention** of an understanding person
Intimate
Into Ac 74-3 to take this **intimate** and confidential step.
Th Fam Af 125-13 take advantage of **intimate** information.
Th Fam Af 125-19 we do not relate **intimate** experiences
Intolerable
Th Is a So 25-31 consciousness of our **intolerable** situation
Intolerance
We Ag 50-3 We talked of **intolerance,**
Wo Wi Ot 103-3 We are careful never to show **intolerance**
Wo Wi Ot 103-8 A spirit of **intolerance** might repel
Th Fam Af 135-14 her **intolerance** finally threw him into
A Vi Fo You 160-30 the absence of **intolerance** of any kind,
Intolerant
We Ag 50-4 while we were **intolerant** ourselves.

Intoxicated

Th Is A So 21-16 He is seldom mildly **intoxicated.**

Th Is A So 21-32 fellow who goes to bed so **intoxicated** he

Mo Ab Al 35-18 became so violent when **intoxicated**

Intoxication

Th Fam Af 128-31 have indulged in spiritual **intoxication.**

Intuitive

Into Ac 86-30 an **intuitive** thought or a decision.

Intuitively

Into Ac 84-8 **intuitively** know how to handle situations

Inventory

Ho It Wo 59-15 Made a searching and fearless moral **inventory**

Ho It Wo 59-27 Continued to take personal **inventory**

Ho It Wo 64-8 started upon a personal **inventory**

Ho It Wo 64-10 business which takes no regular **inventory**

Ho It Wo 64-11 **inventory** is a fact finding

Ho It Wo 67-20 the **inventory** was ours,

Ho It Wo 70-23 thorough about our personal **inventory**

Ho It Wo 71-4 made a decision and an **inventory**

Into Ac 72-1 Having made our personal **inventory**

Into Ac 72-7 weak items in our personal **inventory.**

Into Ac 73-4 They took **inventory** all right,

Into Ac 75-4 We have a written **inventory,**

Into Ac 76-19 We made it when we took **inventory.**

Into Ac 84-17 continue to take personal **inventory**

Ho It Wo 64-8 we started upon a personal **inventory,**

Ho It Wo 64-10 which takes no regular **inventory** usually goes

Ho It Wo 67-20 The **inventory** was ours, not the other man's.

Ho It Wo 70-24 thorough about our personal **inventory,**

Ho It Wo 71-4 an **inventory** of your grosser handicaps,

Into Ac 72-1 Having made our personal **inventory,**

Into Ac 73-7 weak items in our personal **inventory.**

Into Ac 73-4 They took **inventory** all right,

Into Ac 75-4 a written **inventory** and we are prepared

Into Ac 84-17 we continue to take personal **inventory**

Invited

A Vi Fo Yo 155-26 he **invited** our friend to his home.

Involve

Into Ac 81-25 no right to **involve** another person.

Involved

Into Ac 81-13 A man so **involved** often feels very remorseful

Irate

A Vi Fo You 161-19 to his **irate** parents,

Irony

To Emp 137-15 What **irony** - I became an alcoholic

Irrational

To Emp 140-22 an alcoholic is strangely **irrational.**

Irresponsibility

Th Fam Af 129-30 **irresponsibility** toward the family,

Irresponsible

To Emp 139-29 be so weak, stupid and **irresponsible.**

Irritation

To Wives 117-21 snags you will encounter are **irritation,**

Th Fam Af 126-11 and may show **irritation** when reproved

Th Fam Af 128-9 then with **irritation.**

Isolates

To Wives 119-29 many times **isolates** the wife

Th Fam Af 131-10 Drinking **isolates** most homes from the

Issue

Th Fam Af 135-22 was wrong to make a burning **issue** out of

J

Jail

Into Ac 78-27 might land us in **jail** if it were known

Into Ac 79-12 or face **jail,** but we are willing.

Into Ac 79-26 in **jail** he could provide nothing

Into Ac 79-31 willing to go to **jail** if she insisted.

Jay-walking

More Ab Al 37-30 with a passion, say, for **jay-walking**

Mo Ab Al 38-7 stop **jay-walking** for good

Mo Ab Al 38-13 to get the **jay-walking** idea out

Mo Ab Al 38-21 substituted alcoholism for **jay-walking**

Jealous

To Wives 119-10 you may become **jealous** of the attention

Jealousy

Mo Ab Al 37-20 worry, depression, **jealousy** or the like.

Into Ac 82-3 upon whom she can vent **jealousy**

Into Ac 82-11 that most terrible human emotion- **jealousy.**

Th Fam Af 131-13 a feeling of **jealousy** may arise.

To Emp 145-19 resentment, **jealousy,** envy, frustration,

Jeopardize

To Emp 147-22 They often **jeopardize** their own positions

Jeopardy

To Wives 105-32 Positions were always in **jeopardy.**

A Vi Fo Yo 155-7 home in **jeopardy,** wife ill,

Jittery

Wo Wi Ot 91-16 Call on him while he is still **jittery.**

A Vi Fo Yo 163-4 I'm **jittery** and alone.

Jitters

Mo Ab Al 39-23 recover from a bad case of **jitters.**

Dr Bob Ni 173-5 beginning to have morning **jitters** at times.

Dr Bob Ni 173-16 the fraternity house because of my **jitters,**

Dr Bob Ni 176-5 doses of sedatives to quiet the **jitters,**

Dr Bob Ni 176-12 by a morning of unbearable **jitters.**

Dr Bob Ni 177-19 getting drunk, morning **jitters,**

Jittery

A Vi Fo You 163-4 I'm **jittery** and alone.

Into Ac 62-3 upon whom she can vent **jealousy.**

Job

To Emp 138-28 or he is minus a **job.**

To Emp 146-31 even if it means the loss of his **job.**

To Emp 148-32 drinks so much that his **job** suffers,

Jobs

A Vi Fo You 161-20 lending money and securing **jobs**

Join

A Vi Fo You 164-24 of what you find and **join** us.

Jolt

To Emp 141-13 It may be just the **jolt** he needs.

Journey

Th Fam Aft 122-25 as they start their **journey,**

Journeys

A Vi Fo Yo 162-21 every alcoholic who **journeys** will find a

Joy

Th Is A Sol 17-15 our **joy** in escape from disaster

Th Fam Af 128-33 **Joy** at our release from a lifetime of

Th Fam Af 132-16 If newcomers could see no **joy** or fun

A Vi Fo You 164-1 the **joy** of helping others to face life again,

Joyous

Th Fam Af 133-3 to be happy, **joyous,** and free.

A Vi Fo You 151-4 It is **joyous** intimacy with friends

Joyousness

Th Is a Sol 17-13 camaraderie, **joyousness,** and democracy

Judge

Ho It Wo 69-33 God alone can **judge** our sex situation.

Ho It Wo 70-2 let God be the final **judge.**

Into Ac 79-23 if he had walked up to the **Judge** and

Judgement

To Wives 107-30 What had become of their **judgement,**

Th Fam Af 135-21 his wife nor anyone else stands in **judgment.**

Jumped

To Emp 136-21 Paul **jumped** from a hotel window

Jumping-off

A Vi Fo Yo 152-10 He will be at the **jumping-off** place.

Justifiable

Into Ac 81-29 Though there may be **justifiable** exceptions,

Justification

Mo Ab Al 37-22 our **justification** for a spree was insanely

Th Fam Af 126-33 each side may have some **justification.**

Th Fam Af 129-26 feel he has spiritual **justification** for so doing.

Justified

Mo Ab Al 37-19 feeling ourselves **justified** by nervousness,

K

Keep

Into Ac 82-16 he needs to do is to **keep** sober.

Into Ac 82-17 Certainly he must **keep** sober,

Into Ac 85-11 so long as we **keep** in fit spiritual

Wo Wi Ot 102-29 Many of us **keep** liquor in our home.

Keep you

A Vi Fo You 164-27 May God bless you and **keep you-**

Keeping

To Emp 141-11 You are not doing him a favor by **keeping** him

Kept Into Ac 86-7 Have we **kept** something to ourselves

Key

Th Fam Af 124-22 the **key** to life and happiness

Kill

Bill's Story 6-18 Should I **kill** myself?

Th Is A So 20-23 ever drank again it would **kill** him,

Ho It Wo 66-29 had power to actually **kill.**

Killjoy

To Wives 111-8 that you are a nag or a **killjoy,**

Killjoys

To Wives 105-30 self-pity made them **killjoys.**

Kind

Into Ac 86-9 Were we **kind** and loving toward all?

Kindliness

Into Ac 83-10 the way of patience, tolerance, **kindliness**

Kindly

Ho It Wo 67-13 a **kindly** and tolerant view of each and every

Wo Wi Ot 97-6 A **kindly** act once in a while

Kindness

Into Ac 82-7 the way of good sense and loving **kindness**

To Emp 141-8 men will try to take advantage of your **kindness.**

King Alcohol

A Vi Fo yo 151-15 we became subjects of **King Alcohol,**

Kissed

To Wives 105-16 In the morning we have **kissed** and made up.

Knees
We Ag 56-23 he tumbled out of bed to his **knees.**
Knocks
Wo Wi Ot 98-15 Some of us have taken very hard **knocks**
Knowledge
Doc's Op xxv-19 that lie outside our synthetic **knowledge.**
Th Is A So 19-22 our combined experience and **knowledge.**
Mo Ab Al 32-3 get a full **knowledge** of your condition.
Mo Ab Al 36-31 had much **knowledge** about himself
Mo Ab Al 40-5 plus the **knowledge** he had acquired,
Ho It Wo 59-31 praying only for **knowledge** of His will for us
Into Ac 85-26 from Him who has all **knowledge** and power.
Wo Wi Ot 93-30 however deep his faith and **knowledge,**
To Emp 139-9 and lack of **knowledge** as to what part

L

Labor
A Vi Fo You 163-9 willingness, patience and **labor.**
Ladies
To Wives 106-8 and even the **ladies** they sometimes brought
Last
To Emp 138-16 this was his **last** chance.
To Emp 144-4 as the **last** word on this subject,
Last drink
Dr Bob Ni 180-3 June 10, 1935, and that was my **last drink.**
Laugh
Th Fam Af 125-22 may criticize or **laugh** at himself
Th Fam Af 132-33 who seldom play, do not **laugh** much.
A Vi Fo You 157-27 both the visitors burst into a **laugh.**
A Vi Fo You 157-28 Damn little to **laugh** about that I can see.
Laughed
A Vi Fo You 160-20 who **laughed** at their own misfortunes
A Vi Fo Yo 161-24 these are **laughed** out of countenance.

Laughter

Th Fam Af 125-12 **laughter** at the expense of other people,

Th Fam Af 132-26 cheerfulness and **laughter** make for useful-

Lawyer

A Vi Fo You 156-27 was once a well-known **lawyer** in town,

A Vi Fo You 158-9 the **lawyer** gave his life to the care

A Vi Fo You 159-4 room recently vacated by the **lawyer.**

Learn

To Wives 121-6 **learn** these things the hard way.

Learned

Into Ac 73-8 they had not **learned** enough of humility,

Leave

To Wives 111-3 and you have to **leave** him temporarily

Leave of absence

To Emp 138-14 from a three month **leave of absence,**

Lecture

Wo Wi Ot 91-29 careful not to moralize or **lecture.**

To Wives 121-2 We may have seemed to **lecture.**

To Wives 121-4 care for people who **lecture** us.

Left off

Mo Ab Al 33-8 where he had **left off** at thirty.

Lend

A Vi Fo You 162-27 enables us to **lend** a hand,

Lending

A Vi Fo You 161-20 **lending** money and securing jobs

Length

Ho It Wo 58-17 willing to go to any **length**

To Wives 115-7 need not discuss your husband at **length,**

To Emp 140-12 sickness is discussed at **length**

Lengths

Into Ac 76-26 we would go to any **lengths** for victory

Into Ac 79-8 we have decided to to any **lengths** to find

Less likely

Th Fam Af 130-4 He will be **less likely** to drink again,

Lessen

To Wives 120-18 may **lessen** your husband's chance

Letter

To Emp 136-25 as I opened a **letter** which lay on my desk,

Liberation

We Ag 55-4 a spiritual **liberation** from this world,

Licked

Mo Ab Al 42-14 and if I were really **licked** this time.

Lie

To Wives 115-32 should not cause you to **lie** to people

Lies

To Wives 105-8 We have told innumerable **lies** to protect

Life

Doc's Op xxiv-15 just because we were maladjusted to **life,**

Doc's Op xxix-7 had lost everything worthwhile in **life**

Bill's Story 1-6 I was part of **life** at last,

Bill's Story 11-21 a level of **life** better than the best he had

Bill's Story 16-8 or would not, see our way of **life.**

Th Is a so 18-6 all the things worth while in **life.**

Th Is A So 25-9 the hopelessness and futility of **life**

Th Is A So 25-19 our whole attitude toward **life,**

Th Is A So 25-27 where **life** was becoming impossible,

Th Is A So 28-8 A new **life** has been given us

Mo Ab Al 43-2 more useful than the **life** I lived before.

Mo Ab Al 43-3 My old manner of **life** was by no means

We Ag 49-13 that **life** originated out of nothing,

We Ag 49-26 have a logical idea of what **life** is all about.

We Ag 51-3 were making heavy going of **life.**

We Ag 54-22 Imagine **life** without faith!

We Ag 54-23 but pure reason, it wouldn't be **life.**

We Ag 54-24 But we believed in **life-**

Ho It Wo 60-22 decided to turn our will and our **life** over to God

Ho It Wo 60-26 any **life** run on self-will can hardly be a success.

Ho It Wo 61-12 **life** doesn't treat him right.

Ho It Wo 63-8 what we could contribute to **life.**

Ho It Wo 63-10 we could face **life** successfully,

Ho It Wo 63-19 Thy love, and Thy way of **life.**

Ho It Wo 66-10 a **life** which includes deep resentment leads

Into Ac 73-10 told someone else all their **life** story.

Into Ac 73-11 the alcoholic leads a double **life.**

Into Ac 84-7 outlook upon **life** will change.

Into Ac 88-7 trying to arrange **life** to suit ourselves.

Wo Wi Ot 89-8 **Life** will take on new meaning.

Wo Wi Ot 97-28 should be offered your way of **life.**
Wo Wi Ot 99-21 fully understand his new way of **life.**
Wo Wi Ot 102-20 withdrawing from **life** little by little.
Wo Wi Ot 102-27 Keep on the firing line of **life**
To Wives 108-28 Is it right to let him ruin your **life**
To Wives 111-17 to have a full and useful **life,**
To Wife 114-26 sometimes you must start **life** anew.
To Wives 114-28 women adopt a spiritual way of **life**
To Wives 116-16 how much better **life** is
To Wives 120-2 think of what you can put into **life**
To Wives 120-5 You will lose the old **life**
Th Fam Af 122-19 take from the family **life**
Th Fam Af 124-19 makes **life** seem so worth while
Th Fam Af 124-22 the key to **life** and happiness
Th Fam Af 129-6 for the rest of his **life**
Th Fam Af 130-18 a **life** of sane and happy usefulness.
Th Fam Af 131-22 an effective part in the new **life.**
Th Fam Af 132-17 insist on enjoying **life.**
Th Fam Af 133-4 that this **life** is a vale of tears,
To Emp 146-9 a **life** which knows no alcohol,
A Vi Fo You 151-4 a feeling that **life** is good.
A Vi Fo You 151-9 yearning to enjoy **life**
A Vi Fo You 151-14 from society, from **life** itself.
A Vi Fo You 152-6 cannot picture **life** without alcohol.
A Vi Fo You 152-20 **Life** will mean something at last.
A Vi Fo You 153-3 survive and rediscover **life.**
A Vi Fo You 156-16 **life** was not easy for the two friends.
A Vi Fo You 158-9 the lawyer gave his **life** to the care
A Vi Fo You 159-13 had found something brand new in **life.**
A Vi Fo You 161-16 But **life** among Alcoholics Anonymous
A Vi Fo You 164-2 helping others to face **life** again.
Life-and-death
Into Ac 75-7 we are engaged upon a **life-and-death** errand.
Lifetime
Into Ac 84-23 It should continue for our **lifetime.**
Th Fam Af 127-13 square the account in his **lifetime.**
Th Fam Af 128-33 from a **lifetime** of frustration
Lifelong
Mo Ab Al 42-27 throw several **lifelong** conceptions out

A Vi Fo You 152-31 you will make **lifelong** friends
Like
Ho It Wo 58-15 what we used to be **like,**
Ho It wo 58-15 and what we are **like** now.
Likeable
To Emp 139-33 fast-thinking, imaginative and **likeable?**
Lips
A Vi Fo Yo 160-12 to hear the **lips** of their husbands
Liquor
Doc's Op xxvi-1 physical craving for **liquor,**
Bill's Story 1-7 midst of the excitement I discovered **liquor.**
Bill's Story 3-31 **Liquor** caught up with me
Bill's Story 5-3 **Liquor** ceased to be a luxury;
Bill's Story 7-16 when it comes to combating **liquor**
Th Is a So 20-18 That fellow can't handle his **liquor.**
Th Is A So 20-30 trouble in giving up **liquor** entirely
Th Is A So 21-12 lose all control of his **liquor** consumption,
Th Is A So 21-26 concerning everything except **liquor,**
Th Is A So 22-3 he may have **liquor** concealed
Th Is A So 22-7 sedative and **liquor** to quiet his nerves
Mo Ab Al 32-15 and quieted himself with more **liquor.**
Mo Ab Al 34-5 let him try leaving **liquor** alone for one year.
Ho It Wo 64-5 Our **liquor** was but a symptom.
Into Ac 85-3 our new attitude toward **liquor**
Wo Wi Ot 91-28 troubles **liquor** has caused you,
Wo Wi Ot 102-22 just because your friends drink **liquor.**
Wo Wi Ot 102-29 Many of us keep **liquor** in our homes.
To Wives 109-6 He is positive he can handle his **liquor,**
To Wives 110-31 all about **liquor** as a social lubricant.
To Wives 118-21 once his **liquor** problem is solved,
Th Fam Af 13-29 **Liquor** incapacitated father
To Emp 138-28 this chap is either through with **liquor**
To Emp 139-21 take your **liquor** or leave it alone.
To Emp 139-25 To you, **liquor** is no real problem.
To Emp 143-9 and no longer craves **liquor.**
A Vi Fo Yo 152-15 I know I must get along without **liquor,**
A Vi Fo Yo 155-28 control of his **liquor** situation,
Dr Bob Ni 174-8 a great deal more hard **liquor**
Dr Bob Ni 175-20 of **liquor** as their exchequers permitted,

Dr Bob Ni 175-33 the fear of running out of **liquor.**

Dr Bob Ni 176-2 I would run out of **liquor.**

Dr Bob Ni 176-21 get a large supply of **liquor** and smuggle it

Dr Bob Ni 177-14 but in order to get more **liquor**

Dr Bob Ni 177-18 getting **liquor,** smuggling it home,

Dr Bob Ni 179-27 I bought some **liquor** on the way to the depot.

Dr Bob Ni 181-8 I did not get over my craving for **liquor**

Dr Bob Ni 181-16 and pour **liquor** down my throat.

Dr Bob Ni 181-24 to quit drinking **liquor** for good

Liquor problem

Dr Bob Ni 178-27 an answer to my **liquor problem.**

Listed

Ho It Wo 64-29 We **listed** people, institutions or principles

Live

We Ag 44-14 to **live** on a spiritual basis

We Ag 45-10 find a power by which we could **live,**

Ho It wo 60-29 Most people try to **live** by self-propulsion.

Ho It Wo 62-22 but we could not **live** up to them

Ho It Wo 66-20 If we were to **live,** we had to be free of anger.

Ho It Wo 69-21 and help us to **live** up to them.

Into Ac 76-23 to **live** on self-will

Into Ac 83-11 not a theory. We have to **live** it.

Into Ac 83-12 a desire to **live** upon spiritual principles

Wo Wi Ot 96-10 to **live** and be happy.

To Wives 117-17 you will be learning to **live.**

To Wives 118-7 trying to **live** on aq spiritual basis,

To Wives 118-16 **Live** and let **live** is the rule.

To Wives 119-30 and a great cause to **live** for

Th Fam Af 135-27 **Live** and let **live**

To Emp 146-32 must be honest if he would **live** at all.

Lived

We Ag 56-18 felt as though he **lived** in hell.

To Wives 116-17 when **lived** on a spiritual plane.

Th Fam Af 135-5 families who have **lived** with a drinker.

A Vi Fo Yo 155-18 he **lived** in constant worry

Lives

Doc's Op xxvi-18 if they are to re-create their **lives.**

Bill's Story 15-27 resume a vital place in the **lives** of

Th Is A so 18-7 It engulfs all whose **lives** touch the sufferer's.

Th Is A So 18-9 warped **lives** of blameless children,
Th Is A So 25-20 The central fact of our **lives** today
Th Is A So 25-22 entered into our hearts and **lives**
Th Is A So 27-20 guiding forces of the **lives** of these men
Th Is A So 29-10 actually happened in their **lives.**
We Ag 51-8 most important fact of their **lives,**
Ho It Wo 60-17 could not manage our own **lives.**
Ho It Wo 65-31 We went back through our **lives.**
Ho It Wo 67-28 touches about every aspect of our **lives.**
Into Ac 72-25 keep to themselves certain facts about their **lives.**
Into Ac 77-2 trying to put our **lives** in order
Into Ac 82-25 like a tornado roaring it's way through the **lives**
Wo Wi Ot 89-14 is the bright spot of our **lives.**
Wo Wi Ot 103-9 whose **lives** could have been saved,
To Wives 108-28 and the **lives** of your children?
To Wives 116-31 in every department of our **lives.**
To Wives 120-4 your **lives** will be fuller
Th Fam Af 130-11 the power of God in our **lives.**

Living
Doc's Op xxix-8 and was only **living,** one might say, to drink.
Bill's Story 2-22 **Living** modestly, my wife and I saved $1,000.
Bill's Story 13-31 a way of **living** which answered all my
Bill's Story 15-18 a design for **living** that works in rough going.
Bill's Story 15-21 The joy of **living** we really have,
Th Is A So 25-9 futility of life as we had been **living** it.
Th Is A So 28-9 "A design for **living**" that really works.
Th Is A So 28-17 the children of a **living** Creator
Mo Ab Al 43-1 have since been brought into a way of **living**
We Ag 50-28 change in their way of **living** and thinking.
We Ag 51-4 why **living** was so unsatisfactory.
We Ag 52-18 we couldn't make a **living,**
We Ag 54-20 **living** by faith and little else.
Into Ac 81-32 Our design for **living** is not a one-way street.
Wo Wi Ot 98-27 new principles by which he is **living,**
To Wives 108-6 been **living** in that strange world of alcoholism
To Wives 119-28 have been **living** too much alone,
Th Fam Af 122-22 Years of **living** with an alcoholic
Th Fam Af 124-4 conflict with the new way of **living.**
Th Fam Af 133-13 a spiritual mode of **living** is a most

A Vi Fo Yo 159-24 into a spiritual way of **living,**
Dr Bob Ni 180-18 the first **living** human with whom I had ever
Living death
To Emp 150-3 have been saved from a **living death.**
Lock
To Wives 114-22 the kind thing is to **lock** them up,
Logic
We Ag 53-3 **Logic** is great stuff.
Loneliness
Bill's Story 8-8 **loneliness** and despair I found
Wo Wi Ot 89-9 to watch **loneliness** vanish,
A Vi Fo You 151-16 vapor that is **loneliness** settled down.
A Vi Fo You 152-9 Then he will know **loneliness**
Lonely
Into Ac 81-7 the husband begins to feel **lonely,**
To Wives 111-11 This may lead to **lonely** evenings for you.
A Vi Fo You 154-18 and would have a **lonely** weekend.
Lopsided
Th Fam Af 129-10 that his spiritual growth is **lopsided,**
Lose
To Wives 109-19 he is beginning to **lose** his friends.
To Wives 116-6 afraid your husband will **lose** his position.
To Wives 120-4 You will **lose** the old life
Loss
Mo Ab Al 36-28 the **loss** of family and position,
To Emp 146-31 even if it means the **loss** of his job.
Lost
Ho It Wo 62-3 alcoholic who has **lost** all and is locked up.
Into Ac 80-26 and it all would be **lost** anyhow.
Th Fam Af 126-17 to make up for **lost** time.
To Emp 137-13 exceptional men **lost** to this world
Love
Bill's Story 1-5 Here was **love,** applause, war;
Th Is A Sol 21-3 ill health- falling in **love**
We Ag 54-19 capacity for faith, or **love,** or worship
We Ag 56-28 Presence of Infinite Power and **Love.**
Into Ac 83-10 tolerance, kindliness and **love.**
Into Ac 84-29 **Love** and tolerance of others is our code.
To Wives 105-14 retaliatory **love** affairs with other men.

To Wives 106-13 tried to hold the **love** of our children,
To Wives 107-16 could be no **love** in such persons,
To Wives 107-28 even if they did not **love** their families,
To Wives 108-8 see that he really does **love** you
To Wives 118-14 understanding and **love** are the watchwords.
To Wives 118-27 that **love** and loyalty could not cure
To Wives 119-25 counsel and **love** of a woman who has
Th Fam Af 122-7 ground of tolerance, understanding and **love.**
Th Fam Af 124-26 or his wife have had **love** affairs.
Th Fam Af 125-17 temper such talk by a spirit of **love**
Th Fam Af 127-9 tolerance, **love** and spiritual understanding.
Th Fam Af 127-22 show unselfishness and **love**
Th Fam Af 128-23 not see why their **love** and devotion
A Vi Fo You 153-4 **Love** thy neighbor as thyself.
Loved
We Ag 54-12 Who of us had not **loved** something or somebody?
To Wives 106-33 that settled down on our **loved** ones-
To Wives 107-14 men who **loved** their wives and children
Loves
We Ag 54-14 these feelings, these **loves,** these worships,
Loving
Bill's Story 12-11 however **loving** his sway may be.
Th Is a Sol 28-7 the **loving** and powerful hand of God.
Into Ac 82-7 good sense and **loving** kindness
Into Ac 86-9 Were we kind and **loving** toward all?
A Vi Fo You 160-10 to find **loving** and understanding
A Vi Fo You 161-6 their **loving** and All Powerful Creator.
Loyal
Into Ac 81-14 married to a **loyal** and courageous girl
Loyalty
To Wives 105-5 our **loyalty** and the desire that our husbands
To Wives 118-27 love and **loyalty** could not cure
To Emp 145-17 will command undying **loyalty.**
Lucky
Wo Wi Ot 98-29 if he is **lucky** enough to have a home.
Lukewarm
To Wives 113-4 If he is **lukewarm**
Lunacy
Bill's Story 3-1 thought a **lunacy** commission should be appointed.

Lust
Ho It Wo 68-33 that sex is a **lust** of our lower nature,
Luxury
Ho It Wo 66-22 the dubious **luxury** of normal men,

M

Mad
A Vi Fo Yo 151-15 shivering denizens of his **mad** realm,
Made
Into Ac 78-12 We have **made** our demonstration,
Madly
Th Is A So 22-1 searches **madly** for the bottle he misplaced
Madness
Bill's Story 6-25 morning terror and **madness** were on me.
Maintenance
Ho It Wo 66-14 **maintenance** and growth of a spiritual
Into Ac 85-17 contingent on the **maintenance** of our spiritual
Majority
To Wives 114-16 The **majority** have never returned.
Make-believe
Th Fam Af 130-8 the world of spiritual **make-believe**
Maker
Ho It Wo 63-14 Many of us said to our **Maker,**
Making a scene
Dr Bob Ni 173-17 for fear of **making a scene**
Malady
Wo Wi Ot 92-22 alcoholism as an illness, a fatal **malady.**
To Emp 138-10 talking about alcoholism, the **malady,**
Malicious
To Emp 145-26 a **malicious** individual was always making
Manage
Ho It wo 60-17 could not **manage** our own lives.
Mangled
More Ab Al 43-10 have to be pretty badly **mangled** before they

Manic-depressive
Doc's Op xxviii-18 There is the **manic-depressive** type
Manifested
Ho It Wo 64-20 **manifested** in various ways,
Manner
Ho It Wo 58-9 a **manner** of living which demands
Many
Th Is A So 19-17 **Many** could recover if they had the
Th Is A So 20 15 How **many** times people have said
Th Is A So 28-32 **Many** who once were in this class
Mo Ab Al 31-8 **many** who are real alcoholics
Mo Ab Al 34-22 **Many** of us felt that we had plenty of
Mo Ab Al 36-13 I had eaten there **many** times
We Ag 47-24 we accepted **many** things on faith
We Ag 48-2 **Many** of us have been so touchy
We Ag 49-28 **many** spiritually-minded persons
Into Ac 87-26 There are **many** helpful books
Wo Wi Ot 102-29 **Many** of us keep liquor in our homes.
To Emp 139-19 to become quite sure of **many** things
To Emp 149-13 may harbor **many** actual or potential
A Vi Fo You 153-18 **Many**, we are sure, will rise
A Vi Fo You 161-15 Fellowship will number **many** hundreds.
A Vi Fo Yo 162-3 **Many** of us have felt for the first time,
March
A Vi Fo Yo 153-18 will rise to their feet and **march** on.
Marked
Th Fam Af 123-30 has been **marked** by escapades,
Marriage
Ho It Wo 69-2 who bewail the institution of **marriage;**
Married
Into Ac 81-14 **married** to a loyal and courageous girl
Marshalled
We Ag 45-7 as **marshalled** by the will,
Martyr
Into Ac 79-15 be the hasty and foolish **martyr** who
Maudlin
To Wives 105-1 We have been driven to **maudlin** sympathy,

Maximum

Into Ac 77-3 of **maximum** service to God

Master

Bill's Story 8-12 Alcohol was my **master.**

Mastered

Ho It Wo 66-30 these resentments must be **mastered,**

Mastery

A Vi Fo Yo 156-2 that God might give him **mastery.**

Materialize

Into Ac 84-14 They will always **materialize** if we work for

Measure up

To Wives 118-22 to feel that he will now **measure up**

Measures

Bill's Story 15-14 when all other **measures** failed

Ho It Wo 59-4 Half **measures** availed us nothing.

Into Ac 86-17 what corrective **measures** should be taken

Medicine

Dr Bob Ni 173-7 was to take up the study of **medicine,.**

Meditation

Ho It Wo 59-29 Sought through prayer and **meditation**

Ho It Wo 69-30 In **meditation,** we ask God what we should

Into Ac 83-8 asking each morning in **meditation**

Into Ac 85-32 Step eleven suggests prayer and **meditation.**

Into Ac 87-10 the period of **meditation** with a prayer

A Vi Fo You 164-13 Ask Him in your morning **meditation**

Meet

A Vi Fo You 164-25 you will surely **meet** some of us

Meeting

A Vi Fo You 159-33 one night a week for a **meeting**

Melt

Into Ac 78-7 feuds of years' standing **melt** away

Member

Th Fam Af 127-26 each **member** of a resentful family

Th Fam Af 135-18 he is now a most effective **member**

A Vi Fo You 163-10 A.A. **member** who was living in a large

Members

Doc's Op xxiii-6 with the sufferings of our **members**

Th Fam Af 122-6 All **members** of the family

Th Fam Af 125-24 **Members** of a family should watch

A Vi Fo You 162-14 may now see scores of **members.**

Membership

Th Fam Af 131-29 or take **membership** in a religious body.

Dr Bob Ni 173-12 **membership** in one of the drinking societies

Memories

Into Ac 73-19 These **memories** are a nightmare.

Into Ac 73-21 he pushes these **memories** far inside himself.

Mend

Th Fam Af 135-17 and **mend** his spiritual fences.

Mental

Doc's Op xxviii-3 craving beyond their **mental** control

Doc's Op xxix-6 pathological **mental** deterioration.

Mo Ab Al 42-7 those strange **mental** blank spots.

We Ag 54-8 What a state of **mental** goose-flesh

Wo Wi Ot 92-3 Show him the **mental** twist which leads

Wo Wi Ot 92-7 He will match your **mental** inconsistencies

Wo Wi Ot 92-11 how the queer **mental** condition

To Wives 106-31 The alarming physical and **mental** symptoms

To Wives 114-10 his **mental** condition too abnormal or

To Emp 146-8 with physical and **mental** readjustment

Mental state

A Vi Fo You 157-21 the **mental state** preceding the first drink.

Mentally

Ho It Wo 64-26 **mentally** and physically ill,

Ho It Wo 64-28 straighten out **mentally** and physically

To Wives 109-3 may be slowing him up **mentally**

To Emp 141-27 You can see that he is **mentally** and physically

Merriment

Th Fam Af 132-28 shocked when we burst into **merriment**

Message

Doc's Op xxvi-14 The **message** which can interest and hold

Into Ac 77-10 opportunity to carry a beneficial **message.**

Wo Wi Ot 89-5 Carry this **message** to other alcoholics!

Method

To Emp 143-4 Whatever the **method,** it's object is

Methods

Doc's Op xxiii-26 other **methods** had failed completely.

Th Is A So 27-24 the **methods** which I employed are

Mo Ab Al 31-17 some of the **methods** we have tried.

Into Ac 72-26 they have turned to easier **methods.**

Mettle

To Emp 146-7 be on his **mettle** to make good.

Middle of the road solution

Th Is A So 25-26 there is no **middle of the road solution.**

Mild

To Emp 139-23 you can go on a **mild** bender,

Milk

Mo Ab Al 36-19 an ounce of whiskey in my **milk.**

Mind

Doc's Op xxiv-13 quite as abnormal as his **mind.**

Th Is A So 23-6 problem of the alcoholic centers in his **mind,**

Th Is A So 26-13 of the inner workings of his **mind**

Th Is A So 27-6 You have the **mind** of a chronic alcoholic.

Th Is A So 27-8 where that state of **mind** existed

Mo Ab Al 32-18 He made up his **mind** that until he had been

Mo Ab Al 41-10 the thought came to **mind** that it would be nice

Mo Ab Al 41-33 that if I had an alcoholic **mind,** the time and

Mo Ab Al 42-6 from that moment that I had an alcoholic **mind.**

Into Ac 87-2 becomes a working part of the **mind.**

Wo Wi Ot 95-19 until he changes his **mind.**

To Wives 113-7 seed has been planted in his **mind.**

To Emp 140-32 abnormal action of alcohol on his **mind.**

To Emp 143-5 thoroughly clear **mind** and body

Minds

We Ag 57-10 God restored us all to our right **minds.**

Th Fam Af 132-11 cannot make up other's **minds** for them.

Th Fam Af 134-19 their young **minds** were impressionable

A Vi Fo You 161-27 hearts and **minds** attuned to the

Minister

Th Fam Af 132-6 to many a priest, **minister,** or rabbi,

Th Fam Af 132-7 to **minister** to our troubled world.

Ministers

Wo Wi Ot 89-21 **Ministers** and doctors are competent

Miracle

We Ag 57-6 but a **miracle** of healing?

Th Fam Af 124-30 The **miracle** of reconciliation was at hand.

Th Fam Af 128-21 accomplished the **miracle** where they

A Vi Fo You 151-10 that some new **miracle** of control
Miracles
Bill's Story 11-28 My ideas about **miracles**
Bill's Story 11-30 **miracles** directly across the
Th Fam Af 133-15 are **miracles** of mental health.
Th Fam Af 133-26 God has wrought **miracles** among us.
A Vi Fo You 153-13 The age of **miracles** is still with us.
A Vi Fo You 161-5 They had seen **miracles,**
Miraculous
Th Is A So 25-22 in a way which is indeed **miraculous.**
We Ag 50-20 accomplished the **miraculous**
We Ag 55-14 **miraculous** demonstrations of that power
Mire
Th Fam Af 132-20 When we see a man sinking into the **mire**
Misdeeds
Th Fam Af 124-25 possible to dig up past **misdeeds**
Miserable
Bill's Story 8-18 stumble along to a **miserable** end.
Dr Bob Ni 178-16 and I was thoroughly **miserable.**
Misery
We Ag 52-17 we were a prey to **misery** and depression,
Th Fam Af 124-23 you can avert death and **misery** for them.
Th Fam Af 133-6 clear that we made our own **misery.**
Th Fam Af 133-7 the deliberate manufacture of **misery.**
A Vi Fo you 163-27 others from the stream of **misery**
Misfortune
Ho It Wo 67-31 circumstances which brought us **misfortune**
Misfortunes
A Vi Fo You 160-20 laughed at their own **misfortunes**
Misgivings
Into Ac 76-28 Probably there are still some **misgivings.**
Misled
To Emp 148-7 1487 and will no longer be **misled** by ordinary
Mistake
To Wives 119-21 We find it a real **mistake** to dampen
Mistakes
Ho It Wo 67-16 resolutely looked for our own **mistakes.**
Into Ac 84-18 set right any new **mistakes**
To Wives 104-19 We want to analyze **mistakes** we have made.

To Wives 117-17 You will make **mistakes,**

Th Fam Af 124-17 willing to bring former **mistakes,**

Misunderstanding

Th Is A So 18-7 It brings **misunderstanding,** fierce resentment,

Th Is A So 20-28 world of ignorance and **misunderstanding.**

To Emp 142-5 it was because of **misunderstanding.**

Misunderstood

To Wives 111-11 He will tell you he is **misunderstood.**

Misused

Th Fam Af 126-21 Having been neglected and **misused**

Moderate

Th Is A So 21-5 this man can also stop or **moderate,**

Mo Ab Al 39-5 are able to stop or **moderate,**

To Wives 109-10 Some will **moderate** or stop altogether,

To Wives 112-6 in his power to stop or **moderate.**

Moderate drinker

Th Is A So 20-9 start off as a **moderate drinker;**

To Emp 139-20 As a **moderate drinker** you can take your

Moderately

Mo Ab Al 34-16 who are unable to drink **moderately**

To Wives 109-27 how he can drink **moderately** next time.

To Emp 139-15 Those who drink **moderately** may be

Moderating

To Wives 109-18 various means of **moderating** or staying dry

Moderation

Dr Bob Ni 175-27 I drank with **moderation** at first,

Modest

Ho It Wo 61-7 even **modest** and sel-sacrificing.

Mold

Ho It Wo 69-20 We asked God to **mold** our ideals

Moments

Bill's Story 1-5 **moments** sublime with intervals

Mo Ab Al 43-4 would not exchange it's best **moments** for the

Ho It Wo 66-8 Our **moments** of triumph were short-lived.

Money

Into Ac 78-14 Most alcoholics owe **money.**

Into Ac 80-7 accepted a sum of **money** from a bitterly-hated

Into Ac 80-9 denied having received the **money**

Wo Wi Ot 96-30 not trying to impose upon you for **money,**

Wo Wi Ot 97-10 It may mean sharing your **money,**
Wo Wi Ot 98-3 The men who cry for **money**
Th Fam Af 123-25 never have much **money** again.
Th Fam Af 126-7 their **money** troubles are about to be solved,
Dr Bob Ni 176-2 stay sober enough to earn **money,**
Dr Bob Ni 177-21 for me to earn more **money,**
Monopoly
Wo Wi Ot 95-29 We have no **monopoly** on God;
Moral
Bill's Story 7-24 declining **moral** and bodily health
Bill's Story 11-3 His **moral** reaching- most excellent.
We Ag 45-17 to be spiritual as well as **moral.**
To Emp 137-24 feels a **moral** responsibility for the
Moralize
Wo Wi Ot 91-29 being careful not to **moralize,**
Morning
To Wives 109-22 He sometimes drinks in the **morning**
A Vi Fo You 164-13 Ask Him in your **morning** meditation
Dr Bob Ni 176-12 by a **morning** of unbearable jitters.
Morphine
Th Is A So 22-10 **morphine** or some sedative with which to
Most
Bill's Story 2-29 **most** people lost money in stocks
Bill's Story 14-13 God comes to **most** men gradually,
Th Is A So 28-29 **most** of us favor such memberships.
Mo Ab Al 30-1 **Most** of us have been unwilling to admit
Mo Ab Al 33-4 **Most** of us have believed that if we
We Ag 51-7 Presence of God today is the **most** important
Into Ac 78-14 **Most** alcoholics owe money.
Mother
Th Fam Af 130-30 that **mother** became head of the house.
Th Fam Af 131-2 **Mother** made all the plans
Th Fam Af 131-17 **mother** and children demand that he
Th Fam Af 134-21 has done to them and their **mother.**
Motive
Wo Wi Ot 102-4 that your **motive** in going is thoroughly good.
Motives
Th Is A So 27-21 new set of conceptions and **motives** begin to
Into Ac 86-23 dishonest or self-seeking **motives.**

Into Ac 86-27 thinking is cleared of wrong **motives.**
Mottos
Th Fam Af 135-24 We have three little **mottos**
Much
Into Ac 85-24 **Much** has already been said
Th Fam Af 127-24 he did **much** to make them so.
Mumbling
Into Ac 83-2 A remorseful **mumbling** that we are sorry
Must
Into Ac 74-5 denomination which requires confession **must,**
Wo Wi Ot 89-11 an experience you **must** not miss.
Wo Wi Ot 101-2 we **must** avoid moving pictures
Myself
Bill's Story 1-22 I fancied **myself** a leader,
Bill's Story 6-6 I told **myself** I would manage better
Bill's Story 6-19 Should I kill **myself?**
Bill's Story 6-27 cursing **myself** for a weakling.
Bill's Story 13-1 clamors, mostly those within **myself.**
Bill's Story 13-6 I humbly offered **myself** to God,
Bill's Story 13-8 I placed **myself** unreservedly under His care
Bill's Story 13-9 that of **myself** I was nothing;
Mo Ab Al 42-13 then asked me if I thought **myself** alcoholic
We Ag 47-16 is a Power greater than **myself?**
Mystified
Th Fam Af 126-29 The family is **mystified.**

N

Nadir
A Vi Fo Yo 155-5 nearing the **nadir** of alcoholic dispair.
Nag
To Wives 111-8 gets the idea that you are a **nag**
Nagged
Wo Wi Ot 91-15 without being **nagged** by his family.

Th Fam Af 135-13 so she **nagged,** and her intolerance finally
Naturally
Ho It Wo 58-8 **naturally** incapable of grasping
Nature
Th Is A Sol 21-18 resembles his normal **nature** but little.
Ho It Wo 59-18 the exact **nature** of our wrongs.
Into Ac 72-11 the exact **nature** of our defects.
Nausea
Dr Bob Ni 172-23 with a great deal of morning-after **nausea.**
Near-wreck
To Wives 110-2 his home is a **near-wreck**
Nearness
Into Ac 75-16 We begin to feel the **nearness** of our Creator.
Necessary
Into Ac 72-19 thought it **necessary** to go much further.
Into Ac 73-9 in the sense we find it **necessary,**
Into Ac 79-26 be willing to do that if **necessary,**
To Wives 109-7 that drinking is **necessary** in his business.
To Wives 111-5 Patience and good temper are **necessary.**
To Emp 146-15 work is **necessary** to maintain his sobriety.
A Vi Fo Yo 158-11 willing to do anything **necessary.**
Necessity
Bill's Story 5-3 be a luxury; it became a **necessity.**
Bill's Story 14-28 absolute **necessity** of demonstrating these
Th Is A So 19-25 Of **necessity** there will have to be discussion
Mo Ab Al 34-26 no matter how great the **necessity** or the wish.
Into Ac 74-24 great **necessity** for discussing ourselves
Need
Dr Bob Ni 180-31 others who want and **need** it badly.
Needed
Ho It Wo 63-3 He provided what we **needed,**
Needs
Th Is A Sol 20-3 and how we may help meet their **needs.**
Ho It Wo 70-20 We think of their **needs** and work for them.
Neglect
Th Fam Af 129-29 displays a certain amount of **neglect**
Neglected
Th Fam Af 126-9 as they find themselves **neglected.**
Th Fam Af 126-21 Having been **neglected** and misused

Neglectful

To Wives 119-16 that he becomes really **neglectful.**

Neighbor

A Vi Fo Yo 153-4 Love thy **neighbor** as thyself.

Nerve

Th Fam Af 126-17 He is straining every **nerve**

Nerves

Mo Ab Al 39-26 the hospital to rest his **nerves.**

Dr Bob Ni 175-3 my **nerves** did the same thing.

Nervous

Mo Ab Al 32-14 He was very **nervous** in the morning

Mo Ab Al 35-16 except for a **nervous** disposition.

Nervousness

Mo Ab Al 37-20 feeling ourselves justified by **nervousness,**

To Wives 109-23 to hold his **nervousness** in check.

Neurotic

Th Fam Aft 122-23 to make any wife or child **neurotic.**

Neutrality

Into Ac 85-7 placed in a position of **neutrality-**

Never

Mo Ab Al 31-18 **never** drinking alone,

Mo Ab Al 31-19 **never** drinking in the morning,

Mo Ab Al 31-20 **never** having it in the house,

Mo Ab Al 31-20 **never** drinking during business hours,

Mo Ab Al 39-29 It **never** occurred to him that

We Ag 46-31 **never** exclusive or forbidding to those who

To Wives 114-16 The majority have **never** returned.

To Wives 117-28 **Never** forget that resentment is a deadly

To Wives 120-22 We **never, never** try to arrange a man's life

Th Fam Af 123-24 he will **never** have much money again.

A Vi Fo Yo 151-7 **Never** could we recapture the great

A Vi Fo Yo 158-2 sworn that I'd **never** touch another drop

A Vi Fo You 158-21 He **never** drank again.

New

Bill's Story 12-2 His roots grasped a **new** soil.

Bill's Story 12-28 A **new** world came into view.

Bill's Story 14-1 and maintain the **new** order of things,

Th Is A So 28-8 A **new** life has been given us

We Ag 46-28 a **new** sense of power and direction,

Ho It Wo 63-8 As we felt **new** power flow in,

Wo Wi Ot 100-11 live in a **new** and wonderful world,

To Emp 150-2 They have a **new** attitude,

New-found

To Wives 117-10 In spite of your **new-found** happiness,

New friends

A Vi Fo You 152-26 You are going to meet these **new friends**

A Vi Fo You 161-3 They knew they had a host of **new friends;**

New life

Th Is A So 28-8 A **new life** has been given us

Th Fam Af 126-1 enthralled by his **new life**

New man

Wo Wi Ot 100-5 you and the **new man** must walk day by day

Th Fam Af 134-27 will see that he is a **new man**

New People

A Vi Fo You 160-4 where **new people** might bring their

Newcomer

Th Fam Af 133-29 indispensable in treating a **newcomer**

A Vi Fo You 159-31 present their discovery to some **newcomer.**

Newcomers

Into Ac 72-23 **newcomers** have tried to keep to themselves

Wo Wi Ot 89-13 Frequent contact with **newcomers**

Th Fam Af 132-15 If **newcomers** could see no joy or fun

Newspaper clipping

To Emp 137-1 a **newspaper clipping** fell out.

Nightmare

Into Ac 73-19 These memories are a **nightmare.**

Dr Bob Ni 177-18 It was a really horrible **nightmare,**

Nicer

To Wives 116-28 capable of being **nicer** if

A Vi Fo Yo 157-25 but I'm a **nobody** now.

Nobody

A Vi Fo You 157-25 but I'm a **nobody** now.

Non-denominational

Th Fam Af 132-10 as **non-denominational** people,

Normal

Doc's Op xxvi-34 seems the only **normal** one

Doc's Op xxviii-21 entirely **normal** in every respect except

Th Is A Sol 21-18 resembles his **normal** nature but little.
Th Is A Sol 22-25 reacts differently from **normal** people.
Wo Wi Ot 92-12 first drink prevents **normal** functioning
To Wives 113-26 is otherwise a **normal** individual,
Th Fam Af 131-11 laid aside for years all **normal** activities-
To Emp 140-23 **Normal** drinkers are not so affected,
To Emp 141-1 model of honesty when **normal,**
To Emp 150-2 produce as mich as five **normal** salesman.
A Vi Fo You 151-1 For most **normal** folks, drinking means
Normal men
Ho It Wo 66-22 the dubious luxury of **normal men,**
Normally
Th Is A Sol 17-8 people who **normally** would not mix.
Mo Ab al 33-6 we could therefore drink **normally.**
Nothing
Th Is A So 18-24 little or **nothing** can be accomplished.
Th Is A So 18-29 **nothing** whatever except the sincere desire
Th Is A So 28-21 will find here **nothing** disturbing
Mo Ab Al 36-29 to say **nothing** of that intense mental
Mo Ab Al 40-4 that he could do **nothing** about it himself.
Mo Ab Al 41-2 so there was **nothing** new about that.
Mo Ab Al 41-11 That was all. **Nothing** more.
We Ag 54-28 electrons, created out of **nothing,** meaning **nothing,**
Ho It Wo 65-31 **Nothing** counted but thoroughness and honesty.
Into Ac 77-33 realizing that **nothing** worth while
Into Ac 79-26 in jail he could provide **nothing**
Wo Wi Ot 89-1 **nothing** will so much insure immunity
Th Fam Af 13-17 We have found **nothing** incompatible
Th Fam Af 130-24 **Nothing** will help the man who is off
Th Fam Af 131-24 who know **nothing** of alcoholism
Th Fam Af 132-9 there is **nothing** obligatory about it.
To Emp 138-23 had had **nothing** to drink whatever for
To Emp 139-2 There was **nothing** to do but wait.
To Emp 141-14 that **nothing** my company could have done
A Vi Fo Yo 159-2 it seemed as if **nothing** could be done for
Nothingness
We Ag 54-29 whirling on to a destiny of **nothingness?**
Number one
Ho It Wo 64-23 Resentment is the **number one** offender.

Numbers
A Vi Fo Yo 159-21 They grew in **numbers.**
Nurses
A Vi Fo Yo 156-23 He's just beaten up a couple of **nurses.**

O

Obeyed
Th Fam Af 131-3 father usually **obeyed.**
Obituary
To Emp 137-1 It was the **obituary** of one of the best salesmen
Object
We Ag 45-14 it's main **object** is to enable you to find
Objectionable
Into Ac 76-4 which we have admitted are **objectionable.**
Obligation
To Emp 147-11 you should feel under no **obligation** to keep
Obligations
Th Fam Af 129-12 does not include his family **obligations**
Oblivion
Th Is Sol 19-16 hundreds are dropping into **oblivion** every day.
A Vi Fo Yo 151-20 then would come **oblivion**
Obsession
Th Is A So 23-24 There is the **obsession** that somehow, someday
Mo Ab Al 30-8 great **obsession** of every abnormal drinker.
A Vi Fo Yo 151-9 a heartbreaking **obsession**
A Vi Fo Yo 155-20 the familiar alcoholic **obsession**
Obstacles
Into Ac 73-4 to discover the **obstacles** in our path.
Off his head
A Vi Fo Yo 156-23 Goes **off his head** completely when he's
Offended
Wo Wi Ot 94-17 You should not be **offended** if he wants
Offender
Ho It Wo 64-23 Resentment is the number one **offender.**

Offer
Ho It Wo 63-14 God, I **offer** myself to Thee-
Old game
A Vi Fo Yo 152-5 will presently try the **old game** again,
Old habits
Dr Bob Ni 175-29 to drift back into my **old habits**
Old pleasures
A Vi Fo Yo 151-6 The **old** pleasures were gone
Omitted
Into Ac 75-28 we ask if we have **omitted** anything,
Omnipotence
Th Fam Af 133-9 to demonstrate His **omnipotence.**
One
To Wives 108-33 **One:** Your husband may be only a heavy
One half
Dr Bob Ni 181-26 go about it with **one half** the zeal
One-way
Into Ac 81-32 Our design for living is not a **one-way** street.
Open minded
We Ag 48-8 became as **open minded** on spiritual matters
Opinion
To Wives 117-32 an honest difference of **opinion.**
Opinions
Ho It Wo 68-31 we find human **opinions** running to extremes-
Opportunity
Th Is A So 19-17 recover if they had the **opportunity** we have
Into Ac 74-29 go through with it at the first **opportunity.**
Wo Wi Ot 96-9 an **opportunity** to live and be happy.
Th Fam Af 133- 8 cheerfully capitalize it as an **opportunity**
To Emp 138-9 an **opportunity** to be helpful,
To Emp 138-26 an **opportunity** to hear my story?
To Emp 147-24 given an **opportunity** to get well.
A Vi Fo You 164-3 has had his **opportunity** to recover-
Ordained
Into Ac 74-9 someone **ordained** by an established religion.
Ordeal
Th Fam Af 125-4 survived this **ordeal** without relapse,
Order
Into Ac 77-2 trying to put our lives in **order.**

A Vi Fo You 164-16 if your own house is in **order.**
Organization
To Emp 139-31 the alcoholic in your **organization**
Ostracized
Dr Bob Ni 177-9 we became more or less **ostracized** by
Other woman
To Wives 106-20 to live with the **other woman** forever.
Others
Doc's Op xxiii-21 they must do likewise with still **others.**
Doc's Op xxiii-24 one hundred **others** appear to have recovered.
Bill's Story 13-27 bore on my usefulness to **others.**
Bill's Story 14-27 They in turn might work with **others.**
Bill's Story 14-30 imperative to work with **others**
Bill's Story 15-1 through work and self-sacrifice for **others,**
Th Is A so 20-2 upon our constant thought of **others**
Into Ac 74-22 but always considerate of **others.**
Into Ac 79-16 sacrifice **others** to save himself
Into Ac 82-25 roaring his way through the lives of **others.**
Into Ac 86-12 thinking of what we could do for **others,**
Into Ac 86-16 diminish our usefulness to **others.**
Wo Wi Ot 90-25 try to help **others**
Wo Wi Ot 97-5 Helping **others** is the foundation
Wo Wi Ot 102-24 be of maximum helpfulness to **others,**
To Wives 120-1 sense of responsibility for **others.**
Th Fam Af 122-13 that the **others** concede to him.
Th Fam Af 124-18 Showing **others** who suffer how we
Th Fam Af 124-23 life and happiness for **others.**
Th Fam Af 127-27 and admits them to the **others,**
Th Fam Af 132-31 been given the power to help **others.**
A Vi Fo You 158-26 had to give to **others** what they had
A Vi Fo You 161-27 to the welfare of **others,**
A Vi Fo You 164-1 the joy of helping **others**
Dr Bob Ni 180-7 different from what **others** had done or said?
Dr Bob Ni 180-31 **others** who want and need it badly.
Ourself
Into Ac 74-22 we must be hard on **ourself,**
Ourselves
Th Is A So 24-17 handle **ourselves** like other people.
Th Is a So 24-25 pounded on the bar and said to **ourselves,**

Th Is A So 25-24 which we could never do by **ourselves.**
Th Is A So 29-15 disclosing **ourselves** and our problems
Mo Ab Al 37-15 Next day we would ask **ourselves,**
Mo Ab Al 37-19 feeling **ourselves** justified by nervousness,
We Ag 45-11 a Power greater than **ourselves.**
We Ag 46-2 dependence upon a power beyond **ourselves**
We Ag 47-9 we found **ourselves** accepting many things
We Ag 47-14 We needed to ask **ourselves** but one short
We Ag 48-1 found **ourselves** handicapped by obstinacy,
We Ag 50-4 while we were intolerant **ourselves.**
We Ag 54-10 things, money, **ourselves?**
We Ag 55-9 Actually we were fooling **ourselves,**
Ho It Wo 62-5 are not most of concerned with **ourselves,**
Ho It Wo 62-15 They arise out of **ourselves,**
Ho It Wo 63-6 less and less interested in **ourselves,**
Ho It Wo 63-22 abandon **ourselves** utterly to Him.
Ho It Wo 64-4 the things in **ourselves** which had been blocking
Ho It Wo 64-31 We asked **ourselves** why we were angry.
Ho It Wo 66-6 then we were sore at **ourselves.**
Ho It Wo 66-17 we shut **ourselves** off from the sunlight of
Ho It Wo 67-2 they, like **ourselves,** were sick too.
Ho It Wo 67-32 did not we, **ourselves,** set the ball rolling?
Ho It Wo 70-20 This takes us out of **ourselves.**
Ho It Wo 71-1 for us what we could not do for **ourselves.**
Into Ac 72-16 admitting these things to **ourselves.**
Into Ac 72-20 discussing **ourselves** with another person
Into Ac 74-25 discussing **ourselves** with someone,
Into Ac 74-28 if we hold **ourselves** in complete readiness to
Into Ac 76-20 We subjected **ourselves** to a drastic self
Into Ac 76-24 and run the show **ourselves.**
Into Ac 77-3 fit **ourselves** to be of maximum service to God
Into Ac 77-8 Why lay **ourselves** open to being branded fanatics
Into Ac 79-7 Reminding **ourselves** that we have decided
Into Ac 83-21 can honestly say to **ourselves**
Into Ac 84-11 what we could not do for **ourselves.**
Into Ac 86-11 Were we thinking of **ourselves**
Into Ac 87-15 make no request for **ourselves** only.
Into Ac 88-7 trying to arrange life to suit **ourselves.**
Wo Wi Ot 100-9 when we put **ourselves** in God's hands

To Wives 121-3 for we **ourselves** don't always care
Outcome
Into Ac 80-24 had to place the **outcome** in God's hands
Outgrow
Ho It Wo 68-27 we commence to **outgrow** fear.
Th Fam Af 125-28 to **outgrow** that serious handicap.
Outline
Wo Wi Ot 94-4 **Outline** the program of action,
Outsiders
Th Fam Af 132-27 **Outsiders** are sometimes shocked
A Vi Fo You 160-5 **Outsiders** became interested.
Over-anxious
Wo Wi Ot 91-1 urge them not to be **over-anxious,**
Over-concentration
Th Fam Af 127-14 **over-concentration** on financial success.
Over-indulged
Th Fam Af 134-8 that they have **over-indulged,**
Overcome
Doc's Op xxviii-2 they were drinking to **overcome** a craving
Bill's Story 15-30 which has not been **overcome**
We Ag 44-26 were sufficient to **overcome** alcoholism
Ho It Wo 64-27 When the spiritual malady is **overcome,**
Into Ac 72-21 we may not **overcome** drinking.
To Wives 104-21 too great to be **overcome.**
To Wives 117-20 will emerge when they are **overcome.**
Th Fam Af 132-25 we are soon **overcome** by them.
Overhauling
Ho It Wo 68-28 Many of us needed an **overhauling** there.
Overlook
To Emp 141-28 You are willing to **overlook** his past
Overnight
Th Fam Af 133-11 does not often recover **overnight**
Overwhelmed
Bill's Story 8-11 I had been **overwhelmed.**
We Ag 56-23 he was **overwhelmed** by a conviction of the
Owe
Into Ac 77-14 Most alcoholics **owe** money.
Owes
To Wives 118-10 he **owes** you more than sobriety.

Th Fam Aft 123-14 God, they believe, almost **owes** this
Th Fam Af 124-14 **owes** something to those who have not,
Th Fam Af 126-22 They think father **owes** them more
To Emp 145-11 If he **owes** you money

P

Paced
A Vi Fo Yo 154-11 he **paced** a hotel lobby wondering how
Padded
To Emp 145-5 he has **padded** his expense account
Painful
To Wives 121-5 some of it is **painful.**
Th Fam Af 124-12 This **painful** past may be of infinite value
Painfully
Th Fam Af 135-17 He had to **painfully** admit
A Vi Fo Yo 155-10 **Painfully** aware of being somehow abnormal
Painstaking
Into Ac 83-29 are **painstaking** about this phase of our
Panacea
Dr. Bob Ni 171-20 the great **panacea** for all human ills.
Pant-leg
Dr Bob Ni 177-5 the **pant-leg** and stocking racket were out!
Paradoxically
Ho It Wo 68-20 **Paradoxically,** it is the way of strength.
Paralyzing
To Wives 116-5 There is another **paralyzing** fear.
Parental
Dr Bob Ni 172-11 was free from **parental** domination,
Parties
To Wives 110-29 **parties** which would be dull without liquor.
Pass it on
Dr Bob Ni 181-4 took time to **pass it on** to me.
Passed out
Dr Bob Ni 179-9 went upstairs and **passed out.**

Passing on
Dr Bob Ni 180-30 **passing on** what I learned to others
Passion
Wo Wi Ot 95-9 do not exhibit any **passion** for crusade
Past
Into Ac 77-32 done our utmost to straighten out the **past.**
Into Ac 83-32 We will not regret the **past**
Into Ac 84-20 as we cleaned up the **past.**
Wo Wi Ot 94-6 how you straightened out your **past**
Th Fam Af 124-2 forgetfulness of the **past.**
Th Fam Af 124-7 turn the **past** to good account.
Th Fam Af 124-10 **past** then becomes the principle asset
Th Fam Af 124-12 This painful **past** may be of infinite value
Th Fam Af 124-21 the dark **past** is the greatest possession
Th Fam Af 126-21 and misused in the **past,**
Th Fam Af 132-23 relive the horrors of our **past.**
Th Fam Af 132-29 tragic experience out of the **past.**
To Emp 140-15 for what he has done in the **past?**
To Emp 147-33 your **past** will be forgotten
A Vi Fo You 151-8 recapture the great moments of the **past.**
A Vi Fo You 164-23 the wreckage of your **past.**
Path
Wo Wi Ot 100-6 the **path** of spiritual progress.
Pathetic
Th Fam Af 134-22 **pathetic** hardness and cynicism.
Patience
Ho It Wo 67-4 the same tolerance, pity, and **patience**
Ho It Wo 70-28 We have begun to learn tolerance, **patience**
Into Ac 82-21 the **patience** mothers and wives have had
Into Ac 83-9 show us the way of **patience,**
To Wives 108-23 no amount of **patience** will make any
To Wives 111-4 **Patience** and good temper are most necessary.
To Wives 111-26 your reasonableness and **patience.**
To Wives 118-13 **Patience,** tolerance, understanding and
To Emp 138-1 has there been a lack of **patience**
A Vi Fo You 163-8 willingness, **patience** and labor.
Patient
Ho It Wo 61-6 kind, considerate, **patient,**
Wo Wi Ot 90-6 They should be **patient,**

To Wives 105-10 we have been **patient.**

To Wives 112-18 This may take **patient** waiting,

To Wives 118-25 Be **patient.**

To Emp 144-16 will tell the **patient** the truth about his condition,

A Vi Fo Yo 162-3 one of our number was a **patient** there.

Patiently

To Wives 107-2 we have **patiently** and wearily climbed,

Pause

Into Ac 87-31 As we go through the day we **pause,**

Pay

To Emp 143-13 later be deducted from his **pay.**

Dr Bob Ni 174-31 I was beginning to **pay** very dearly

Paying my debt

Dr Bob Ni 181-3 **paying my debt** to the man who took time to

Peace

Bill's Story 8-22 happiness, **peace,** and usefulness,

Bill's Story 14-10 followed such a **peace** and serenity

Bill's Story 16-17 a widening circle of **peace** on earth

We Ag 50-31 a new power, **peace,** happiness

Ho It Wo 63-9 as we enjoyed **peace** of mind

Into Ac 75-15 We can be alone at perfect **peace**

Into Ac 84-1 and we will know **peace.**

Pedestal

Th Fam Aft 122-4 and placed on a **pedestal.**

People

To Wives 119-14 he should work with other **people**

To Wives 121-4 **people** who lecture us.

Th Fam Af 125-13 at the expense of other **people,**

Th Fam Af 125-27 We alcoholics are sensitive **people.**

A Vi Fo Yo 152-14 like some righteous **people** I see?

A Vi Fo Yo 156-7 **people** he had hurt.

Pepper

Ho It Wo 69-8 have us all on a straight **pepper** diet.

Perfect

Ho It Wo 60-8 anything like **perfect** adherence to these

Into Ac 75-15 We can be alone at **perfect** peace and ease.

Th Fam Af 129-12 may not be so **perfect** after all.

Perfection

Ho It Wo 60-12 progress rather than spiritual **perfection.**

Perfectly

Into Ac 79-31 He said he was **perfectly** willing to go to jail

A Vi Fo Yo 158-10 and said he was **perfectly** willing

Performed

Ho It Wo 63-4 and **performed** His work well.

Perish

Bill's Story 16-13 in and through us, or we **perish.**

Permission

Into Ac 80-3 If we have obtained **permission,**

Persevere

To Emp 144-24 we think that if you **persevere**

Persevered

Into Ac 73-1 Having **persevered** with the rest of the program.

Person

Th Fam Af 129-21 now that he has become a superior **person**

Personal

Bill's Story 10-30 when they talked of a God **personal** to me,

Bill's Story 12-6 there might be a God **personal** to me

Th Is A So 28-26 an entirely **personal** which each one decides

Th Is A So 19-5 followed by forty-three **personal** experiences.

We Ag 52-16 trouble with **personal** relationships

Ho It Wo 59-27 Continued to take **personal** inventory

Ho It Wo 60-14 our **personal** adventures before and after

Ho It Wo 63-33 of which is a **personal** housecleaning,

Ho It Wo 64-8 we started upon a **personal** inventory.

Ho It Wo 64-33 our **personal** relationships (including sex)

Into Ac 79-10 no matter what the **personal** consequences

Persons

Th Fam Af 135-12 one of those **persons** who really feels

Persuader

We Ag 48-10 alcohol was a great **persuader.**

Petty

A Vi Fo You 161-24 **petty** rivalries and jealousies-

Phase

Th Fam Af 129-14 is but a **phase** of his development,

Phenomenon

Mo Ab Al 37-11 the curious mental **phenomenon** that parallel

Phobia

Dr Bob Ni 177-12 My **phobia** for sleeplessness

Phobias

Dr Bob Ni 175-32 I developed two distinct **phobias.**

Physical

To Emp 143-2 The matter of **physical** treatment

To Emp 143-16 **physical** treatment is but a small part

To Emp 146-8 **physical** and mental readjustment

Physically

Ho It Wo 64-26 mentally and **physically** ill,

Ho It Wo 64-28 we straighten out mentally and **physically.**

To Emp 141-28 he is mentally and **physically** sick.

Picture

To Wives 118-19 a **picture** of the ideal man.

Pig

Dr Bob Ni 178-1 looked like a **pig,** and was uncomfortable

Pitiful

Mo Ab Al 30-20 which led in time to **pitiful** and

Pity

Ho It Wo 67-4 the same tolerance, **pity**, and patience that

Plague

Th Fam af 124-26 a blight, a veritable **plague.**

Plagued

Th Fam Af 123-28 family will be **plagued** by spectres from

Planted

To Wives 113-7 The seed has been **planted** in his mind.

Th Fam Af 130-14 to be firmly **planted** on earth.

Plastered

Dr Bob Ni 179-7 and I had come home **plastered,**

Play

Ho It Wo 68-14 We are in the world to **play** the role

Th Fam Aft 122-16 each wants to **play** the lead?

Th Fam Af 131-21 if the family is going to **play** an

Th Fam Af 132-33 who seldom **play,** do not laugh much.

Th Fam Af 133-1 let each family **play** together

To Emp 146-11 You may need to encourage him to **play**

Playing

Ho It Wo 62-27 we had to quit **playing** God.

Plea

To Emp 136-19 I still expected a **plea** for clemency,

Pleasure

Wo Wi Ot 102-11 try yo increase the **pleasure** of those there;

Th Fam Af 132-3 new avenues of usefulness and **pleasure.**

Dr Bob Ni 181-2 2. It is a **pleasure.**

Pleasures

Wo Wi Ot 97-9 great interference with your **pleasures,**

A Vi Fo You 151-6 The old **pleasures** were gone.

Plight

Mo Ab Al 43-16 the average alcoholic's **plight**

A Vi Fo You 155-23 admitting his **plight** to people

Plunge

Th Fam Af 125-32 He may either **plunge** into a frantic

Poison

Ho It Wo 66-23 for alcoholics these things are **poison.**

Poisoning

A Vi Fo You 157-18 was told of the acute **poisoning**

Police

Wo Wi Ot 97-19 may have to send for the **police**

Possessed

Th Fam Af 123-33 The family may be **possessed** by the idea

Possession

Th Fam Af 124-21 the dark past is the greatest **possession**

Possible

We Ag 55-6 God made these things **possible,**

We Ag 56-16 Is it **possible** that all the religious people I have

Postpone

Into Ac 75-2 not use this as a mere excuse to **postpone.**

Postponed

Into Ac 74-27 If that is so, this step may be **postponed.**

Postponement

Into Ac 83-23 a valid reason for **postponement** in some

Potential

Mo Ab Al 33-27 **Potential** female alcoholics often turn

Mo Ab Al 33-32 large numbers of **potential** alcoholics

Mo Ab Al 34-11 you may yet be a **potential** alcoholic.

Mo Ab Al 39-7 But the actual or **potential** alcoholic,

To Emp 149-14 many actual or **potential** alcoholics.

Pour

Dr Bob Ni 181-16 and **pour** liquor down my throat.

Power

Doc's Op xxv-32 **power** which pulls chronic

Doc's Op xxvi-17 a **power** greater than themselves

Th Is A Sol 24-7 lost the **power** of choice in drink.

We Ag 50-18 **Power** greater than themselves

Doc's Op xxvii-23 more than human **power** is needed

Doc's Op xxix-30 have the "will **power**" to resist

Bill's Story 11-10 and since, the **power**

Bill's Story 11-22 Had this **power** originated in him?

Bill's Story 11-23 had been no more **power**

Bill's Story 10-16 **Power** greater than myself

Bill's Story 12-20 **Power** greater than myself

We Ag 47-16 **Power** greater than myself

Th Is A Sol 23-31 assert his **power** of will.

The Is A Sol 24-7 lost the **power** of choice

Th Is A Sol 24-8 so-called will **power**

Mo Ab Al 33-17 on their own will **power**

Mo Ab Al 34-2,4 quit on our will **power**

Mo Ab Al 34-21 the **power** to choose whether

Mo Ab Al 40-27 of exercising my will **power**

Mo Ab Al 42-6 I saw that will **power** and self-

Mo Ab Al 43-20 must come from a Higher **Power**

We Ag 45-6 the needed **power** wasn't there

We Ag 45-9 Lack of **power,** that was our dilemma

We Ag 45-10 find a **power** by which we could live

We Ag 45-11 a **Power** greater than ourselves.

We Ag 45-12 how were we to find this **Power?**

We Ag 45-14 to find a **power** greater than yourself

We Ag 46-2 a **power** beyond ourselves

We Ag 46-17 believe in a **Power** greater than ourselves

We Ag 46-20 that **Power,** which is God

We Ag 46-28 a new sense of **power** and direction

We Ag 48-15 **Power** greater than himself

We Ag 50-10 the **Power** which is greater than himself

We Ag 50-18 **Power** greater than himself

We Ag 50-19 This **Power** has in each case

We Ag 50-26 attitude toward that **Power,**
We Ag 50-31 **power,** peace, happiness, and sense of
We Ag 53-4 were given the **power** to reason
We Ag 55-13 faith in a **Power** greater than ourselves
We Ag 55-15 **power** in human lives
We Ag 56-28 Infinite **Power** and Love.
Ho It Wo 59-2 there is One who has all **power-**
Ho It Wo 59-11 believe that a **power** greater than ourselves
Ho It Wo 59-32 and the **power** to carry that out.
Ho It Wo 60-18 That probably no human **power**
Ho It Wo 62-25 trying on our own **power**
Ho It Wo 63-8 As we felt new **power** flow in,
Ho It Wo 63-18,19 those I would help of thy **power**
Ho It Wo 66-28 had **power** to actually kill.
Into Ac 85-22 exercise our will **power** along this
Into Ac 85-26 has all knowledge and **power.**
Wo Wi Ot 92-13 functioning of the will **power.**
Wo Wi Ot 93-9 willing to believe in a **Power** greater
Wo Wi Ot 100-10,11 the dictates of a Higher **Power**
To Wives 112-6 have confidence in his **power** to stop
To Wives 118-8 every thing in his **power** to avoid disagreement
To Wives 118-33 not possibly have had any **power.**
Th Fam Af 132-30 have been given the **power** to help others.
To Emp 138-29 If he has your will **power** and guts
A Vi Fo You 158-24 and is a **power** in the church
A Vi Fo You 163-6 of **power** much greater than yourself.
Power of God
Bill's Story 13-32 Belief in the **power of God,**
We Ag 52-26 stop doubting the **power of God.**
To Wives 114-17 The **power of God** goes deep.
Th Fam Af 130-11 the **power of God** in our lives.
A Vi Fo You 162-4 the Presence and **power of God**
Powerful
Th Is a Sol 24-2 the most **powerful** desire to stop drinking
Th Is A Sol 28-7 the loving and **powerful** hand of God.
Ho It Wo 58-25 alcohol- cunning, baffling, **powerful!**
Ho It Wo 63-3 Being all **powerful,** He provided
To Wives 113-32 had spectacular and **powerful** recoveries.
The Fam Af 130-17 between a **powerful** spiritual experience

Th Fam Af 133-13 spiritual mode of living is a most **powerful**

A Vi Fo You 161-7 loving and All **Powerful** Creator.

Powerless

Ho It Wo 59-9 We admitted we were **powerless**

Powers

Ho It Wo 69-22 our sex **powers** were God given

Practical

Wo Wi Ot 89-1 **Practical** experience shows that nothing will

A Vi Fo You 160-29 **practical** approach to his problems,

Practice

Wo Wi Ot 97-29 **practice** spiritual principles

Praise

Into Ac 78-9 enemies sometimes **praise** what we are doing

Th Fam Af 127-4 Let them **praise** his progress.

Pray

Bill's Story 13-25 Never was I to **pray** for myself

Ho It Wo 70-15 We earnestly **pray** for the right ideal,

Into Ac 76-10 I **pray** that you now remove from me

Into Ac 82-8 Each might **pray** about it,

Into Ac 87-17 never to **pray** for our own selfish ends.

Prayed

To Wives 105-10 We have **prayed,** we have begged,

A Vi Fo You 158-1 I've **prayed** to God on hangover mornings

Prayer

Ho It wo 59-29 Sought through **prayer** and meditation

Into Ac 85-32 Step eleven suggests **prayer** and meditation.

Into Ac 85-33 shouldn't be shy on this matter of **prayer.**

Into Ac 87-11 a **prayer** that we be shown

Prayer meeting

Dr Bob Ni 172-9 Wednesday evening **prayer meeting.**

Prayers

Into Ac 87-25 memorize a few set **prayers**

Praying

Ho It Wo 59-31 **praying** only for knowledge of

Precedes

Mo Ab Al 40-20 insanity which **precedes** that first drink

Predicament

A Vi Fo Yo 154-9 his **predicament** was dangerous.

Prejudice

Bill's Story 12-4 the vestiges of my old **prejudice.**

Bull's Story 12-27 Scales of pride and **prejudice** fell from

We Ag 45-27 shared his honest doubt and **prejudice.**

We Ag 46-16 able to lay aside **prejudice**

We Ag 47-4 Do not let any **prejudice** you may have

We Ag 48-2 sensitiveness, and unreasoning **prejudice.**

We Ag 49-22 beg you to lay aside **prejudice,**

We Ag 55-24 helps sweep away **prejudice,**

Into Ac 77-1 We might **prejudice** them.

Wo Wi Ot 89-20 Unfortunately a lot of **prejudice** exists.

Wo Wi Ot 93-13 There is no arousing any **prejudice**

A Vi Fo You 162-7 it might **prejudice** his own work,

Prejudiced

We Ag 48-12 we hope no one else will be **prejudiced**

Prejudices

Bill's Story 1-8 the **prejudices** of my people concerning drink.

To Emp 139-14 strong opinions, perhaps **prejudices.**

Premeditation

Mo Ab Al 37-26 during the period of **premeditation**

Prepared

Into Ac 75-4 we are **prepared** for a long talk.

Presence

A Vi Fo You 162-4 the **Presence** and Power of God

Present

A Vi Fo Yo 159-31 how they might **present** their discovery

Pressure

Wo Wi Ot 91-14 prospect will see he is under no **pressure.**

Prevented

To Wives 120-31 If a repetition is to be **prevented,**

Price

A Vi Fo Yo 155-17 but the **price** seemed high

Pride

Bill's Story 8-1 **pride.** I, who had thought

Bill's Story 12-27 Scales of **pride** and prejudice

Th Is A Sol 25-5 the leveling of our **pride**

Ho It Wo 65-27 **Pride**- personal

Into Ac 75-11 We pocket our **pride** and go to it,

To Wives 104-23,24 long rendezvous with hurt **pride,**

To Wives 105-8,9 lies to protect our **pride**
To Wives 116-20 we were afflicted with **pride,**
Th fam Af 125-3 new victory over hurt **pride** could be won.
Dr Bob Ni 181-19 any other form of intellectual **pride**
Prime object
A Vi Fo Yo 160-3 the **prime object** was to provide
Principal
Th Fam Af 124-10 past thus becomes the **principal** asset
Principle
To Wives 111-1 The first **principle** of success
To Wives 115-20 The same **principle** applies in dealing
Th Fam Af 125-18 Another **principle** we observe carefully
Th Fam Af 128-2 will become the guiding **principle.**
Principles
Bill's Story 14-29 these **principles** in all my affairs.
Th Is a Sol 19-7 important demonstration of our **principles**
Mo Ab Al 42-33 spiritual **principles** would solve all my
We Ag 47-23 make use of spiritual **principles**
Ho It wo 60-3 and to practice these **principles** in all
Ho It Wo 60-8 perfect adherence to these **principles.**
Ho It Wo 60-10 The **principles** we have set down
Ho It Wo 64-30 we listed people, institutions or **principles**
Into Ac 79-6 there are some general **principles** which we
Into Ac 83-13 a desire to live upon spiritual **principles**
Into Ac 87-26 emphasize the **principles** we have been
Wo Wi Ot 93-10 that he live by spiritual **principles.**
Wo Wi Ot 93-12 language to describe spiritual **principles.**
Wo Wi Ot 94-2 dealing only with general **principles**
Wo Wi Ot 97-29 accept and practice spiritual **principles,**
Wo Wi Ot 98-26 explained to them the new **principles**
Wo Wi Ot 98-28 put those **principles** into action at home.
To Wives 112-21 If you act upon these **principles,**
To Wives 112-23 The same **principles** which apply to
To Wives 116-23 began to apply spiritual **principles** in
To Wives 116-30 we try to put spiritual **principles** to work
To Wives 121-14 it uses the general **principles** of the AA
Th Fam Af 130-21 do well to examine the **principles**
Th Fam Af 130-23 to approve these simple **principles,**
To Emp 139-5 Without mush ado he accepted the **principles**

A Vi Fo You 156-30 The use of spiritual **principles** in such
Private room
A Vi Fo Yo 157-2 Put him in a **private room.**
Probed
To Emp 142-19 be thoroughly **probed** on these points.
Problem
Doc's Op xxvii-20 Faced with this **problem,**
Doc's Op xxvii-27 little impression upon the **problem**
Doc's Op xxix-32 His alcoholic **problem** was so complex,
Th Is A Sol 17-4 They have solved the drink **problem.**
Th Is a Sol 19-14 the **problem** would hardly be scratched.
Th Is A Sol 19-21 setting forth the **problem** as we see it.
Th Is a Sol 19-24 concerned with a drinking **problem.**
Th Is A Sol 23-6 the main **problem** of the alcoholic
Th Is A Sol 25-11 in whom the **problem** had been solved,
Mo Ab Al 32-32 Every means of solving his **problem**
Mo Ab Al 35-3 this is the crux of the **problem.**
Mo Ab Al 39-32 a spiritual remedy for his **problem.**
Mo Ab Al 42-9 that a **problem** had them hopelessly
We Ag 45-15 which will solve your **problem.**
We Ag 56-32 His alcoholic **problem** was taken away.
Ho It Wo 68-9 didn't fully solve the fear **problem.**
Ho It Wo 69-29 as we would treat any other **problem.**
Into Ac 74-11 quick to see and understand our **problem.**
Into Ac 75-19 The feeling that the drink **problem** has
Into Ac 82-12 may decide that the **problem** be attacked
Into Ac 85-9 the **problem** has been removed.
Wo Wi Ot 98-23 Now, the domestic **problem:**
Wo Wi Ot 101-15 he would escape the alcohol **problem.**
Wo Wi Ot 103-16 the gravity of the alcoholic **problem,**
To Wives 104-11 whose **problem** has been solved,
To Wives 108-31 The **problem** with which you struggle
To Wives 111-28 friendly talk about his alcoholic **problem.**
To Wives 115-26 home of every **problem** drinker
To Wives 117-7 the pressing **problem** of drink
To Wives 118-22 once his liquor **problem** is solved,
To Wives 119-6 alcohol is no longer a **problem**
To Wives 120-28 removed your husband's liquor **problem**
To Wives 120-32 to be prevented, place the **problem,**

Th Fam Af 124-13 families still struggling with their **problem.**

Th Fam Af 126-6 rushes headlong at his economic **problem**

To Emp 139-25 To you, liquor is no real **problem.**

To Emp 144-1 the employee may resolve his **problem.**

To Emp 148-7 at least he will understand the **problem**

To Emp 149-1 we don't have any alcoholic **problem.**

To Emp 149-16 how prevalent this **problem** is.

To Emp 149-17 organization has no alcoholic **problem,**

A Vi Fo You 151-26 As ex-**problem** drinkers,

A Vi Fo You 160-11 among women who knew her **problem,**

Problems

Doc's Op xxvi-11 their **problems** pile up on them

Doc's Op xxvi-23 the solving of these **problems** become a part

Doc's Op xxvii-13 who had so many **problems**

Bill's Story 13-15 acquainted him with my **problems**

Bill's Story 13-25 meet my **problems** as he would have me

Bill's Story 13-32 which answered all my **problems..**

Bill's Story 15-8 to a solution of their **problems.**

Th Is A Sol 26-22 with respect to other **problems.**

Th Is A sol 29-15 disclosing ourselves and our **problems**

Mo Ab Al 40-24 licking my other personal **problems,**

Mo Ab Al 41-4 have any pressing **problems** or worries.

Mo Ab Al 42-33 would solve all my **problems.**

Mo Ab Al 43-11 commence to solve their **problems.**

We Ag 45-21 as we discuss his alcoholic **problems**

We Ag 55-5 people who rose above their **problems.**

Ho It Wo 69-10 We all have sex **problems.**

Into Ac 87-13 whatever we need to take care of such **problems.**

Wo Wi Ot 90-9 Get an idea of his behavior, his **problems,**

Wo Wi Ot 100-26 in solving your own domestic **problems,**

Wo Wi Ot 103-19 After all. Our **problems** were of our own

To Wives 116-18 He can solve your **problems** too.

To Wives 116-32 we find it solves our **problems** too;

To Wives 117-8 But all **problems** will not be solved

To Wives 117-12 old **problems** will still be with you.

To Wives 118-2 you can dispose of serious **problems** easier

To Wives 121-18 indicate the **problems** such people may face.

Th Fam Af 126-3 certain family **problems** will arise.

Th Fam Af 131-26 The **problems** of the community might

To Emp 144-32 If he feels free to discuss his **problems**
A Vi Fo You 156-1 he would have to face his **problems**
A Vi Fo You 160-4 new people might bring their **problems.**
A Vi Fo You 160-29 very practical approach to his **problems,**
Process
Mo Ab Al 42-19 The **process** snuffed out the last flicker of
Mo Ab Al 42-29 my mind to go through with the **process,**
We Ag 48-12 Sometimes this was a tedious **process;**
Th Fam Aft 122-8 This involves a **process** of deflation.
Profound
Th Fam Af 130-28 will be other **profound** changes
Program
Bill's Story 9-30 a practical **program** of action.
Th Is A Sol 19-23 useful **program** for anyone concerned
Mo Ab Al 42-21 spiritual answer and **program** of action
Mo Ab Al 41-25 but the **program** of action,
Ho It Wo 58-4 give themselves to this simple **program,**
Ho It Wo 59-8 suggested as a **program** of recovery:
Into Ac 72-12 the fifth step in the **program** of recovery
Into Ac 73-2 Having persevered with the rest of the **program,**
Into Ac Ot 94-4 Outline the **program** of action,
Wo Wi Ot 94-26 why he need not follow all of the **program.**
Wo Wi Ot 96-17 with the Twelve Steps of the **program** of
Wo Wi Ot 99-27 continue his **program** day by day.
To Wives 113-6 Avoid urging him to follow our **program.**
To Wives 113-19 and he may go for the **program** at once.
To Wives 117-1 We urge you to try our **program,**
To Wives 121-15 principles of the AA **program** as a guide
Th Fam Af 126-30 he is falling down on his spiritual **program.**
Th Fam Af 130-26 wife who adopts a sane spiritual **program,**
To Emp 147-3 conscientiously following the **program** of
Progress
Into Ac 78-8 Rarely do we fail to make satisfactory **progress.**
Progressive
Mo Ab Al 30-22 in the grip of a **progressive** illness.
Prolonged
Dr Bob Ni 173-20 after a **prolonged** period of drinking,
Promises
Into Ac 84-12 Are these extravagant **promises?**

To Emp 148-8 no longer be misled by ordinary **promises.**
Dr Bob Ni 177-23 **promises** which seldom kept me sober
Promising
A Vi Fo Yo 156-30 none too **promising.**
Proof
We Ag 48-28 but no perfect visual **proof.**
We Ag 48-29 that visual **proof** is the weakest **proof?**
Proposals
Into Ac 75-27 Carefully reading the first five **proposals**
Prospect
Wo Wi Ot 90-1 When you discover a **prospect**
Wo Wi Ot 91-13 **prospect** will see he is under no pressure.
Wo Wi Ot 96-1 Do not be discouraged if your **prospect**
A Vi Fo Yo 156-21 a first class alcoholic **prospect.**
Protect
To Wives 115-31 Your desire to **protect** him
Protection
Ho It Wo 59-5 We asked his **protection** and care
To Wives 115-21 Unless they actually need **protection**
Prove
Mo Ab Al 31-11 try to **prove** themselves exceptions
We Ag 54-24 We could not **prove** life in the sense
Proved
We Ag 55-2 people who **proved** that man could never fly?
A Vi Fo Yo 163-18 The doctor **proved** to be able
Proven
We Ag 47-19 It has been repeatedly **proven** among us
Proves
A Vi Fo Yo 153-14 Our own recovery **proves** that.
Provocation
Th Fam Af 124-31 under one **provocation** or another,
To Emp 146-3 defend a man from needless **provocation**
Provided
Ho It Wo 63-3 He **provided** what we needed,
Psychiatrist
A Vi Fo Yo 163-16 in touch with a prominent **psychiatrist**
Psychic
Doc's Op xxvii-8 experience an entire **psychic** change
Doc's Op xxvii-11 once a **psychic** change has occurred,

Doc's Op xxvii-24 to produce the essential **psychic** change.
Pulling
Th Fam Aft 123-16 years in **pulling** down the structure
Purpose
Th Fam Af 125-6 good and useful **purpose** is to be served,
Th Fam Af 130-9 replaced by a great sense of **purpose,**
Put
To Wives 120-2 what you can **put** into life

Q

Quarrels
Wo Wi Ot 100-15 not to participate in their **quarrels.**
Quart
Dr Bob Ni 175-6 I would get my friends to smuggle me a **quart,**
Dr Bob Ni 179-20 bought several **quarts** on my way to the hotel.
Quiet
Into Ac 75-23 find a place where we can be **quiet** for an hour.
Quiets
Ho It Wo 70-21 It **quiets** the imperious urge,
Quit
Mo Ab Al 34-3 beyond the point where we could **quit** on our
Mo Ab Al 34-19 Whether such a person can **quit** upon a
Mo Ab Al 39-29 his mind to **quit** drinking altogether.
We Ag 44-5 you find you cannot **quit** entirely,
Ho It Wo 62-27 we had **quit** playing God.
Wo Wi Ot 90-20 ask him if he wants to **quit** for good
To Emp 141-25 He wants to **quit** drinking
To Emp 142-12 do not want to **quit.**
Dr Bob Ni 181-23 to **quit** drinking liquor for good and all,
Quitting
Mo Ab Al 34-29 The experiment of **quitting** for a period
Dr Bob Ni 173-24 **quitting** school was very foolish

R

Racket
A Vi Fo Yo 158-8 trying to fight this booze **racket** alone.
Radically
To Wives 117-2 as the **radically** changed attitude
Raised from the dead
Bull's Story 11-19 in effect, **raised from the dead,**
Rare
Th Fam Af 125-14 these are **rare** occurrences.
Rarely
Ho It Wo 58-1 **Rarely** have we seen a person fail
Into Ac 78-8 **Rarely** do we fail to make satisfactory progress.
React
Th Fam Af 128-17 family may **react** unfavorably.
Reaction
To Wives 114-7 His **reaction** may be one of enthusiasm.
Reactions
To Emp 139-17 and understanding your own **reactions,**
Read
Wo Wi Ot 95-22 ask him to **read** this book
Readiness
Into Ac 74-28 if we hold ourselves in complete **readiness** to
Readjustment
Th Fam Aft 122-5 Successful **readjustment** means
To Emp 146-8 physical and mental **readjustment**
Ready
Into Ac 76-8 When **ready,** we say something like this:
Reality
Doc's Op xxiv-16 we were in full flight from **reality,**
We Ag 48-32 are not inward **reality** at all.
Realize
Into Ac 84-10 suddenly **realize** that God is doing for us
Reason
Mo Ab Al 42-2 trivial **reason** for having a drink.
We Ag 49-4 We have no **reason** to doubt it.
We Ag 51-9 they present a powerful **reason** why

We Ag 51-12 Almost everyone knows the **reason.**

We Ag 53-23 far over the Bridge of **Reason** toward the

We Ag 53-27 grateful that **Reason** had brought us so far.

We Ag 54-4 faithful to the God of **Reason.**

We Ag 54-15 have to do with pure **reason?**

We Ag 54-23 Were nothing left but pure **reason,**

We Ag 54-32 we saw that **reason** isn't everything.

We Ag 54-33 Neither is **reason,** as most of us use it,

Into Ac 72-22 The best **reason** first:

Into Ac 73-3 We think the **reason** is that they never

Into Ac 83-23 there may be a valid **reason** for

Wo Wi Ot 97-26 there is no **reason** why you should neglect

Wo Wi Ot 99-32 never come back for one **reason** or another.

Wo Wi Ot 101-24 if we have a legitimate **reason** for being

Wo Wi Ot 101-31 **reason** for going into this place?

Th Fam Af 134-11 unless the **reason** is understood

To Emp 140-6 whether the **reason** be for humanitarian or

To Emp 148-10 will have no further **reason** for covering up

Reasonable

We Ag 48-24 without a **reasonable** assumption

We Ag 49-27 we used to have no **reasonable** conception

To Emp 137-32 at work long beyond a **reasonable** period.

To Emp 146-14 A **reasonable** amount of latitude will be

We Ag 49-27 have no **reasonable** conception whatever.

We Ag 53-9 **reasonable** approach and interpretation.

We Ag 53-11 we think our present faith is **reasonable,**

To Emp 137-32 at work long beyond a **reasonable** period.

To Emp 146-14 A **reasonable** amount of latitude

Reasonableness

We Ag 48-11 It finally beat us into a state of **reasonableness.**

To Wives 111-26 come to appreciate your **reasonableness**

Reasonably

To Wives 110-33 has it's advantages when **reasonably** used.

Reasoned

Mo Ab Al 35-6 Friends who have **reasoned** with him

Mo Ab Al 40-22 I **reasoned** I was not so far advanced

Reasoning

Mo Ab Al 37-12 with our sound **reasoning** there inevitably

Mo Ab Al 37-14 Our sound **reasoning** failed to hold

We Ag 54-1 believe in our own **reasoning?**
Reasons
Bill's Story 2-30 I discovered many more **reasons** later on.
Mo Ab Al 36-32 Yet all **reasons** for not drinking were
We Ag 48-16 We think there are good **reasons.**
We Ag 51-2 they show the underlying **reasons**
Into Ac 72-21 when we see good **reasons** why we should
Wo Wi Ot 94-25 Your candidate may give **reasons** why he
Rebel
Wo Wi Ot 94-26 He may **rebel** at the thought
Rebellious
We Ag 56-2 he became **rebellious** at what he thought an
Reborn
Ho It Wo 63-12 We were **reborn.**
Recapture
A Vi Fo Yo 151-7 Never could we **recapture** the great
Receipt
Into Ac 80-8 giving him no **receipt** for it.
Receptive
Wo Wi Ot 91-16 may be more **receptive** when depressed.
Recluse
To Wives 115-3 you become a trembling **recluse,**
Reconciliation
Th Fam Af 124-30 miracle of **reconciliation** was at hand.
Reconciled
Into Ac 72 20 We will be more **reconciled** todiscussing
Reconstruction
Into Ac 83-1 there is a long period of **reconstruction** ahead.
Record
Mo Ab Al 35-14 had a commendable World War **record.**
Recover
Th Is A Sol 19-17 Many could **recover** if
Th Is A Sol 26-19 why he could not **recover**
Th Is a Sol 27-7 one single case **recover**
Mo Ab Al 39-22 had gone to **recover** from
Ho It Wo 58-2,3 Those who do not **recover**
Ho It Wo 58-12 but many of them do **recover** if
Wo Wi Ot 89-9 To watch people **recover,**
Wo Wi Ot 89-16 drinkers who want to **recover.**

Wo Wi Ot 92-20 little chance he can **recover** by himself.

Wo Wi Ot 96-8 cannot **recover** by himself.

Wo Wi Ot 97-30 head of the family will **recover.**

Wo Wi Ot 99-30 cannot **recover** unless he has his family

Th Fam Af 126-18 He is striving to **recover** fortune

Th Fam Af 133-11 does not often **recover** overnight

Th Fam Af 135-2 has to if he would **recover.**

To Emp 142-31 that your man wants to **recover**

To Emp 143-22 confidence in his ability to **recover?**

To Emp 146-30 And is still trying to **recover,**

A Vi Fo You 158-23 He has helped other men **recover,**

A Vi Fo You 162-11 willing and able to **recover**

A Vi Fo You 164-3 has had his opportunity to **recover**

Recovered

Doc's Op xxiii-24 appear to have **recovered.**

Doc's Op xxix-5 but partially **recovered** from

Th Is A Sol 17-3 Nearly all have **recovered**

Th Is A Sol 20-7 we have **recovered** from

Th Is A Sol 29-4 how we **recovered.**

We Ag 45-1 would have **recovered** long ago

Wo Wi Ot 90-23 you as a person who has **recovered.**

Wo Wi Ot 96-14 who have since **recovered,**

To Wives 113-8 men, much like himself, have **recovered.**

Th Fam Af 132-30 We have **recovered,** and have been given

Th Fam Af 133-14 We, who have **recovered** from serious

To Emp 146-21 An alcoholic who has **recovered,**

Recoveries

Doc's Op xxvii-25 **recoveries** resulting from psychiatric

To Wives 113-32 had spectacular and powerful **recoveries.**

Recovering

Th Fam Af 122-2 with the husband who is **recovering.**

Recovers

Mo Ab Al 30-17 alcoholic ever **recovers** control.

To Emp 149-29 The right kind of man, the kind who **recovers,**

Recovery

Doc's Op xxiii-3 the plan of **recovery**

Doc's Op xxiii-18 a possible means of **recovery.**

Doc's Op xxvii-8,9 little hope of his **recovery.**

Mo Ab Al 30-13 first step in **recovery.**
Mo Ab Al 31-2,3 there has been brief **recovery**
Ho It Wo 59-8 a program of **recovery:**
Into Ac 72-12 Fifth Step in the program of **recovery**
Into Ac 73-32 and their chance for **recovery!**
Wo Wi Ot 90-25 as part of their own **recovery,**
Wo Wi Ot 94-8,9 a vital part in your own **recovery.**
Wo Wi Ot 96-17,18 Twelve Steps of the program of **recovery**
Wo Wi Ot 97-1,2 his destruction rather than his **recovery.**
Wo Wi Ot 97-5 foundation stone of your **recovery.**
Wo Wi Ot 99-20 should be sure of his **recovery.**
Wo Wi Ot 99-33 **recovery** is not dependent upon people.
To Wives 113-13 hurry him the longer his **recovery**
To Wives 120-19 lessen your husband's chance of **recovery.**
Th Fam Af 125-31 At the beginning of **recovery**
Th Fam Af 127-15 Although financial **recovery** is on the way
To Emp 139-6 on the road to **recovery.**
To Emp 143-21 We had to place **recovery** above everything,
To Emp 143-22 without **recovery** we would have lost both
To Emp 145-33 decreased the man's chance of **recovery.**
To Emp 147-3 following the program of **recovery**
A Vi Fo You 153-14 Our own **recovery** proves that!
Rectify
Th Fam Af 124-9 to face and **rectify** errors
Rediscover
A Vi Fo yo 153-3 survive and **rediscover** life.
Redouble
To Wives 120-13 he must **redouble** his spiritual activities
Re-establish
Th Fam Af 134-17 to **re-establish** friendly relations
Reflected
To Wives 118-15 they will be **reflected** back to you
Reflection
Into Ac 86-15 remorse, or morbid **reflection,**
Reformer
Wo Wi Ot 89-19 as an evangelist or **reformer.**
Reforming
To Wives 111-20 your heart on **reforming** your husband.

Refusal

A Vi Fo Yo 158-33 much shocked by their son's **refusal**

Regain

To Wives 104-5 women **regain** their health as readily as men

Regard

Dr Bob Ni 172-27 without **regard** for the rights.

Regret

Ho It Wo 64-14 promptly and without **regret.**

Into Ac 77-28 and expressing our **regret.**

Into Ac 83-32 We will not **regret** the past

Regulate

Mo Ab Al 32-29 He tried to **regulate** his drinking

Rehabilitation

Doc's Op xxiii-19 As part of his **rehabilitation** he commenced

Doc's Op xxvi-28 the **rehabilitation** of these men

Doc's Op xxix-27 Following his physical **rehabilitation,**

Bill's Story 7-9 the mental and physical **rehabilitation** of

To Emp 148-18 permit the **rehabilitation** of good men.

Rejected

We Ag 45-30 **rejected** this particular conception because it

Rejection

We Ag 45-32 With that **rejection** we imagined we had

Relapse

Th Is A So 26-14 that **relapse** was unthinkable.

Mo Ab Al 31-3 followed always by a still worse **relapse.**

Mo Ab Al 35-2 the mental states that precede a **relapse**

To Wives 120-11 better that he have no **relapse** at all,

Th Fam Af 125-5 survived this ordeal without **relapse,**

Relate

Th Fam Af 125-19 we do not **relate** intimate experiences

Relation

We Ag 47-8 our first conscious **relation** with God as we

Relations

Ho It Wo 65-5 our personal, or sex **relations,**

Wo Wi Ot 98-24 or just strained **relations.**

Th Fam Af 134-18 friendly **relations** with his children.

Relationship

Th is A So 28-18 form a **relationship** upon simple and

Th Is A So 29-8 established his **relationship** with God.

Into Ac 72-3 a new **relationship** with our Creator,

Wo Wi Ot 100-1 dependent upon his **relationship** with God.

A Vi Fo You 164-17 your **relationship** with Him is right

Relationships

We Ag 52-16 having trouble with personal **relationships,**

Ho It Wo 64-33 our personal **relationships** (including sex)

Into Ac 82-26 Sweet **relationships** are dead.

Relax

Into Ac 86-31 We **relax** and take it easy.

Release

We Ag 55-7 We had seen spiritual **release,**

Th Fam Af 128-33 Joy at our **release** from a lifetime of

A Vi Fo You 151-3 It means **release** from care, boredom,

A Vi Fo You 152-19 - " "

A Vi Fo You 154-16 would find companionship and **release.**

A Vi Fo Yo 159-30 happy in their **release,**

Reliance

Doc's Op xxvi-11 their **reliance** upon things human,

A Vi Fo You 164-8 your real **reliance** is always upon Him.

Relief

Doc's Op xxviii-30 The only **relief** we have to suggest

Dr Bob Ni 174-32 physically and, in hope of **relief,**

Relieve

Ho It Wo 63-16 **Relieve** me of the bondage of self,

Relieved

Mo Ab Al 42-30 my alcoholic condition was **relieved,**

Dr Bob Ni 180-24 **relieved** of the terrible curse

Religion

Bill's Story 9-20 I've got **religion.**

Bill's Story 9-23 **religion.** He had that starry eyed look.

We Ag 49-22 even against organized **religion**

Into Ac 74-9 someone ordained by an established **religion**

Wo Wi Ot 93-27 not there to instruct him in **religion.**

Th Fam Af 132-2 If he does not argue about **religion,**

Religious

Bill's Story 9-30 of a simple **religious** idea

Bill's Story 11-7 that **religious** dispute had

Bill's Story 11-25 to look as though **religious** people

Th Is A Sol 17-7 **religious** backgrounds

Th Is A Sol 19-26 psychiatric, social and **religious**
Th Is A Sol 27-30 while his **religious** convictions
Th Is A Sol 28-11 Varieties of **Religious** Experience
Th Is A Sol 28-20 Those having **religious** affiliations
Th Is A Sol 28-24 **religious** bodies our members identify
Th Is A Sol 28-28 Not all of us join **religious** bodies
Mo Ab Al 43-22,23 Though not a **religious** person
We Ag 56-3 an overdose of **religious** education.
We Ag 56-17 **religious** people I have known
Into Ac 74-4 Those of us belonging to a **religious**
Into Ac 74-7,8 Though we have no **religious** connection
Into Ac 77-7 that we have gone **religious.**
Into Ac 77-9 being branded fanatics or **religious** bores?
Into Ac 87-22, Wo Wi Ot 93-18 to a **religious** denomination
Into Ac 87-24 members of **religious** bodies,
Into Ac 87-29 to see where **religious** people are right.
Wo Wi Ot 90-11 and his **religious** leanings.
Wo Wi Ot 93-19 His **religious** education and training
Th Fam Af 128-5 He becomes a **religious** enthusiast.
Th Fam Af 128-14 mother, who has been **religious** all her life,
Th Fam Af 131-28 family has no **religious** connections,
Th Fam Af 131-29 membership in a **religious** body.
Th Fam Af 131-30 Alcoholics who have derided **religious**
A Vi Fo You 158-32 They were deeply **religious** people,
Relive
Th Fam Af 132-23 **relive** the horrors of our past.
Rely
Ho It Wo 68-16 and humbly **rely** on Him,
Relying
Ho It Wo 68-13 trusting and **relying** upon God.
Remark
Th Fam Af 125-26 one careless, inconsiderate **remark**
Remarkable
Ho It Wo 63-2 all sorts of **remarkable** things followed.
Wo Wi Ot 100-6 **remarkable** things will happen.
Th Fam Af 133-16 have seen **remarkable** transformations
Remedy
Doc's Op xxiv-3 may well have a **remedy** for thousands
To Wives 112-33 will be shy of a spiritual **remedy,**

To Wives 118-17 willingness to **remedy** your own defects,

To Emp 137-33 employers have tried every known **remedy.**

To Emp 144-10 though he does not go for this **remedy.**

Remember

Th Fam Af 127-5 Let them **remember** that his drinking

A Vi Fo You 164-7 **remember** that your real reliance is

Remorse

Bill's Story 6-8 The **remorse,** horror and hopelessness

Ho It Wo 66-5 Sometimes it was **remorse**

Into Ac 86-14 not to drift into worry, **remorse** or

To Wives 106-32 the deepening pall of **remorse,**

Remorseful

Doc's Op xxvii-6 emerging **remorseful,** with a firm

Doc's Op xxviii-11 They are over-**remorseful**

Into Ac 81-13 often feels very **remorseful**

Into Ac 83-2 A **remorseful** mumbling that we are sorry

To Wives 109-24 He is **remorseful** after serious drinking bouts

Remove

Ho It Wo 59-19 ready to have God **remove** all these defects

Ho It Wo 59-21 Humbly asked Him to **remove** our shortcomings

Ho It Wo 68-25 We ask Him to **remove** our fear

Ho It Wo 71-2 God can **remove** whatever self-will has blocked

Into Ac 76-4 now ready to let God **remove** from us all the

Into Ac 76-10 I pray that you now **remove** from me every

Removed

To Wives 120-28 God has either **removed** your husband's

Rendezvous

To Wives 104-23 We have had long **rendezvous** with hurt pride

Renewed

Bill's Story 5-13 which **renewed** my wife's hope.

Renewing

Bill's Story 5-33 **Renewing** my resolve, I tried again.

Renews

Th Fam Af 131-12 When he **renews** interest in such things

Repair

Into Ac 76-21 **repair** the damage done in the past.

Th Fam Af 127-6 damage that may take long to **repair.**

Repaired

A Vi Fo Yo 156-15 have been **repaired** in four.

Repetition

To Wives 120-31 If a **repetition** is to be prevented,

Represented

Th Is A So 17-6 many of it's occupations are **represented,**

Reprieve

Into Ac 85-16 What we really have is a daily **reprieve**

Reproved

Th Fam Af 126-11 may show irritation when **reproved**

Reputation

Into Ac 73-14 He wants to enjoy a certain **reputation,**

Into Ac 79-11 We may lose our position or **reputation**

Into Ac 80-11 destroying the **reputation** of another.

Into Ac 80-16 would destroy the **reputation** of his partner,

Th Fam Af 126-18 striving to recover fortune and **reputation**

To Emp 148-22 waste of time, men and **reputation.**

Reputations

To Wives 105-9 and our husband's **reputations.**

Repute

A Vi Fo You 153-8 bad **repute** and hopelessness?

Requires

Into Ac 72-8 This **requires** action on our part,

Required

Bill's Story 12-20 Nothing more was **required** of me to make

Into Ac 79-11 We may lose our position or **reputation**

Rescue

Th Is A So 17-12 the moment after **rescue** from shipwreck

Resentful

Ho It wo 65-8 I'm **resentful** at:

Into Ac 81-5 a wife gets worn out, **resentful** and

Into Ac 86-6 Were we **resentful,** selfish, dishonest

To Wives 116-3 be careful not to be **resentful**

To Wives 117-32 not to disagree in a **resentful** or critical

To Wives 119-4 When **resentful** thoughts come,

Th Fam Af 122-14 the more **resentful** they become.

Th Fam Af 127-26 As each member of a **resentful** family

Th Fam Af 127-30 self-justification or **resentful** criticism.

Resentment

Bill's Story 13-16 toward whom I felt **resentment.**

Bill's Story 15-11,12 self-pity and **resentment**

Th Is A Sol 18-8 fierce **resentment,** financial

Ho It Wo 64-23 **Resentment** is the "number one" offender.

Ho It Wo 66-10 a life which includes deep **resentment**

Ho It Wo 66-15 this business of **resentment**

Ho It Wo 68-4 even though we had no **resentment**

Into Ac 79-18 Because of **resentment** and drinking,

Into Ac 84-24 dishonesty, **resentment** and fear.

Wo Wi Ot 100-19 warn against rousing **resentment**

To Wives 105-1 to bitter **resentment.**

To Wives 117-29 Never forget that **resentment** is a deadly

To Wives 118-27 **resentment** that love and loyalty could not

The Fam Aft 126-27 **Resentment** grows.

To Emp 145-18 enemies if alcoholics are **resentment,** jealousy

Resentments

Ho It Wo 62-5 ourselves, our **resentments**, or our

Ho It Wo 64-28,29 In dealing with **resentments**

Ho It Wo 66-30 these **resentments** must be mastered,

Ho It Wo 70-24,25 listed and analyzed our **resentments.**

To Wives 117-22 hurt feelings and **resentments.**

Reservation

Ho It Wo 63-28 voicing it without **reservation.**

Resign

To Emp 148-3 I think you ought to **resign.**

Resolutely

Ho It Wo 67-15 we **resolutely** looked for our own mistakes.

Resolutions

Mo Ab Al 34-14 after making their **resolutions;**

Resolves

To Wives 107-18 surprise us with fresh **resolves**

Respected

Th Fam Aft 122-12 having his or her wishes **respected.**

A Vi Fo Yo 153-7 happy, **respected,** and useful

A Vi Fo Yo 158-22 a **respected** and useful member

Responsibilities

Wo Wi Ot 97-3 Never avoid these **responsibilities,**

Th Fam Af 130-31 She met these **responsibilities** gallantly.

To Emp 137-26 he tries to meet these **responsibilities.**

A Vi Fo Yo 154-28 But what about his **responsibilities-**
Responsibility
To Wives 120-1 sense of **responsibility** for others.
Responsible
Into Ac 83-7 our own actions are partly **responsible.**
To Emp 143-13 better for him to feel fully **responsible.**
Restore
Ho It Wo 59-12 could **restore** us to sanity.
Restored
We Ag 57-4 God had **restored** his sanity.
We Ag 57-10 God has **restored** us all to our right minds.
Th Fam Af 123-23 hard work to be **restored** financially,
A Vi Fo You 161-26 being **restored** and united under one God,
Result
Into Ac 78-4 we will be gratified with the **result.**
To Wives 106-22 The unexpected **result** was that
Results
Th Fam Af 134-32 Marvelous **results** often follow
To Emp 138-11 and described the symptoms and **results**
To Emp 144-6 are you not looking for **results** rather than
Retaining
To Emp 14-3 would he be worth **retaining?**
Retaliate
Ho It Wo 61-25 make each of them wish to **retaliate,**
Ho It Wo 62-9 the toes of our fellows and they **retaliate.**
Retaliation
Ho It Wo 67-9 We avoid **retaliation** or argument.
Retreat
Th Fam Af 129-25 he may **retreat** further into himself
Return
Th Is A So 25-29 no **return** through human aid,
To Emp 143-32 To **return** to the subject matter of this book:
To Emp 144-28 On your employee's **return**, talk with him.
Returned
A Vi Fo Yo 154-32 His sanity **returned**
Reunited
To Wives 119-6 After all, your family is **reunited,**

Reveal

To Emp 145-5 **reveal** that he has padded

Revelation

We Ag 57-11 To this man, the **revelation** was sudden.

Revolted

Into Ac 73-17 he is **revolted** at certain episodes

Revolutionary

We Ag 50-27 a **revolutionary** change to their way of living

Revulsion

To Emp 141-2 his **revulsion** will be terrible.

Rid

Ho It Wo 62-20 entirely getting **rid** of self

Ridicule

Th Fam Af 125-23 but criticism or **ridicule** coming from

Right

Into Ac 87-29 see where religious are **right.**

A Vi Fo You 164-18 that your relationship with Him is **right,**

Right person

Into Ac 74-30 that we talk with the **right person.**

Righteous

A Vi Fo You 152-14 like some **righteous** people I see?

Rights

Dr Bob Ni 172-27 without regard for the **rights,** wishes

Rigorous honesty

Ho It Wo 58-10 which demands **rigorous honesty.**

To Emp 145-9 as you know, demands **rigorous honesty.**

Riot

Ho It Wo 62-16 extreme example of self-will run **riot,**

Rise

A Vi Fo You 153-18 will **rise** to their feet and march on.

Risk

To Wives 112-5 **risk** he takes if he drinks too much.

Risks

Into Ac 80-22 it was better to take those **risks** than to stand

Road

To Wives 114-28 their **road** will be smoother.

Road of Happy Destiny

A Vi Fo You 164-26 as you trudge the **Road of Happy Destiny.**

Roaring

A Vi Fo You 155-29 he went on a **roaring** bender.

Rocky

To Wives 104-22 We have traveled a **rocky** road,

Romantic

Th Fam aft 123-7 They remember when father was **romantic,**

Rough

In Ac 72-5 we have ascertained in a **rough** way

Ruin

A Vi Fo You 156-9 for this might mean **ruin,**

Ruined

Th Fam Aft 123-18 are now **ruined** or damaged.

Rule

Mo Ab Al 31-11 prove themselves exceptions to the **rule,**

Into Ac 74-21 The **rule** is we must be hard on ourself,

Wo Wi Ot 90-33 no specific **rule** can be given.

Wo Wi Ot 99-26 no **rule** can be laid down.

Wo Wi Ot 101-23 our **rule** is not to avoid a place where

To Wives 118-16 Live and let live is the **rule.**

Ruptured

To Emp 140-21 spinal fluid actually **ruptured** the brain.

S

Sacrifice

Into Ac 79-16 **sacrifice** others to save himself

Safe

Into Ac 85-7 of neutrality- **safe** and protected.

Saints

Ho It Wo 60-8 We are not **saints.**

Salesmen

To Emp 150-2 as much as five normal **salesmen.**

Sally

A Vi Fo Yo 152-1 we smile at such a **sally.**

Salvaging

To Emp 139-10 in **salvaging** their sick employees.

To Emp 140-5 Is he worth **salvaging?**

Sane

Bill's Story 14-16 to ask if I were still **sane.**

Th Fam Af 130-18 a life of **sane** and happy usefulness.

Th Fam Af 130-26 wife who adopts a **sane** spiritual program,

Sanely

Into Ac 85-1 react **sanely** normally,

Sanity

Bill's Story 7-3 People feared for my **sanity.**

We Ag 57-4,5 God had restored his **sanity.**

Ho It Wo 59-12 could restore us to **sanity.**

Ho It Wo 70-17 for **sanity**, and for the strength to do

Into Ac 84-31 by this time **sanity** will have returned.

A Vi Fo You 154-32 His **sanity** returned and he thanked God.

Satisfactory

A Vi Fo Yo 152-21 The most **satisfactory** years

Satisfied

Th Fam Af 134-4 would be **satisfied** by candy.

Save

Ho It Wo 67-7 God **save** me from being angry.

Into Ac 74-19 have no right to **save** our own skin

Into Ac 79-16 sacrifice others to **save** himself

Saved

Wo Wi Ot 103-9 whose lives could have been **saved,**

To Emp 150-3 they have been **saved** from a living death.

Scale

Into Ac 84-2 No matter how far down the **scale** we have gone

Scandalous

Th Fam Af 125-12 there might be **scandalous** gossip,

Scarcely

Th Fam Af 127-13 He can **scarcely** square the account

Scared

Dr Bob Ni 175-15 thoroughly **scared** by what happened,

School

Dr Bob Ni 173-24 quitting **school** was very foolish,

Scotch

Dr Bob Ni 179-19 I drank all the **scotch** they had on the train

Scrapes

To Emp 140-30 these **scrapes** can generally charged,

A Vi Fo You 161-18 Cleaning up old **scrapes,**

Screaming

To Wives 107-7 **screaming** delirium and insanity.

Search

We Ag 55-25 to **search** diligently within yourself,

Searched

Ho It Wo 64-18 we **searched** out the flaws in our make-up

Secret

Into Ac 80-10 having a **secret** and exciting affair with

Security

Th Fam Aft 123-7 of happiness and **security**

Sedatives

Dr Bob Ni 176-5 fill up on large doses of **sedatives**

Dr Bob Ni 177-20 taking large doses of **sedatives**

Seed

To Wives 113-6 The **seed** has been planted

To Wives 117-9 **seed** has started to sprout in

Seldom

Dr Bob Ni 176-14 very **seldom** did I receive patients.

Self-appraisal

Into Ac 72-18 find a solitary **self-appraisal** sufficient.

Into Ac 76-20 to a drastic **self-appraisal.**

Wo Wi Ot 94-5 made a **self-appraisal,**

Self-centered

Ho It Wo 61-28 Our actor is **self-centered**

To Wives 116-21 to make up the **self-centered** person;

Th Fam Af 124-2 We think that such a view is **self-centered**

Self-centeredness

Bill's Story 14-4 destruction of **self-centeredness**

Ho It Wo 62-6 Selfishness- **self-centeredness!**

Ho It Wo 62-24 reduce our **self-centeredness** much

Self-confidence

Ho It Wo 68-8 once had great **self-confidence,**

Self-confident

Mo Ab Al 40-26 every right to be **self-confident**

Self-conscious

To Wives 115-15 You will no longer be **self-conscious**

Dr Bob Ni 178-14 I was **self-conscious** and ill at ease
Self-consciousness
To Wives 115-18 lack of **self-consciousness** will do wonders
Self-control
Th Is A Sol 26-20 to regain **self-control**
Self-deception
Mo Ab Al 31-10 every form of **self-deception**
Self-delusion
Ho It Wo 62-8 fear, **self-delusion**, self-seeking
Self-destruction
We Ag 56-9 the point of **self-destruction.**
Self-discipline
Mo Ab Al 32-25 sobriety and **self-discipline**
Self-esteem
Ho It Wo 64-30 it was found that our **self-esteem**
Ho It Wo 65-4 Was it our **self-esteem**
Ho It Wo 65-10,12,14,16,21,29 **Self-esteem** (fear)
Sel-evident
Bill's Story 9-32 and the result was **self-evident.**
Self-imposed
We Ag 53-15 crushed by a **self-imposed** crisis
Self-justification
Th Fam Af 127-30 **self-justification** or resentful criticism.
Self-knowledge
Bill's Story 7-22 was the answer - **self-knowledge**
Mo Ab Al 39-9 on the basis of **self-knowledge**
Mo Ab Al 40-6 **Self-knowledge** would fix it.
Mo Ab Al 42-7 **Self-knowledge** would not help
Self-pity
Bill's Story 8-9 that bitter morass of **self-pity**
Bill's Story 15-11 by waves of **self-pity** and resentment
Ho It Wo 62-5 our resentments, or our **self-pity?**
Ho It Wo 62-8 self-delusion, self-seeking, and **self-pity**
Into Ac 84-4 uselessness and **self-pity** will disappear.
Into Ac 86-22 that it be divorced from **self-pity**
Into Ac 88-4 **self-pity** or foolish decisions.
To Wives 104-34 frustration, **self-pity**, misunderstanding,
To Wives 105-30 their **self-pity** made them killjoys.
To Wives 116-20 with pride, **self-pity**, vanity and all

Th Fam Af 127-30 heated argument, **self-pity,**
Self-pitying
Ho It Wo 61-18 angry, indignant, **self-pitying.**
Self-propulsion
Ho It Wo 60-29 try to live by **self-propulsion.**
Self-reliance
Doc's Op xxix-16 brimming over with **self-reliance**
Ho It Wo 68-6 Wasn't it because **self-reliance** failed us?
Ho It Wo 68-6,7 **Self-reliance** was as good as far as
Self-respect
Dr Bob Ni 180-26 I have regained my **self-respect**
Self-revealing
Th Is A Sol 29-11 consider these **self-revealing**
Self-sacrifice
Bill's Story 15-1 work and **self-sacrifice** for others
Wo Wi Ot 93-26 by **self-sacrifice** an unselfish
Self-sacrificing
Ho It Wo 61-7 modest and **self-sacrificing.**
To Wives 105-7 We have been unselfish and **self-sacrificing.**
Self-searching
Th Is A Sol 25-4 none of us liked the **self-searching**
Self-seeker
Ho It Wo 61-19 Is he not really a **self-seeker**
Self-seeking
Ho It Wo 62-8 **self-seeking,** and self-pity
Ho It Wo 67-17 dishonest, **self-seeking** and frightened?
Into Ac 84-6 **Self-seeking** will slip away.
Into Ac 86-23 dishonest or **self-seeking** motives
Self-sufficiency
We Ag 52-32 the idea that **self-sufficiency** would
Self-will
Ho It Wo 60-26 any life run on **self-will** can hardly
Ho It Wo 62-16 example of **self-will** run riot,
Ho It Wo 71-2,3 God can remove whatever **self-will** has
Into Ac 76-23 our effort to live on **self-will**
Into Ac 87-14 for freedom from **self-will**
Selfish
Th Is A Sol 21-27 dishonest and **selfish.**
Ho It Wo 61-8 egotistical, **selfish** and dishonest.

Ho It Wo 67-16, 69-13 Where had we been **selfish,**

Ho It Wo 69-20 was it **selfish** or not?

Into Ac 82-27 **Selfish** and inconsiderate habits

Into Ac 84-5 lose interest in **selfish** things

Into Ac 86-6 Were we resentful, **selfish,** dishonest

Into Ac 87-17 never tp pray for our own **selfish** ends.

To Wives 116-22 we were not above **selfishness**

Selfishly

Ho It Wo 69-23 neither to be used lightly or **selfishly**

Selfishness

Ho It Wo 62-6 **Selfishness**- self-centeredness!

Ho It Wo 62-18 must be rid of this **selfishness.**

Into Ac 84-23,24 Continue to watch for **selfishness,**

Dr. Bob Ni 172-4 engendered the **selfishness** which played

Selves

Mo Ab Al 30-12 concede to our innermost **selves** that we were

To Wives 107-20 would be their old sweet **selves,**

Sense

Th Fam Af 130-10 replaced by a great **sense** of purpose,

Dr Bob Ni 181-1 1, **Sense** of duty.

Sensible

Th Is A So 21-25 He is often perfectly **sensible**

Mo Ab Al 42-26 program of action, though entirely **sensible,**

Into Ac 83-25 We should be **sensible,**

To Emp 148-24 We think we are **sensible** when we urge

Sensitive

Th Fam Af 125-27 We alcoholics are **sensitive** people.

Separate

To Wives 121-13 **separate** from Alcoholics Anonymous,

Th Fam Af 125-2 to **separate** for a time

Serenity

Bill's Story 14-10 peace and **serenity** as I had

Ho It Wo 68-17 to match calamity with **serenity.**

Into Ac 84-1 comprehend the word **serenity**

Serious

Bill's Story 3-22 drinking assumed more **serious** proportions

Mo Ab Al 34-9 becoming **serious** drinkers again later.

Mo Ab Al 35-30 alcoholic and in a **serious** condition.

Mo Ab Al 37-25 there was little **serious** or effective thought

We Ag 56-8 ever more **serious** alcoholism,

Wo Wi Ot 91-27 If he is in a **serious** mood

To Wives 112-20 the wife of another **serious** drinker.

To Wives 118-2 you can dispose of **serious** problems

To Wives 118-5 This is getting **serious.**

Th Fam Af 125-28 to outgrow that **serious** handicap.

Th Fam Af 133-15 have recovered from **serious** drinking,

Th Fam Af 135-22 his more **serious** ailments were being

To Emp 141-16 realize how **serious** my situation was.

To Emp 147-23 trying to help **serious** drinkers who should

To Emp 148-24 plug up this sometimes **serious** leak.

A Vi Fo Yo 151-24 Now and then a **serious** drinker,

Sermon

Into Ac 80-27 After the **sermon**, he quietly got up

Serve

Into Ac 85-20 How can I best **serve** thee-

Service

Into Ac 77-4 be of maximum **service** to God

Services

To Emp 146-19 make use of his **services** with other employees

Seven

A Vi Fo Yo 159-27 these three had succeeded with **seven** more.

Severe

To Emp 142-28 This may seem **severe,** but it is

Sex

Ho It Wo 68-28 Now about **sex.**

Ho It Wo 68-32 cry that **sex** is a lust of our lower nature,

Ho It Wo 69-1 who cry for **sex** and more **sex;**

Ho It Wo 69-10 We all have **sex** problems.

Ho It Wo 69-19 sound ideal for future **sex** life.

Ho It Wo 69-22 that our **sex** powers were God-given

Ho It Wo 69-29 we treat **sex** as we would any other problem.

Ho It Wo 69-33 God alone can judge our **sex** situation.

Ho It Wo 70-3 fanatical about **sex** as others are loose.

Ho It Wo 70-15 To sum up about **sex:**

Into Ac 80-3 drinking does complicate **sex** relations

Th Fam Af 134-7 A word about **sex** relations.

Sexually

Th Fam Af 134-7 Alcohol is so **sexually** stimulating

Shadow of a doubt

Th Fam Af 135-4 status beyond the **shadow of a doubt.**

Shaking

Bill's Story 5-8 early in the morning **shaking** violently.

Shaky

Wo Wi Ot 102-7 if you are **shaky,** you had better work with

Shameful

Th Fam af 123-31 humiliating, **shameful** or tragic.

Shared

Th Is A So 17-17 The feeling of having **shared**

A Vi Fo Yo 159-17 They **shared** their homes,

Sharing

Wo Wi Ot 97-10 It may mean **sharing** your money and

Shield

To Wives 120-23 to **shield** him from temptation.

Shielded

To Emp 147-2 he will be **shielded** from temptation to drink.

Shivering

Vi Fo yo 151-15 **shivering** denizens of his mad realm,

Shocked

Th Fam Af 132-37 Outsiders are sometimes **shocked**

To Emp 149-11 He might be **shocked** if he knew

A Vi Fo Yo 158-32 much **shocked** by their son's refusal

Shocking

To Emp 145-4 proceeds to tell you **shocking** things?

Shockingly

Into Ac 82-20 he has so **shockingly** treated.

Shortness of breath

Dr Bob Ni 178-2 uncomfortable from **shortness of breath.**

Shoulder

A Vi Fo You 153-1 commence **shoulder** to **shoulder** your common

Short

Ho It Wo 70-5 Suppose we fall **short** of the chosen ideal

Into Ac 78-28 We may be **short** in our accounts

Shortcomings

Th Is A So 19-31 tolerance of other people's **shortcomings**

Th Is A So 25-6 the confession of **shortcomings** which

We Ag 50-2 sometimes used their **shortcomings**

Ho It Wo 59-21 asked Him to remove our **shortcomings**

Th Fam af 127-27 begins to see his **shortcomings**

Shortcuts

Th Fam Aft 123-1 alluring **shortcuts** and by-paths

Shotgun

To Emp 137-4 the trigger of a loaded **shotgun-**

Showing

Th Fam Af 124-18 **Showing** others who suffer how we

Shrink

Into Ac 80-5 drastic step is indicated we must not **shrink.**

Shut

Ho It Wo 66-17 we **shut** ourselves off from the sunlight of

Sick

Ho It Wo 66-33 were perhaps spiritually **sick.**

Ho It Wo 67-2 they, like ourselves, were **sick** too.

Ho It Wo 67-6 This is a **sick** man.

Ho It Wo 70-30 we look on them as **sick** people.

Wo Wi Ot 90-6 they are dealing with a **sick** person.

Wo Wi Ot 92-2 learned that you were **sick.**

Wo Wi Ot 100-18 that he has been a very **sick** person

Wo Wi Ot 101-17 to shield the **sick** man from temptation

To Wives 107-12 that we were dealing with **sick** men.

To Wives 108-18 another very **sick** unreasonable person.

To Wives 115-11 that he is a **sick** person,

Th Fam Af 130-32 to treat father as a **sick** or wayward child.

To Emp 139-10 in salvaging their **sick** employees.

To Emp 141-28 he is mentally and physically **sick.**

To Emp 147-31 an alcoholic, you are a mighty **sick** man.

To Emp 149-20 refers to alcoholics, **sick** people,

A Vi Fo You 153-19 approach still other **sick** ones

A Vi Fo You 157-22 Yes that's me, said the **sick** man,

A Vi Fo You 164-15 for the man who is still **sick.**

Sickened

Doc's Op xxiv-19 our bodies were **sickened** as well.

To Wives 108-12 usually because he is warped and **sickened**

Sickness

Th Is A So 18-3 in a way no other human **sickness** can.

To Emp 140-11 where the alcoholic **sickness** is discussed

Sign
To Wives 120-18 The slightest **sign** of fear
Silly
To Wives 116-29 But it was a **silly** idea
Simple
Doc's Op xxvii-16 to follow a few **simple** rules.
Bill;s Story 14-3 **Simple**, but not easy; a price had to be paid.
Th Is A So 27-2 maintain a certain **simple** attitude.
Th Is A So 28-19 form a relationship upon **simple**
We Ag 46-29 provided we took other **simple** steps.
We Ag 47-20 that upon this **simple** cornerstone
We Ag 50-33 met a few **simple** requirements.
We Ag 52-25 a **simple** reliance upon the Spirit of the Universe,
We Ag 57-7 Yet it's elements are **simple.**
Ho It Wo 58-4 give themselves to this **simple** program.
Ho It Wo 62-31 Most good ideas are **simple,**
Into Ac 88-10 let Go discipline us in the **simple** way we have
Th Fam Af 130-22 approve these **simple** principles,
Sincere
Doc's Op xxvii-17 cried out to me in **sincere** and despairing
Th Is a Sol 18-30 the **sincere** desire to be helpful;
Into Ac 77-12 a **sincere** desire to set right the wrong.
To Emp 149-11 at this gentleman's **sincere** opinion.
Sincerely
Ho It Wo 63-1 When we **sincerely** took such a position
Wo Wi Ot 95-21 If he is **sincerely** interested
Dr Bob Ni 181-24 and **sincerely** feel that you must have
Sincerity
Mo Ab Al 37-16 in all earnestness and **sincerity**
To Wives 117-14 The faith and **sincerity** of both you and
Sinful
Th Fam Af 135-13 something rather **sinful** about these
Sink
A Vi Fo You 163-30 Some of them may **sink** and perhaps
Sinking
Th Fam Af 132-20 When we see a man **sinking** into the mire
Sins
Bill's Story 13-11 faced my **sins** and became willing

Situation

Ho It Wo 70-16 for guidance in each questionable **situation,**

Into Ac 79-32 the whole **situation** has long since been

To Wives 104-20 no **situation** is too difficult

To Wives 114-18 You may have the reverse **situation**

Sixth sense

Into Ac 85-30 begun to develop this vital **sixth sense.**

Skeletons

Th Fam Af 123-32 to bury these **skeletons** in a dark closet

Th Fam Af 125-9 keep few **skeletons** in the closet.

Skin

Into Ac 74-19 to save our own **skin** at another person's

Skip

Into Ac 72-22 If we **skip** this vital step

Slander

Into Ac 80-24 guilty of such ruinous **slander.**

Sleeping

Dr Bob Ni 175-32 the fear of not **sleeping,**

Sleeplessness

Dr Bob Ni 177-13 My phobia for **sleeplessness** demanded

Slip

Wo Wi Ot 100-4 seen others **slip** when the family came back

To Emp 139-3 the man did **slip** and was fired.

Dr Bob Ni 181-6 for myself against a possible **slip.**

Slow

Into Ac 78-22 Our drinking has made us **slow** to pay.

Slowly

We Ag 57-12 Some of us grow into it more **slowly.**

Slyly

To Emp 145-29 he was **slyly** carrying tales.

Smash

Wo Wi Ot 97-15 A drunk may **smash** the furniture

Smelled

Dr Bob Ni 178-3 after one was all **smelled** up with beer

Smile

To Wives 118-5 of either to **smile** and say,

Smoother

To Wives 114-28 their road will be **smoother.**

Smuggle

Dr Bob Ni 175-6 I would get my friends to **smuggle** me a quart,

Dr Bob Ni 176-21 supply of liquor and **smuggle** it home

Snags

To Wives 117-21 Some of the **snags** you will encounter

Sober

Bill's Story 4-31 or hardly draw a **sober** breath.

Wo Wi Ot 99-13 **sober**, considerate, and helpful

To Wives 116-1 when he is **sober** and in good spirits.

Th Fam Af 127-3 They should be thankful he is **sober**

Th Fam Af 131-3 When **sober**, father usually obeyed.

A Vi Fo You 154-8 weak, and **sober** but a few months,

A Vi Fo You 154-21 had he not been **sober** six months now?

A Vi Fo You 156-25 a grand chap when he's **sober,**

A Vi Fo You 159-15 if they would remain **sober,**

Dr Bob Ni 176-1 if I did not stay **sober** enough to earn money,

Dr Bob Ni 177-15 I had to stay **sober** during the day,

Dr Bob Ni 177-24 promises which seldom kept me **sober**

Dr Bob Ni 179-22 stayed **sober** Monday till after the dinner

Sobriety

Bill's Story 5-12 there were periods of **sobriety**

Mo Ab Al 33-11 period of **sobriety**

Into Ac 82-29 when he says that **sobriety** is enough.

Wo Wi Ot 100-24 the blessed fact of his **sobriety.**

Wo Wi Ot 101-10 His only chance for **sobriety**

To Wives 118-10 he owes you more than **sobriety.**

To Wives 119-15 to maintain his own **sobriety.**

Th Fam Af 128-7 As soon as his **sobriety** begins

Th Fam Af 129-33 will do more to insure his **sobriety**

A Vi Fo You 152-6 for he isn't happy about his **sobriety**

Sociability

A Vi Fo You 160-2 Aside from fellowship and **sociability,**

Social lubricant

To Wives 110-31 liquor as a **social lubricant.**

Softer

Ho It Wo 58-20 could find an easier, **softer** way.

Soil

To Wives 117-9 started to sprout in a new **soil,**

Solid

Wo Wi Ot 102-3 be sure you are on **solid** spiritual ground

Solution

Th Is A Sol 17-22 discovered a common **solution**

Th Is A Sol 25-4 There is a **solution**

Th Is A Sol 25-26 no middle-of-the-road **solution**

Mo Ab Al 43-25 virtually no other **solution.**

Wo Wi Ot 91-9 in the way of a **solution.**

Wo Wi Ot 92-29 because you offer a **solution.**

Wo Wi Ot 95-16 If he is not interested in your **solution,**

To Wives 104-12 not yet found a happy **solution.**

To Wives 117-6 find a **solution** for the pressing problem

To Emp 141-19 the **solution** contained in this book,

To Emp 145-8 if he has accepted our **solution**

Solve

Doc's Op xxvi-13 astonishingly difficult to **solve.**

Mo Ab Al 42-33 spiritual principles would **solve** all my

Mo Ab Al 43-10 commence to **solve** their problems.

We Ag 45-15 which will **solve** your problem.

Ho It Wo 68-9 it didn't fully **solve** the fear problem.

To Wives 116-17 If God can **solve** the age-old riddle

To Wives 116-18 He can **solve** your problems too.

Solved

Th Is A Sol 17-4 They have **solved** the drink problem.

Th Is A Sol 25-11 in whom the problem had been **solved,**

To Wives 118-22 once his liquor problem is **solved**

To Wives 117-8 all problems will not be **solved**

To Wives 118-22 once his liquor problem is **solved,**

Th Fam Af 126-8 troubles are about to be **solved,**

Solves

To Wives 116-32 we find it **solves** our problems too.

Solving

Doc's Op xxvi-22 let the **solving** of these problems

Doc's Op he despaired of ever **solving** them,

Mo Ab Al 32-32 Every means of **solving** his problem

Somebody

A Vi Fo Yo 157-24 You fellows are **somebody.**

Someone

Into Ac 74-20 **someone** who will understand.

Into Ac 74-25 discussing ourselves with **someone,**
Something
A Vi Fo Yo 164-16 you cannot transmit **something** you haven't
Son
To Wives 104-9 who see their **son** wasting away.
Sophomore
Dr Bob Ni 173-19 bad to worse until **sophomore** spring
Sordid
Wo Wi Ot 102-26 to visit the most **sordid** spot on earth
A Vi Fo Yo 151-18 Some of us sought out **sordid** places,
Sorry
Ho It Wo 70-8 If we are **sorry** for what we have done,
Into Ac 78-22 let these people know we are **sorry.**
Into Ac 81-7 begins to feel lonely, **sorry** for himself.
Into Ac 81-26 We are **sorry** for what we have done
Into Ac 83-3 A remorseful mumbling that we are **sorry**
To Wives 118-6 I'm **sorry** I got disturbed.
Dr Bob Ni 181-21 I feel **sorry** for you.
Sought
We Ag 57-13 He has come to all who honestly **sought** Him.
Ho It Wo 59-29 **Sought** through prayer and meditation
Ho It Wo 60-20 That God could and would if He were **sought.**
Sound minds
Th Fam Af 133-25 enjoy **sound minds** and bodies.
Source
A Vi Fo You 163-6 tapped a **source** of power
Special
Th Is A Sol 21-27 He often possesses **special** abilities,
Spectacular
To Wives 113-32 had **spectacular** and powerful recoveries.
Spectres
Th Fam Af 123-28 family will be plagued by **spectres** from
Spinal fluid
To Emp 140-21 pressure of the **spinal fluid** actually ruptured
Spineless
To Emp 139-26 the **spineless** and the stupid.
Spirit
Bill's Story 10-26 had to believe in a **Spirit**
Bill's Story 12-9 **Spirit** of Nature

We Ag 46-26, 52-15, Into Ac 75-21 **Spirit** of the Universe
We Ag 46-31 the Realm of **Spirit** is broad,
We Ag 51-24 about the realm of the **spirit**
Ho It Wo 66-18 sunlight of the **Spirit.**
Into Ac 77-26 a helpful and forgiving **spirit,**
Into Ac 84-20,21 entered the world of the **Spirit.**
Into Ac 85-27,28 the flow of His **Spirit** into us.
Wo Wi Ot 24 a new attitude and **spirit** all around.
Wo Wi Ot 103-6 looks for the **spirit** among us
Wo Wi Ot 103-8 A **spirit** of intolerance
To Wives 117-32,33 in a resentful or critical **spirit.**
Th Fam Af 125-16 a **spirit** of love and tolerance.
A Vi Fo You 164-25 Fellowship of the **Spirit,**
Spiritual
Doc's Op xxiv-28 solution on the **spiritual** as well
Bill's Story 15-1 **spiritual** life through work and
Th Is A Sol 25-12 simple kit of **spiritual** tools
Th Is A Sol 25-17 deep and effective **spiritual** experiences
Th Is a Sol 25-32 to accept **spiritual** help
Th Is A Sol 27-4 without **spiritual** help
Th Is A Sol 27-15 vital **spiritual** experiences
Th Is A Sol 27-32 vital **spiritual** experience
Th Is A Sol 29-2 to a **spiritual** experience
Mo Ab Al 39-33 **spiritual** remedy for his problem.
Mo Ab Al 42-21 they outlined the **spiritual** answer
Mo Ab Al 42-32 **spiritual** principles would solve all
Mo Ab Al 43-23,24 respect for the **spiritual** approach
We Ag 44-8 only a **spiritual** experience will conquer
We Ag 44-14 or to live on a **spiritual** basis
We Ag 44-20 we must find a **spiritual** basis of life
We Ag 45-17 a book which we believe to be **spiritual**
We Ag 45-22 falls when we speak of **spiritual** matters
We Ag 47-3 other **spiritual** expressions which
We Ag 47-4,5 have against **spiritual** terms deter you
We Ag 47-7 needed to commence **spiritual** growth
We Ag 47-21 effective **spiritual** structure can be built
We Ag 47-23 not make use of **spiritual** principles unless
We Ag 47-25 When people presented us with **spiritual**
We Ag 48-4 **spiritual** things made us bristle

We Ag 48-8 open minded on **spiritual** matters
We Ag 49-28 cynically dissecting **spiritual** beliefs
We Ag 50-7 never gave the **spiritual** side of life
We Ag 55-4 **spiritual** liberation from this world,
We Ag 55-6,7 We had seen **spiritual** release,
We Ag 56-12 had known a **spiritual** experience.
Ho It Wo 60-1 Having had a **spiritual** awakening
Ho It wo 60-9 willing to grow along **spiritual** lines
Ho It Wo 60-11 We claim **spiritual** progress
Ho It Wo 60-11,12 rather than **spiritual** perfection.
Ho It Wo 63-23 desirable to take this **spiritual** step
Ho It Wo 63-24 friend, or **spiritual** adviser.
Ho It Wo 64-25 forms of **spiritual** disease,
Ho It Wo 64-27 When the **spiritual** malady is overcome,
Ho It Wo 66-14,15 growth of a **spiritual** experience
Into Ac 75-17 We may have had certain **spiritual** beliefs
Into Ac 75-18 begin to have a **spiritual** experience.
Into Ac 76-31 some of them on a **spiritual** basis
Into Ac 76-33 should not emphasize the **spiritual** feature
Into Ac 77-14 our talk of **spiritual** discoveries
Into Ac 79-8 any lengths to find a **spiritual** experience,
Into Ac 83-11 The **spiritual** life is not a theory.
Into Ac 83-12,13 to live upon **spiritual** principles
Into Ac 83-14,15 to them about **spiritual** matters.
Into Ac 85-12 in fit **spiritual** condition.
Into Ac 85-13 the **spiritual** program of action
Into Ac 85-17 maintenance of our **spiritual** condition
Wo Wi Ot 93-4 Stress the **spiritual** feature freely.
Wo Wi Ot 93-10 that he live by **spiritual** principles.
Wo Wi Ot 93-12 to describe **spiritual** principles.
Wo Wi Ot 95-11 from any moral or **spiritual** hilltop;
Wo Wi Ot 95-11,12 the kit of **spiritual** tools
Wo Wi Ot 95-28 prefers some other **spiritual** approach
Wo Wi Ot 97-29 and practice **spiritual** principles,
Wo Wi Ot 98-31 concentrate on his own **spiritual**
Wo Wi Ot 100-6 the path of **spiritual** progress.
Wo Wi Ot 101-9 the matter with his **spiritual** status.
Wo Wi Ot 102-3,4 solid, **spiritual** ground
To Wives 112-32,33 will be shy of a **spiritual** remedy,

To Wives 114-28 adopt a **spiritual** way of life
To Wives 116-17 when lived on a **spiritual** plane.
To Wives 116-23 began to apply **spiritual** principles
To Wives 116-30 put **spiritual** principles to work
To Wives 118-7 trying to live on a **spiritual** basis,
To Wives 119-2 he could have a **spiritual** experience.
To Wives 120-13,14 must redouble his **spiritual** activities
To Wives 120-15 not remind him of his **spiritual** deficiency-
Th Fam Af 124-28 In the first flush of **spiritual** experience
Th Fam Af 126-30 falling down on his **spiritual** program.
Th Fam Af 127-9 love, and **spiritual** understanding.
Th Fam Af 127-17 always followed **spiritual** progress;
Th Fam Af 128-4 a stirring **spiritual** experience
Th Fam Af 128-10 There is talk about **spiritual** matters
Th Fam Af 128-24 Dad is not **spiritual** after all,
Th Fam Af 128-31 We have indulged in **spiritual** intoxication.
Th Fam Af 129-10 that his **spiritual** growth is lopsided.
Th Fam Af 129-11 a **spiritual** life which does not include
Th Fam Af 129-16 vagaries of dad's **spiritual** infancy
Th Fam Af 129-25 feel he has **spiritual** justification
Th Fam Af 129-27,28 not agree with dad's **spiritual** activities
Th Fam Af 130-4 success ahead of **spiritual** development.
Th Fam Af 130-7,8 the world of **spiritual** make believe
Th Fam Af 130-17 a powerful **spiritual** experience
Th Fam Af 130-19 family has **spiritual** convictions or not,
Th Fam Af 130-25 man who is off on a **spiritual** tangent
Th Fam Af 130-26 wife who adopts a sane **spiritual** program,
Th Fam Af 131-32 Being possessed of a **spiritual** experience
Th Fam Af 133-13 convinced that a **spiritual** mode of living
Th Fam Af 135-1 whether the family goes on a **spiritual** basis
Th Fam Af 135-17 and mend his **spiritual** fences.
A Vi Fo You 156-30 The use of **spiritual** principles
A Vi Fo You 159-6 The way you fellows put this **spiritual** stuff
A Vi Fo You 159-24 into a **spiritual** way of living,
A Vi Fo You 160-1 interested in a **spiritual** way of life.
A Vi Fo You 162-11 to recover on a **spiritual** basis.
Dr Bob Ni 178-18 it was something of a **spiritual** nature,
Dr Bob Ni 180-15 that is to say the **spiritual** approach.

Spiritual disease
Ho It Wo 64-25 From it stem all forms of **spiritual disease,**
Spiritual experience
A Vi Fo You 155-15 A **spiritual experience**, he conceded,
A Vi Fo you 157-30 spoke of their **spiritual experience**
A Vi Fo you 158-14 had begun to have a **spiritual experience.**
Spirituality
Ho It Wo 68-19 laugh at those who think **spirituality**
Th Fam Af 128-16 had better get his brand of **spirituality**
Spiritually
We Ag 49-30 many **spiritually**-minded persons
Ho It Wo 64-26 we have been **spiritually** sick.
Ho It Wo 66-33 were perhaps **spiritually** sick.
Wo Wi Ot 100-31 Assuming we are **spiritually** fit,
A Vi Fo You 156-18 they must keep **spiritually** active.
Spree
Doc's Op xxvii-5 the well-known stages of a **spree,**
Mo Ab Al 32-13 doing a great deal of **spree** drinking.
Mo Ab Al 35-7 reasoned with him after a **spree**
Mo Ab Al 37-22 our justification for a **spree** was insanely
Wo Wi Ot 90-19 Wait for the end of the **spree,**
Wo Wi Ot 92-4 leads to the first drink of a **spree.**
Wo Wi Ot 99-17 pay the penalty by a **spree.**
To Emp 143-1 who are just getting over a **spree,**
A Vi Fo You 155-29 the **spree** that ended all sprees.
Dr Bob Ni 174-11 I went on a particularly strenuous **spree.**
Sprees
Th Is A So 21-32 by a senseless series of **sprees.**
Into Ac 73-17 the things he does on his **sprees.**
To Wives 106-30 as the **sprees** got closer together.
To Wives 113-22 Cheerfully see him through more **sprees.**
A Vi Fo You 159-1 He suffered horribly from his **sprees,**
Square mile
A Vi Fo You 163-13 more alcoholics per **square mile**
Squarely
A Vi Fo Yo 156-1 face his problems **squarely** that God might
Stability
We Ag 49-29 demonstrating a degree of **stability,**

Stage

To Wives 113-27 your chances are good at this **stage.**

Stand

Into Ac 83-27 As God's people we **stand** on our feet;

Stared glassily

A Vi Fo You 157-5 **stared glassily** at the strangers beside his

Start

To Wives 114-26 sometimes you must **start** life anew.

To Emp 145-2 he will probably be off to a fast **start.**

Starving

To Wives 119-11 have been **starving** for his companionship,

State of mind

Dr Bob Ni 172-28 a **state of mind** which became more

Stealing

Ho It Wo 68-1 fear ought to be classed with **stealing.**

Step

Ho It Wo 63-21 We thought well before taking this **step**

Ho It Wo 63-23 take this spiritual **step** with an understanding

Ho It Wo 63-2 though our decision was a vital and crucial **step,**

Into Ac 72-22 if we skip this vital **step,** we may not overcome

Into Ac 74-4 this intimate and confidential **step.**

Into Ac 74-27 If that is so, this **step** may be postponed,

Into Ac 75-13 once we have taken this **step**

Into Ac 80-4 and the drastic **step** is indicated

Step eleven

Into Ac 85-32 **Step eleven** suggests prayer and meditation.

Step four

Ho It Wo 64-9 This was **step four.**

Step Seven

Into Ac 76-14 We have then completed **step seven.**

Step six

Into Ac 76-2 we then look at **step six.**

Step ten

Into Ac 84-16 This thought brings us to **step ten,**

Step three

Ho It Wo 60-21 Being convinced, we were at **step three,**

Ho It Wo 63-13 We were now at **step three.**

Step twelve

Into Ac 88-13 next chapter is entirely devoted to **step twelve.**

Steps

Ho It Wo 58-18 you are ready to take certain **steps.**

Ho It Wo 59-7 Here are the **steps** we took,

Steps eight and nine

Into Ac 76-16 Let's look at **steps eight and nine.**

Stimulating

Th Fam Af 134-8 Alcohol is so sexually **stimulating**

A Vi Fo You 160-27 the **stimulating** and electric atmosphere

Stirring

Th Fam Af 128-4 a **stirring** spiritual experience.

Stole

Bill's Story 6-24 I **stole** from my wife's slender purse

Stolen

Th Fam Af 128-19 a God who has **stolen** dad's affections.

Stop

Th Is A So 20-21 I should think he'd **stop** for her sake.

Mo Ab Al 31-33 Try to drink and **stop** abruptly.

Mo Ab Al 34-10 Though you may be able to **stop** for

Mo Ab Al 34-17 the question is how to **stop** altogether.

Mo Ab Al 34-18 that the reader desires to **stop.**

Mo Ab Al 40-12 convinced he had to **stop** drinking,

Wo Wi Ot 90-7 any indication that he wants to **stop,**

To Wives 109-25 and tells you he wants to **stop.**

To Wives 109-31 He wants to want to **stop.**

To Wives 110-8 he desperately wants to **stop** but cannot.

To Wives 112-6 confidence in his power to **stop**

To Wives 113-15 Being certain he wants to **stop,**

To Wives 116-12 wants to **stop** drinking forever.

To Wives 116-13 that he can **stop** if he will.

Th Fam Af 135-11 that he was not ready to **stop.**

To Emp 141-9 your man does not want to **stop,**

To Emp 141-21 there are many men who want to **stop,**

To Emp 147-27 Do you want to **stop** drinking or not?

To Emp 148-2 cannot or will not **stop** drinking,

To Emp 148-13 If he wants to **stop,** he should be

To Emp 148-15 cannot or does not want to **stop,**

A Vi Fo Yo 155-9 He had a desperate desire to **stop,**

A Vi Fo Yo 155-15 could **stop** his drinking for long.

A Vi Fo Yo 157-26 I know more than ever I can't **stop.**
Stop drinking
To Emp 142-13 to **stop drinking** forever?
Stopped
To Wives 116-28 if our husbands **stopped** drinking.
To Emp 141-15 could have done would have **stopped** me
Stopping
A Vi Fo You 164-2 there will be no **stopping** until everyone
Stories
Th Fam Af 125-21 to stick to our own **stories.**
Story
A Vi Fo You 160-23 he heard the **story** of some man
Straggle
Th Fam Aft 122-26 may be footsore and may **straggle.**
Strained
Th Fam Aft 122-21 a highly **strained,** abnormal condition.
Straight alcohol
Dr Bob Ni 178-5 fortify my beer with **straight alcohol.**
Straight pepper diet
Ho It Wo 69-8 would have us all on a **straight pepper diet.**
Straightened
To Emp 150-5 moment spent in getting them **straightened** out.
Dr Bob Ni 174-6 endeavor to get me **straightened** around.
Strange
Mo Ab Al 42-7 those **strange** mental blank spots.
To Wives 108-6 that **strange** world of alcoholism
Th Fam Af 128-8 look at their **strange** new dad
Strangely
Mo Ab Al 38-24 we have been **strangely** insane.
To Emp 140-22 an alcoholic is **strangely** irrational.
A Vi Fo You 160-7 at the disposal of this **strangely** assorted
Strangers
To Wives 119-17 Your house is filled with **strangers.**
A Vi Fo You 157-5 stared glassily at the **strangers** beside his
A Vi Fo You 161-4 had known these **strangers** always.
Strapped down
A Vi Fo You 156-28 we've got him **strapped down** tight.
Strength
Bill's Story 13-24 asking only for direction and **strength**

Ho It Wo 68-21 Paradoxically, it is the way of **strength.**

Ho It Wo 70-17 for the **strength** to do the right thing.

Into Ac 76-13 Grant me **strength,**

Into Ac 79-9 we ask that we be given **strength** and direction

Into Ac 85-25 receiving **strength,** inspiration,

Stricken

A Vi Fo You 161-2 do for some **stricken** acquaintance

Striving

Th Fam Af 126-18 He is **striving** to recover fortune

Strong

A Vi Fo Yo 157-33 I used to be **strong** for the church.

Struck

To Wives 106-16 They **struck** the children,

Struggle

Into Ac 86-32 We don't **struggle.**

Struggled

To Wives 118-31 that for which we **struggled** for years.

Struggles

Wo Wi Ot 92-3 the **struggles** you made to stop.

Struggling

Th Fam Af 124-13 still **struggling** with their problem.

Stubbornness

To Emp 140-9 with **stubbornness,** or a weak will?

Stumble

Ho It Wo 70-6 fall short of the chosen ideal and **stumble?**

To Emp 147-6 In case he does **stumble,**

Stumbled

A Vi Fo You 160-15 when next he **stumbled.**

Stumbling

To Wives 113-12 Wait until repeated **stumbling** convinces him

Stupid

To Emp 139-26 the spineless and the **stupid.**

To Emp 139-28 that a man could be so weak, **stupid,**

A Vi Fo Yo 152-12 where I shall be **stupid,**

Stupidity

Wo Wi Ot 103-10 had it not been for such **stupidity.**

Substitute

A Vi Fo Yo 152-16 Yes, there is a **substitute**

Subtle

Into Ac 85-15 alcohol is a **subtle** foe.

Success

To Wives 111-1 The first principle of **success**

Successes

To Emp 144-24 percentage of **successes** will gratify you.

Successful

Wo Wi Ot 95-8 will be most **successful** with alcoholics if

Wo Wi Ot 100-25 **successful** in solving your own domestic

Th Fam Aft 122-5 **Successful** readjustment means

Suffer

Th Is A Sol 17-25 those who **suffer** from alcoholism.

Ho It wo 58-11 There are those too, who **suffer** from grave

To Wives 109-20 His business may **suffer** somewhat.

To Wives 114-24 The wives and children of such men **suffer**

Th Fam Af 124-18 Showing others who **suffer** how

Suffered

Doc's Op xxiv-11 who have **suffered** alcoholic torture

Th Fam Af 126-26 show his contrition for what they **suffered.**

Th Fam Af 127-19 Since the home has **suffered** more than

To Emp 139-1 brother-executive **suffered** from a serious

A Vi Fo You 157-19 acute poisoning from which he **suffered,**

A Vi Fo You 159-1 He **suffered** horribly from his sprees,

Sufferer

Th Is A Sol 23-30 the **sufferer** will rouse himself

Sufferer's

Th Is A Sol 18-7 whose lives touch the **sufferer's.**

Mo Ab Al 34-31 greater service to alcoholic **suffers**

Suffering

Th Is A Sol 22-18 it's attendant **suffering** and humiliation,

Th Is a sol 24-10 the memory of the **suffering**

Mo Ab Al 36-30 intense mental and physical **suffering**

Mo Ab Al 41-24 unbearable mental and physical **suffering.**

We Ag 44-7 may be **suffering** from an illness

Th Fam Af 129-9 he is **suffering** from distortion of values.

A Vi Fo You 155-22 bring still more **suffering** to his family

A Vi Fo You 159-25 relieving much worry and **suffering.**

Sufferings

Doc's Op xxiii-5 the **sufferings** of our members

Suffers

To Emp 148-32 drinks so much that his job **suffers,** we fire him

Sufficient

We Ag 46-23 was **sufficient** to make the approach

Suggested

Ho It Wo 59-7 **suggested** as a program of recovery.

Suggestions

To Emp 144-19 abide by it's **suggestions.**

Suggestive

A Vi Fo You 164-11 Our book is meant to be **suggestive** only.

Suicide

Bill's Story 16-6 One poor chap committed **suicide.**

We Ag 56-5 insanity, fatal illness, **suicide-**

Suitable

Into Ac 74-26 no **suitable** person available.

Summa cum laude

Dr Bob Ni 172-30 was graduated **summa cum laude**

Sunk

A Vi Fo Yo 158-27 what they had found, or be **sunk.**

A Vi Fo You 161-22 or has **sunk** to low to be

Sunlight

Ho It Wo 66-18 from the **sunlight** of the Spirit.

Superior

Th Fam Af 129-21 now that he has become a **superior** person

Supreme

Th Fam Af 124-6 thing of **supreme** value in life.

Supreme Being

We Ag 46-7 How could a **Supreme Being** have anything to do

We Ag 46-8 who could comprehend a **Supreme Being**

Survive

Bill's Story 15-2 he could not **survive** the certain trials.

To Wives 120-14 if he expects to **survive.**

A Vi Fo You 153-3 give of yourself that others may **survive**

Survived

Th Fam af 125-4 **survived** this ordeal without relapse,

Swallowed

Ho It Wo 71-6 **swallowed** and digested some big chunks of truth

Sweep
Into Ac 76-22 **sweep** away the debris
Into Ac 77-32 We are there to **sweep** off our side of the street.
Sweet
To Wives 107-19 they would be their old **sweet** selves,

Sweets
Th Fam Af 133-32 the use of **sweets** was often helpful,
Th Fam Af 134-5 a tendency to eat **sweets**
Swept
We Ag 56-27 he had built through the years were **swept** away.
Sworn
A Vi Fo Yo 158-2 and **sworn** that I'd never touch another drop
Sympathetic
To Wives 115-14 the growth of **sympathetic** understanding.
Th Fam Af 129-16 an understanding and **sympathetic** family,
Symptom
Doc's Op xxviii-24 have one **symptom** in common:
Ho It Wo 64-6 Our liquor was but a **symptom.**
Symptoms
Ho It Wo 67-1 Though we did not like their **symptoms**
Wo Wi Ot 91-21 about your drinking habits, **symptoms,**
To Wives 106-32 alarming physical and mental **symptoms,**

T

Tactful
Into Ac 83-25 We should be sensible, **tactful,**
Tales
To Emp 145-29 he was slyly carrying **tales.**
Talk
We Ag 45-18 that we are going to **talk** about God.
Into Ac 74-30 that we **talk** with the right person.
Into Ac 75-5 we are prepared for a long **talk.**
Wo Wi Ot 91-19 turn the **talk** to some phase of drinking.

Wo Wi Ot 95-10 Never **talk** down to an alcoholic
To Wives 113-22 **Talk** about his condition
To Emp 145-14 Can he **talk** frankly with you
A Vi Fo Yo 154-10 to **talk** with someone, but whom?

Talked
Wo Wi Ot 91-11 you have **talked** with the family,
Talking
To Wives 114-30 and you think everyone is **talking**
Talks
Th Fam Af 127-28 These family **talks** will be constructive
Tangent
Th Fam Af 130-25 who is off on a spiritual **tangent**
Tangible
Wo Wi Ot 99-9 After they have seen **tangible** results,
Taper off
Th Is A So 22-11 some sedative with which to **taper off.**
Tapped
A Vi Fo You 163-5 just now **tapped** a source of power
Tears
Th Fam Af 133-4 that this life is a vale of **tears,**
Teetotaler
To Emp 139-13 a moderate drinker or a **teetotaler,**
Telephone
Wo Wi Ot 97-13 Your **telephone** may jangle at any time
Temper
To Wives 111-5 Patience and good **temper** are necessary.
Th Fam Af 125-16 **temper** such talk by a spirit of love
Temporary
To Emp 141-3 nothing more than **temporary** conditions.
Temporizes
To Emp 142-22 If he **temporizes** and still thinks he can
Temptation
We Ag 57-1 a few brief moments of **temptation** the thought
Into Ac 85-6 neither are we avoiding **temptation.**
Wo Wi Ot 101-17 shield the sick man from **temptation**
To Wives 120-23 to shield him from **temptation.**
To Emp 147-2 shielded from **temptation** to drink.

Tempted

Into Ac 84-33 If **tempted,** we recoil from it as from a hot flame.

To Wives 120-25 so he will not be **tempted**

Tempting

Wo Wi Ot 101-28 This may seem like **tempting** Providence

Tension

Into Ac 73-23 under constant fear and **tension-**

To Wives 115-25 terrible **tension** which grips the home

Terrible

To Wives 115-25 **terrible** tension which grips

To Emp 141-2 his revulsion will be **terrible.**

Terror

A Vi Fo Yo 151-21 **Terror,** Bewilderment, Frustration

Test

To Wives 117-15 will be put to the **test.**

Testimony

We Ag 55-23 If our **testimony** helps sweep away prejudice,

Thank you

To Emp 149-31 and **thank you** to his dying day.

Thanked

A Vi Fo Yo 154-32 His sanity returned and he **thanked** God.

Thankful

Th Fam Af 127-3 They should be **thankful** he is sober

That's me.

A Vi Fo Yo 157-17 **That's me. That's me.** I drink like that.

Themselves

Doc's Op xxiv-5 anything they say about **themselves.**

Doc's Op xxv-32 They believe in **themselves,**

Doc's Op xxvi-17 a power greater than **themselves,**

Mo Ab Al 31-11 will try to prove **themselves** exceptions

Mo Ab Al 33-22 they found **themselves** as helpless as

Ho It Wo 58-4 give **themselves** to this simple program.

Ho It Wo 58-6 incapable of being honest with **themselves.**

Into Ac 72-23 tried to keep to **themselves** certain facts about

Into Ac 73-7 only thought they had humbled **themselves.**

Wo Wi Ot 103-2 ought to decide for **themselves.**

To Wives 1-7=29 how could they be so blind about **themselves?**

Th Fam Af 126-9 as they find **themselves** neglected.

Th Fam Af 133-24 Most of them give freely of **themselves.**

A Vi Fo Yo 159-17 in giving **themselves** for others.

Theory

Into Ac 83-11 The spiritual life is not a **theory.**

Think

Mo Ab Al 37-5 of the ability to **think** straight,

Mo Ab Al 41-25 As soon as I regained my ability to **think,**

Thinking

Bill's Story 13-21 test my **thinking** by the new God Consciousne

Mo Ab Al 47-8 this kind of **thinking** has been characteristic of

We Ag 48-5 This sort of **thinking** had to be abandoned.

We Ag 50-28 change in their way of living and **thinking.**

We Ag 53-13 our former **thinking** was soft and mushy

Ho It Wo 70-4 We avoid hysterical **thinking** or advice.

Into Ac 86-11 Were we **thinking** of ourselves most of the time?

Into Ac 86-12 **thinking** of what we could do for others,

Into Ac 86-21 we ask God to direct our **thinking,**

Into Ac 86-27 when our **thinking** is cleared of wrong motives.

Into Ac 87-7 we find that our **thinking** will,

To Wives 114-30 over what other people are **thinking**

Th Fam Af 133-11 nor do twisted **thinking** and depression

Th Fam Af 134-26 dad's new way of living and **thinking.**

To Emp 140-17 a victim of crooked **thinking,**

A Vi Fo You 158-5 he had been **thinking** it over.

Third day

A Vi Fo Yo 158-9 On the **third day** the lawyer gave his life to

Thorough

Ho It Wo 58-22 to be fearless and **thorough** from the very start.

Thoroughly

Ho It Wo 58-2 who has **thoroughly** followed our path.

Thoroughness

Ho It wo 65-32 Nothing counted but **thoroughness** and honesty.

Thought

We Ag 57-2 the **thought** of drink has never returned

Into Ac 86-31 an intuitive **thought** or a decision.

Into Ac 87-32 and ask for the right **thought** or action.

To Wives 119-24 direct some of your **thought** to the wives

Th Fam af 124-20 Cling to the **thought** that,

To Emp 143-20 will require a transformation of **thought**
Thought-life
Into Ac 86-26 Our **thought-life** will be placed on a much
Thoughtful
Th Fam Aft 123-8 romantic, **thoughtful** and successful.
Th Fam Af 131-25 **thoughtful** consideration given

Thoughts
Into Ac 84-28 turn our **thoughts** to someone we can help.
Into Ac 85-21 **thoughts** which must go with us constantly.
To Wives 119-4 When resentful **thoughts** come,
Thorough
Ho It Wo 58-22 be fearless and **thorough** from the very start.
Thoroughly
To Emp 143-5 object is to **thoroughly** clear mind and body
Thoroughness
Ho It Wo 65-32 Nothing counted but **thoroughness** and honesty.
Threatening
To Wives 106-19 **threatening** to live with the other woman
Three
To Wives 109-32 **Three:** This husband has gone much further
To Emp 137-13 Here were **three** exceptional men lost
A Vi Fo Yo 154-22 could handle say, **three** drinks-
A Vi Fo Yo 157-12 The last **three** times, I got drunk on the way
A Vi Fo Yo 159-10 He was there **three** months.
A Vi Fo Yo 159-26 **three** had succeeded with seven more.
Three alcoholics
A Vi Fo Yo 158-25 there were **three alcoholics** in that town,
Three visitors
A Vi Fo Yo 159-5 He had **three visitors.**
Through
To Emp 136-16 I told him he was **through**-
To Emp 138-27 this chap is either **through** with liquor
Through the wringer
Mo Ab Al 38-20 We, who have been **through the wringer,**
Thunderclouds
To Wives 117-25 great **thunderclouds** of dispute
Tight
Th Is A So 21-22 He has a positive genius for getting **tight**

To Wives 106-21 In desperation, we have even got **tight** ourselves
To Wives 115-29 when as a matter of fact he was **tight.**
Dr Bob Ni 178-21 but still got **tight** every night
Dr Bob Ni 179-21 I got **tight** that night,
Dr Bob Ni 179-23 then proceeded to get **tight** again.
Time
Th Fam Aft 123-18 It will take **time** to clear away
Together
Th Is A So 17-20 would never have held us **together**
To Wives 119-7 are working **together**
Th Fam Af 124-29 and drew closer **together.**
A Vi Fo Yo 152-33 you will escape disaster **together**
Tolerance
Th Is A So 19-31 real **tolerance** of other people's
Ho It Wo 67-3 the same **tolerance,** pity, and patience that
Ho It Wo 70-28 We have begun to learn **tolerance,**
Into Ac 83-10 show us the way of patience, **tolerance,**
Into Ac 84-29 Love and **tolerance** of others is our code.
Th Fam Aft 122-7 **tolerance,** understanding and love
Th am Af 125-17 by a spirit of love and **tolerance.**
Th Fam Af 127-9 **tolerance,** love, and spiritual understanding.
To Emp 138-1 a lack of patience and **tolerance.**
Tolerant
Ho It Wo 67-13 **tolerant** view of each and every one.
Tone
To Wives 119-33 his excess enthusiasm will **tone** down.
Too much
Ho It Wo 59-1 Without help it is **too much** for us.
Tornado
Into Ac 82-24 The alcoholic is like a **tornado** roaring his way
Torture
Doc's Op xxiv-11 who have suffered alcoholic **torture**
Bill's Story 6-30 the physical and mental **torture**
Tortured
Dr Bob Ni 175-3 my stomach **tortured** me,
Tortures
Dr Bob Ni 179-1 subject to the **tortures** we inflict
Touch
A Vi Fo Yo 158-2 sworn that I'd never **touch** another drop

Touches

Ho It Wo 67-27 **touches** about every aspect of our lives.

Tragic

Th Fam Af 123-31 humiliating, shameful or **tragic.**

Th Fam Af 132-14 serious, sometimes **tragic** things.

Th Fam Af 132-28 **tragic** experience out of the past.

Traits

Wo Wi Ot 92-31 if not all, of the **traits** of the alcoholic.

Transcended

A Vi Fo Yo 159-16 It was **transcended** by the happiness

Transformation

To Emp 143-20 will require a **transformation** of thought

Transformations

Th Fam Af 133-16 have seen remarkable **transformations**

Transmit

A Vi Fo Yo 164-16 you cannot **transmit** something you haven't

Travelers

Th Fam Af 130-15 where our fellow **travelers** are,

Treasure

Th Fam Af 129-3 hug the new **treasure** to himself.

Treat

Th Fan Af 130-32 obliged to **treat** father as a sick or wayward

Treated

Doc's Op xxix-4 be **treated** for chronic alcoholism.

Treating

Doc's Op xxv-9 **treating** alcoholic and drug addiction.

Th Fam Af 129-24 Instead of **treating** the family

Th Fam Af 133-28 indispensable in **treating** a newcomer

Treatment

Doc's Op xxiii-11 in the **treatment** of alcoholism

Doc's Op xxiii-17 In the course of his third **treatment**

Doc's Op xxviii-29 by any **treatment** by which we are

Doc's Op xxix-28 he thought the **treatment** a waste of effort,.

Bill's Story 13-4 **Treatment** seemed wise, for I showed

Th Is A So 26-10 finished his **treatment** with unusual

Mo Ab Al 30-27 to be any kind of **treatment** which will make

To Emp 142-17 and that after rest and **treatment** he will be

To Emp 143-11 to advance the cost of **treatment,**

To Emp 143-16 physical **treatment** is but a small part

To Emp 145-30 was sent to a hospital for **treatment.**

A Vi Fo Yo 157-8 We're giving you a **treatment** for

Trembled

A Vi Fo Yo 156-8 He **trembled** as he went about,

Dr Bob Ni 174-12 my hand **trembled** so I could not hold

Trembles

To Wives 104-8 the wife who **trembles** in fear of

Trembling

Bill's Story 8-13 **Trembling,** I stepped from the hospital

To Wives 115-3 you become a **trembling** recluse,

Trigger

To Emp 137-3 he had placed his toe on the **trigger**

Trouble

We Ag 55-4 dogged by **trouble** and frustration.

Ho It Wo 68-2 It seems to cause more **trouble.**

Into Ac 79-4 That's a common form of **trouble** too.

Th Fam Af 133-8 but if **trouble** comes,

A Vi Fo Yo 156-4 feared what his **trouble** had been.

Dr Bob Ni 174-23 I could not get into any **trouble.**

Troubled

Th Fam Af 132-7 to minister to our **troubled** world.

Troubles

Ho It Wo 62-7 That, we think, is the root of our **troubles.**

Ho It Wo 62-14 So our **troubles,** we think, are basically of our

Into Ac 80-32 chances are that we have domestic **troubles.**

Wo Wi Ot 91-28 **troubles** liquor has caused you,

To Wives 119-18 He gets stirred up about their **troubles,**

Th Fam Af 126-7 money **troubles** are about to be solved,

Th Fam Af 131-5 accustomed to wearing the family trousers.

Trudge

A Vi Fo You 164-26 as you **trudge** the Road of Happy Destiny.

True

Doc's Op xxiv-17 These things were **true** to some extent,

Doc's Op xxvi-33 differentiate the **true** from the false

Th Is A Sol 23-27 How **true** this is, few realize.

We Ag 44-19 were not **true** alcoholics

We Ag 47-29 But I cannot accept as surely **true** the many

We Ag 49-13 Were our contentions **true**

We Ag 55-8 liked to tell ourselves it wasn't **true.**

To Wives 109-12 a good number will become **true** alcoholics
To Wives 109-16 He admits this is **true,** but is positive that
To Wives 119-27 It is probably **true** that you and your
To Wives 120-11 as has been **true** with many
Th Fam Af 124-7 That is **true** only if one is willing
A Vi Fo You 162-23 To some extent this already **true.**

Trust
Ho It Wo 68-13 We **trust** infinite God rather than our
Wo Wi Ot 98-22 condition is that he **trust** in God

Trusted
Into Ac 80-30 one of the most **trusted** citizens of his town.
To Emp 146-26 Your man may be **trusted.**

Trusting
Ho It Wo 68-12 basis of **trusting** and relying upon God.

Truth
Th Is A Sol 23-18 Once in a while he may tell the **truth.**
Th Is A Sol 23-19 And the **truth,** strange to say, is usually
Th Is a Sol 23-32 The tragic **truth** is that if the man
Ho It Wo 64-12 is an effort to discover the **truth**
Ho It Wo 71-7 some big chunks of **truth** about yourself.
Into Ac 73-28 seldom told them the whole **truth**
Wo Wi Ot 93-24 an example of the **truth** that faith alone
Wo Wi Ot 98-16 hard knocks to learn this **truth:**
To Wives 106-15 much nearer the **truth** than we realized.
To Emp 144-16 tell the patient the **truth** about his condition.

Trying
Th Fam Af 123-26 for what he is **trying** to get.

Tugboat Annie
Dr Bob Ni 177-5 went to see Wallace Beery in **"Tugboat Annie"**

Turmoil
Into Ac 82-28 have kept the home in **turmoil.**

Twelfth suggestion
Wo Wi Ot 89-4 This our **twelfth suggestion:**

Twelve steps
Into Ac 75-27 which contains the **twelve steps.**
Wo Wi Ot 96-17 prepared to go through with the **twelve steps**

Twenty-four
Into Ac 86-19 think about the **twenty-four** hours ahead.

Twisted
Th Fam Af 133-11 nor do **twisted** thinking and depression
Two
To Wives 109-13 **Two:** Tour husband is showing lack of
Two friends
A Vi Fo You 156-16 life was not easy for the **two friends.**
A Vi Fo You 157-15 the **two friends** told him about their
A Vi Fo You 157-30 the **two friends** spoke of their spiritual
Two large centers
A Vi Fo You 162-26 contact with our **two large centers.**
Two men
Bill's Story 9-28 how **two men** had appeared in court,

U

Unabated
To Emp 137-20 This kind of waste goes on **unabated.**
Unable
Mo Ab Al 34-16 **unable** to drink moderately
Mo Ab Al 39-8 will be absolutely **unable** to stop drinking on
Into Ac 78-28 short in our accounts and **unable** to make good.
To Wives 109-14 **unable** to stay on the water wagon
To Wives 111-21 You may be **unable** to do so,
A Vi Fo Yo 152-7 will be **unable** to imagine life either with
Unafraid
To Wives 111-19 We know women who are **unafraid,**
Unbalanced
Th Fam Af 128-29 He is not so **unbalanced** as they might
Unbearable
To Wives 111-3 though your husband becomes **unbearable**
Uncanny
A Vi Fo You 160-31 the **uncanny** understanding
Uncommunicative
Into Ac 81-5 worn out, resentful and **uncommunicative.**

Unconsciously
Th Fam Aft 122-18 Is he not **unconsciously** trying
Understand
Th Is A So 28-31 of alcoholism, as we **understand** it,
Mo Ab Al 38-30 we **understand** ourselves so well
Into Ac 74-10 person quick to see and **understand** our problem.
Into Ac 74-12 people who do not **understand** alcoholics.
Into Ac 74-21 tell to someone who will **understand,**
Into Ac 74-32 that he fully **understand** and approve
Wo Wi Ot 99-21 **understand** his new way of life.
To Wives 104-18 we **understand** as perhaps few can.
To Wives 121-7 we are anxious that you **understand,**
To Emp 137-14 because I did not **understand** alcoholism
To Emp 141-7 Seeing your attempt to **understand** and help,
To Emp 144-32 If he knows you **understand**
To Emp 148-7 at least he will **understand** the problem
A Vi Fo You 157-14 I can't **understand** it.
A Vi Fo You 164-21 as you **understand** God.
Understanding
Doc's Op xxv-1 better chance of **understanding** and accepting
Th Is A So 17-10 a friendliness, and an **understanding** which
Ho It Wo 63-24 with an **understanding** person.
Into Ac 74-14 for a close-mouthed, **understanding** friend.
Into Ac 82-20 Passing all **understanding** is the patience
Into Ac 84-21 function is to grow in **understanding**
Wo Wi Ot 94-20 quiet and full of human **understanding,**
To Wives 115-14 the growth of sympathetic **understanding.**
To Wives 115-24 promote a better **understanding**
To Wives 118-13 **understanding** and love are the watchwords.
Th Fam Af 127-10 love, and spiritual **understanding.**
Th Fam Af 129-15 an **understanding** and sympathetic family,
To Emp 137-16 intervention of an **understanding** person,
To Emp 139-17 and **understanding** your own reactions,
A Vi Fo You 151-18 hoping to find **understanding**
A Vi Fo You 160-10 loving and **understanding** companionship
A Vi Fo You 160-31 the uncanny **understanding**
A Vi Fo Yo 162-9 **Understanding** our work, he can do this
Understands
Into Ac 81-10 "the girl who **understands**"

Understood
Bill's Story 13-7 God, as I then **understood** Him,
We Ag 47-8 relation with God as we **understood** Him.
Ho It Wo 60-23 to God as we **understood** Him.
To Wives 106-5 they **understood** our men as we did not!
Undisciplined
Into Ac 88-9 We alcoholics are **undisciplined.**
Undoubtedly
To Emp 138-8 was **undoubtedly** alcoholic.
To Emp 139-6 He is **undoubtedly** on the road to recovery.
To Emp 145-13 you can **undoubtedly** make helpful
Undreamed-of-future
To Wives 119-8 toward an **undreamed-of-future**
Undying
To Emp 145-17 will command **undying** loyalty.
Unearth
Th Fam Af 124-32 would **unearth** the old affair
Unexpected
Into Ac 78-5 out of ten the **unexpected** happens.
Unfair
To Emp 146-4 needless provocation and **unfair** criticism.
Unfavorably
Th Fam Af 128-18 family may react **unfavorably.**
Unfit
Dr Bob Ni 176-8 I would be quite **unfit** for work.
Unhappy
Bill's Story 3-25 There were many **unhappy** scenes
We Ag 52-19 we were **unhappy,**
Into Ac 74-18 which will hurt them and make them **unhappy.**
Th Fam Af 123-10 the family may be **unhappy.**
A Vi Fo Yo 151-22 **Unhappy** drinkers who read this
Unhappiness
Ho It Wo 66-11 leads only to futility and **unhappiness.**
To Wives 104-21 no **unhappiness** is too great to overcome.
Th Fam Af 122-15 This makes for discord and **unhappiness.**
Unharmed
Wo Wi Ot 102-28 God will keep you **unharmed.**
United
A Vi Fo You 161-26 and **united** under one God,

Unlimited
Dr Bob Ni 175-24 almost **unlimited** supply the government
Unlovely
Bill's Story 16-4 alcoholic in his cups is an **unlovely** creature
Unloving
To Wives 108-11 only seems to be **unloving** and inconsiderate

Unmanageable
Ho It Wo 59-10 that our lives had become **unmanageable.**
Uniquely
Wo Wi Ot 89-24 you can be **uniquely** useful to other
Unnecessary
To Wives 121-8 avoid these **unnecessary** difficulties.
Unreasonable
We Ag 51-24 some of us just as biased and **unreasonable**
To Wives 108-18 very sick, **unreasonable** person.
To Wives 117-23 husband will sometimes be **unreasonable**
Unreasoning
We Ag 48-2 sensitiveness, and **unreasoning** prejudice.
Unsatisfactory
We Ag 51-4 why living was so **unsatisfactory.**
Unselfish
Wo Wi Ot 93-26 **unselfish** and constructive action.
To Wives 105-7 We have been **unselfish** and self-sacrificing
Unselfishness
Th Fam Af 127-21,22 if he fails to show **unselfishness** and love
Unthinking
Into Ac 82-28 a man is **unthinking** when says that sobriety is
To Wives 107-15 be so **unthinking,** so callous, so cruel?
Unwilling
Doc's Op xxviii-type of man who is **unwilling** to admit
Mo Ab Al 30-1 have been **unwilling** to admit
Into Ac 73-28 **Unwilling** to be honest
Upper room
A Vi Fo You 160-23 in an **upper room** of this house,
Upset
Th Fam Af 134-12 there may be an emotional **upset.**
Dr Bob Ni 181-11 I used to get terribly **upset** when I saw

Urge
Ho It Wo 70-21 It quiets the imperious **urge,**
Useful
Th Is A Sol 19-23 a **useful** program for anyone
Th Is A Sol 20-1 more **useful** to others
Wo Wi Ot 89-24 uniquely **useful** to other alcoholics.
To Wives 111-9 accomplishing anything **useful** may be zero.
To Wives 111-17 to have a full and **useful** life,
Th Fam Af 125-6 unless some good and **useful** purpose
To Emp 136-6 **useful** to business men everywhere.
A Vi Fo You 153-7 happy, respected and **useful** once more.
A Vi Fo You 158-22 a respected and **useful** member of his
Usefulness
Bill's Story 8-23 know happiness, peace, and **usefulness,**
Bill's Story 13-26 on my **usefulness** to others.
We Ag 49-32 stability, happiness, and **usefulness**
Into Ac 76-12 stands in the way of my **usefulness**
Into Ac 86-15 that would diminish our **usefulness** to others.
Th Fam Af 130-18 a life of sane and happy **usefulness.**
Th Fam Af 132-3 new avenues of **usefulness** and pleasure.
Th Fam Af 132-26 and laughter make for **usefulness.**
Uselessness
We Ag 52-19 we had a feeling of **uselessness,**
Into Ac 84-4 That feeling of **uselessness** and self-pity
Utmost
Into Ac 77-31 done our **utmost** to straighten out the past
Utterly
We Ag 45-8 were not sufficient; they failed **utterly.**

V

Vain
Mo Ab Al 30-5 countless **vain** attempts to prove we could drink
We Ag 49-19 Rather **vain** of us, wasn't it?
Dr Bob Ni 174-6 made a long journey in the **vain** endeavor

Vale of tears

Th Fam Af 133-4 that this life is a **vale of tears.**

Valid

Into Ac 83-23 there may be a **valid** reason

Value

Th Fam Af 124-6 thing of supreme **value** in life.

Th Fam Af 124-12 past may be of infinite **value**

Values

Th Fam Af 129-9 suffering from a distortion of **values.**

Vanity

To Wives 116-20 **vanity** and all the things which go to

Vicissitude

We Ag 56-32 No later **vicissitude** has shaken it.

Victim

Ho It Wo 61-20 Is he not a **victim** of the delusion

To Emp 140-17 he has been a **victim** of crooked thinking,

To Emp 146-1 protect the **victim** from this kind of talk.

Victory

Bill's Story 14-9 a sense of **victory**

Ho It Wo 63-18 **victory** over them may bear witness

Into Ac 76-26 any lengths for **victory** over alcohol.

Th Fam Af 125-3 new **victory** over hurt pride

Vigorous

Ho It Wo 63-32 launched out on a course of **vigorous** action,

Violent

Mo Ab Al 35-18 became so **violent** when intoxicated

Wo Wi Ot 91-7 not forcibly unless he is **violent.**

Wo Wi Ot 97-17 fight with him if he is **violent.**

To Wives 110-14 He is **violent,** or appears definitely insane

Violently

We Ag 45-27 Some of us have been **violently** anti-religious.

Virtuous

Ho It Wo 61-5 may sometimes be quite **virtuous.**

Vision

Into Ac 85-19 carry the **vision** of God's will into all

To Wives 118-23 to that cherished **vision.**

Visioned

A Vi Fo You 161-6 They had **visioned** the Great Reality-

Visiting
A Vi Fo You 161-17 and **visiting** hospitals.
Visitors
A Vi Fo You 161-9 hardly accommodate it's weekly **visitors,**
Vital
Ho It wo 64-2 our decision was a **vital** and crucial step,
Into Ac 72-22 If we skip this **vital** step,
Into Ac 85-29 to develop this **vital** sixth sense.
Wo Wi Ot 94-8 a **vital** part in your recovery.

W

Wait
Wo Wi Ot 90-30 **wait** for the end of his next drinking bout.
To Wives 113-20 probably not have long to **wait.**
To Emp 139-2 There was nothing to do but **wait.**
Waiting
To Wives 112-18 This may take patient **waiting,**
Walk
Th Is A So 19-2 take up their beds and **walk** again.
Into Ac 75-29 we shall **walk** a free man at last.
Wo Wi Ot 100-5 **walk** day by day in the path of spiritual
Walked
A Vi Fo Yo 158-15 and **walked** from the hospital a free man.
Walking
Into Ac 75-21 **walking** hand in hand with the Spirit of the
Wall
To Wives 107-27 **wall** had been built around them.
Want
To Emp 141-21 there are many men who **want** to stop,
To Emp 148-15 cannot or does not **want** to stop,
Dr Bob Ni 180-31 others who **want** and need it badly.
Wants
To Wives 109-31 He **wants** to want to stop.

To Emp 141-24 He **wants** to quit drinking

To Emp 142-30 that your man **wants** to recover

To Emp 148-13 If he **wants** to stop,

Ward

A Vi Fo Yo 157-7 I was always in a **ward** before.

Warn

Wo Wi Ot 100-19 **warn** against arousing resentment

Warned

To Emp 136-12 I had **warned** him several times

Warped

Th Is A so 18-9 **warped** lives of blameless children.

To Wives 108-12 usually because he is **warped** and sickened

To Emp 142-11 many alcoholics, being **warped** and drugged,

Warps

A Vi Fo Yo 157-20 and **warps** his mind.

Warrant

Into Ac 79-3 has a **warrant** out for our arrest.

Waste

Wo Wi Ot 90-3 don't **waste** time trying to persuade him.

Wo Wi Ot 96-5 **waste** of time to keep chasing a man

To Emp 137-20 This kind of **waste** goes on unabated.

To Emp 142-28 why **waste** time with him?

To Emp 148-22 **waste** of time, men and reputation.

To Emp 148-25 stop this **waste** and give your

Wasted

Into Ac 87-18 Many of us have **wasted** a lot of time

Wasting

To Wives 104-9 who see their son **wasting** away.

Watchwords

To Wives 118-14 understanding and love are the **watchwords.**

Water wagon

Th Is A So 22-20 Why can't he stay on the **water wagon?**

To Wives 109-14 unable to stay on the **water wagon**

Way out

A Vi Fo Yo 153-22 for those who must find a **way out.**

Way of life

To Wives 117-19 A better **way of life** will emerge

A Vi Fo You 153-26 have adopted this **way of life.**

A Vi Fo You 160-2 in a spiritual **way of life.**

Wayward

Th Fam Af 130-32 to treat father as a sick or **wayward** child.

A Vi Fo You 160-13 how her own **wayward** mate might be

Weak

Th Is A Sol 20-20 His will power must be **weak.**

Into Ac 72-7 the **weak** items in our personal inventory.

To Wives 115-16 though your husband were a **weak** character.

To Wives 120-19 In a **weak** moment he may take

To Emp 139-28 that a man could be so **weak,**

To Emp 140-9 with stubbornness, or a **weak** will?

Weakling

Bill's Story 6-27 cursing myself for a **weakling.**

Weakness

Ho It Wo 68-20 who think spirituality the way of **weakness.**

Wearily

To Wives 107-2 we have patiently and **wearily** climbed,

Wearing

Th Fam Af 131-5 accustomed to **wearing** the family trousers.

Week-end

A Vi Fo Yo 154-18 and would have a lonely **week-end.**

Welcome

Wo Wi Ot 95-2 do not wear out your **welcome.**

Welcomed

A Vi Fo You 161-22 or has sunk to low to be **welcomed**

Welfare

Wo Wi Ot 94-14 **welfare** of other people ahead of his own.

A Vi Fo You 161-27 attuned to the **welfare** of others,

Well

Wo Wi Ot 98-21 can get **well** regardless of anyone.

To Emp 141-20 six months later, a **well** man.

To Emp 142-13 submit to anything to get **well,**

To Emp 142-27 a man who can and will get **well**

A Vi Fo You 154-30 they would not know how to get **well,**

Well-being

Th Fam Af 127-17 material **well-being** always followed

To Emp 137-25 for the **well-being** of his help,

Well-known lawyer

A Vi Fo Yo 156-27 he was once a **well-known lawyer** intown,

Wet brain
Bill's Story 7-29 or I would develop a **wet brain,**
Whiskey
Mo Ab Al 36-19 put an ounce of **whiskey** into my milk
Mo Ab Al 36-20 ordered a **whiskey** and poured it into the milk.
Mo Ab Al 36-23 taking the **whiskey** on a full stomach
Mo Ab Al 36-24 ordered another **whiskey** and poured it into
Mo Ab Al 37-2 that he could take **whiskey** if only he mixed it
Whistling
A Vi Fo Yo 152-2 **whistling** in the dark
Whoopee
To Emp 149-22 the habitual or **whoopee** drinker.
Wife
Bill's Story 2-11 it disturbed my **wife.**
Bill's Story 2-22 my **wife** and I saved $1,000.
Bill's Story 3-27 for loyalty to my **wife**, helped at times
Bill's Story 4-31 **wife** began to work in a department store
Bill's Story 5-25 but my **wife** happily observed
Bill's Story 7-27 My weary and despairing **wife**
Bill's Story 8-5 I thought of my poor **wife.**
Bill's Story 15-6 My **wife** and I abandoned ourselves
Mo Ab al 35-12 has a charming **wife** and family.
Mo Ab Al 38-12 his **wife** gets a divorce
Mo Ab Al 41-20 instead of my **wife.**
Ho It Wo 63-24 an understanding person, such as our **wife,**
Ho It Wo 65-10 His attention to my **wife.**
Ho It Wo 65-11 Told my **wife** of my mistress.
Into Ac 79-19 had not paid alimony to his first **wife.**
Into Ac 79-28 We suggested he write his first **wife** admitting
Into Ac 81-5 a **wife** gets worn out,
Into Ac 81-18 If we are sure our **wife** does not know
Into Ac 81-33 as good for the **wife** as for the husband.
Into Ac 82-19 making good to the **wife** or parents
Into Ac 82-31 To his **wife,** he remarked,
Wo Wi Ot 90-9 most interested in him- usually his **wife.**
Wo Wi Ot 95-25 pushed or prodded by you, his **wife**
Wo Wi Ot 97-14 Your **wife** may sometimes say she is neglected
Wo Wi Ot 98-16 **wife** or no **wife** - we simply do not stop.
Wo Wi Ot 99-20 The **wife** should fully understand

Wo Wi Ot 99-32 In some cases the **wife** will never come back
Wo Wi Ot 100-29 story of how you and your **wife** settled
To Wives 104-8 the **wife** who trembles in fear
To Wives 112-20 help the **wife** of another serious drinker.
Th Fam Af 122-2 certain attitudes a **wife** may take with
Th Fam Af 122-9 The alcoholic, his **wife,** his children
Th Fam Af 122-23 to make any **wife** or child neurotic.
Th Fam Af 124-27 the alcoholic or his **wife** have had
Th Fam Af 130-26 the **wife** who adopts a sane spiritual program
Th Fam Af 135-9 his **wife** commenced to admonish him
Th Fam Af 135-11 His **wife** is one of those persons who
Th Fam Af 135-20 neither his **wife** nor anyone else
To Emp 146-28 When his **wife** next calls saying he is sick,
A Vi Fo You 155-7 home in jeopardy, **wife** ill,
A Vi Fo You 158-11 His **wife** came, scarcely daring to be
A Vi Fo You 160-5 One man and his **wife** placed their large
A Vi Fo You 160-9 Many a distracted **wife** has visited this
A Vi Fo You 161-1 He and his **wife** would leave elated
Dr Bob Ni 177-31 with the permission of my good **wife.**
Wife's
Bill's Story 5-13 renewed my **wife's** hope.
Bill's Story 6-24 I stole from my **wife's** slender purse
Wild
Into Ac 81-20 general way that we have been **wild,**
Will *noun*
Bill's Story 7-15 the **will** is amazingly weakened
Bill's Story 11-16 His human **will** had failed
We Ag 45-7 as marshalled by the **will**
Ho It Wo 59-13 made a decision to turn over our will
Ho It Wo 60-22 decided to turn our **will** and our life
Ho It Wo 70-28 patience and good **will** toward all men
Into Ac 76-24 if we haven't the **will** to do this
Into Ac 85-23 the proper use of the **will.**
To Emp 140-9 with stubborness, or a weak **will?**
Will *God's*
Ho It Wo 59-32 His **will** for us and the power to carry
Ho It Wo 63-20 May I do Thy **will** always.
Ho It Wo 67-7, Into Ac 85-20, 88-2 Thy **will** be done.
Into Ac 85-19 the vision of God's **will**

Will *verb (all others)*

Mo Ab Al 31-11 **will** try to prove themselves
Ho It Wo 58-3 who cannot or **will** not completely
Ho It Wo 63-17 that I may better do thy **will**
Ho It Wo 69-31 The right answer **will** come
Ho It Wo 75-1 that he **will** not try to change our plan.
Into Ac 76-6 cling to something we **will** not let go
Into Ac 77-13 a demonstration of good **will**
Into Ac 84-4 self-pity **will** disappear.
Into Ac 84-4 we **will** lose interest in selfish things
Into Ac 84-6 Self-seeking **will** slip away.
Into Ac 84-7 outlook upon life **will** change.
Into Ac 84-8 We **will** intuitively know how to handle
Into Ac 84-31 sanity **will** have returned.
Into Ac 85-2 We **will** see that our new attitude
Wo Wi Ot 89-8 Life **will** take on new meaning.
Wo Wi Ot 92-6 he **will** understand you at once.
Wo Wi Ot 92-7 He **will** match your mental
Wo Wi Ot 92-29 You **will** soon have your friend admitting
Wo Wi Ot 93-22 he **will** be curious to learn
Wo Wi Ot 94-12 he **will** try to help other alcoholics
Wo Wi Ot 95-8 **will** be most successful with alcoholics
Wo Wi Ot 95-14 you **will** do anything to help.
Wo Wi Ot 97-30 head of the family **will** recover.
Wo Wi Ot 97-31 family **will** find life more bearable.
Wo Wi Ot 102-28 God **will** keep you unharmed.
Wo Wi Ot 103-14 Alcoholics Anonymous **will** help
To Wives 109-10 Some **will** moderate or stop, and some **will** not.
To Wives 109-11,12 **will** become true alcoholics
To Wives 114-20 or **will** not get over alcoholism.
To Wives 115-14,15 You **will** no longer be self-conscious
To Wives 116-13 he can stop if he **will!**
To Wives 117-11 there **will** be ups and downs.
To Wives 117-17 you **will** be learning to live.
To Wives 117-17 You **will** make mistakes,
To Wives 117-20 A better way of life **will** emerge
To Wives 117-22 husband **will** sometimes be unreasonable
To Wives 117-23 you **will** want to criticize.
To Wives 118-15 **will** be reflected back to you

Th Fam Af 123-18 It **will** take time to clear away the wreck.

Th Fam Af 132-2 he **will** make new friends

To Emp 142-31 that he **will** go to any extreme to do so.

To Emp 148-2 if you cannot or **will** not stop drinking,

To Emp 148-20 those who cannot or **will** not stop.

A Vi Fo You 152-9 Then he **will** know loneliness such as

A Vi Fo You 152-33 you **will** escape disaster together, and you **will** commence shoulder to shoulder

A Vi Fo You 153-3 You **will** learn the full meaning

A Vi Fo You 153-18 **will** rise to their feet and march on.

A Vi Fo You 153-19 They **will** approach still other sick ones

A Vi Fo You 164-4 to recover- if he can and **will.**

A Vi Fo You 164-15 The answers **will** come,

A Vi Fo You 164-25 you **will** surely meet some of us as you

Will power

Doc's Op xxix-30 the "**will-power**" to resist the impulse

Th Is A Sol 20-19 His **will power** must be weak.

Th Is A Sol 22-21 common sense and **will power**

Th Is A Sol 23-31 assert his **power** of **will**

Th Is A Sol 24-8 Our so-called **will power** becomes

Mo Ab Al 34-8 so-called **will power**

Mo Ab Al 33-17 on their own **will power**

Mo Ab Al 34-4 quit on our **will power**

Mo Ab Al 40-27 of exercising my **will power**

Mo Ab Al 42-6 I saw that **will power** and self-knowledge

Into Ac 85-22 can exercise our **will power** along this line

Wo Wi Ot 92-13 functioning of the **will power**

To Wives 107-31 their **will power?**

To Emp 138-28 if he has your **will power** and guts

A Vi Fo You 155-14 no amount of **will power** he might muster

Willing

Bill's Story 13-11 became **willing** to have my

Th Is A Sol 26-1 **willing** to make an effort

Th Is A sol 27-1 provided he remains **willing**

Th Is A Sol 28-20 **willing** and honest enough to try

We Ag 47-15 am I even **willing** to believe,

We Ag 47-17 or is **willing** to believe

We Ag 57-7 Circumstances made him **willing**

Ho It Wo 58-17 **willing** to go to any length
Ho It Wo 59-23 became **willing** to make amends
Ho It Wo 60-9 we are **willing** to grow along spiritual
Ho It Wo 67-23 and were **willing** to set these matters
Ho It Wo 69-25 we must be **willing** to grow toward it.
Ho It Wo 69-26 We must be **willing** to make amends
Ho It Wo 70-31 **willing** to straighten out the past
Into Ac 72-19 We **will** be more reconciled
Into Ac 76-7 ask God to help us be **willing.**
Into Ac 76-9 I am now **willing** that you should have
Into Ac 76-18 we are **willing** to make amends.
Into Ac 77-17 we are **willing** to announce our convictions
Into Ac 79-12 face jail, but we are **willing.**
Into Ac 79-25 to be **willing** to do that if necessary,
Into Ac 79-31 was perfectly **willing** to go to jail
Into Ac 81-26 God **willing,** it shall not be repeated.
Wo Wi Ot 92-32 is **willing** to tell him that he is alcoholic,
Wo Wi Ot 93-9 **willing** to believe in a Power greater
Wo Wi Ot 97-33 alcoholic who is able and **willing** to
To Wives 112-13 may be **willing** to talk to one
Th Fam Af 124-7 if one is **willing** to turn the past
Th Fam Af 124-16 **willing** to bring former mistakes,
To Emp 141-28 You are **willing** to overlook his past
A Vi Fo You 152-12 "Yes, I'm **willing**"
A Vi Fo You 153-12 be **willing** to make use of our experience
A Vi Fo You 158-11 **willing** to do anything necessary.
A Vi Fo You 159-19 They were **willing**, by day or night,
A Vi Fo You 162-11 **willing** and able to recover
Willingness
Bill's Story 12-23 **willingness** I might build what I
Bill's Story 12-31 had been a humble **willingness**
Bill's Story 13-17 entire **willingness** to approach
Bill's Story 13-33 plus enough **willingness,**
We Ag 46-16 express even a **willingness** to believe
Into Ac 76-2 emphasized **willingness** as being indispensable
To Wives 118-17 **willingness** to remedy your own defects,
Th Fam Af 124-8 We grow by our **willingness** to face
A Vi Fo You 163-8 a matter of **willingness,** patience

Wise

Wo Wi Ot 90-14 Sometimes it is **wise** to wait till he

Th Fam Af 123-25 But the **wise** family will admire him

Wish

A Vi Fo You 152-9 He will **wish** for the end.

A Vi Fo Yo 153-11 Should you **wish** them above all else,

Wishes

Th Fam Aft 122-12 his or her **wishes** respected.

Witch -burners

Wo Wi Ot 103-7 when he finds we are not **witch-burners**

Withdraw

Wo Wi Ot 102-21 Don't start to **withdraw** again

Withdrawing

Wo Wi Ot 102-19 **withdrawing** from life little by little.

Withdrew

A Vi Fo Yo 151-13 the more we **withdrew** from society,

Withholding

Into Ac 75-13 we have taken this step, **withholding** nothing

Witness

Ho It Wo 63-18 may bear **witness** to those i would help

Wives

Doc's Op xxvi-22 the despairing **wives,** the children;

Th Is A Sol 18-10 sad **wives** and parents

Th Is A Sol 18-17 **wives,** parents and intimate friends

Into Ac 74-17 cannot disclose anything to our **wives**

Into Ac 82-21 the patience mothers and **wives** have had

Into Ac 87-20 we ask our **wives** or friends to join us

Wo Wi Ot 97-11 counseling frantic **wives** and relatives,

To Wives 104-10 Among us are **wives,** relatives and friends

To Wives 104-12 We want the **wives** of Alcoholics Anonymous

To Wives 104-13 to address the **wives** of men who drink too

To Wives 104-17 As **wives** of Alcoholics Anonymous,

To Wives 107-14 men who loved their **wives** and children

To Wives 114-24 The **wives** children of such men suffer

To Wives 116-19 We **wives** found that, like everybody else,

To Wives 119-24 to the **wives** of his new alcoholic friends.

To Wives 121-15 a guide for husbands, **wives,** relatives,

Th Fam Af 125-1 Husbands and **wives** have sometimes

Th Fam Af 127-23 We know there are difficult **wives** and
Woke up
Dr Bob Ni 179-29 I **woke up** at a friend's house,
Woman
Into Ac 81-23 want to know who the **woman** is
Wo Wi Ot 101-13 Ask any **woman** who has sent her husband
To Wives 106-20 to live with the other **woman** forever.
To Wives 105-4 through the mind of every **woman** who has
To Wives 119-25 counsel and love of a **woman** who has
To Emp 137-6 A **woman**'s voice came faintly over long
Women
Doc's Op xxvi-30 Men and **women** drink essentially because
Into Ac 80-33 mixed up with **women** in a fashion
To Wives 104-3 applies quite as much to **women.**
To Wives 104-4 Our activities in behalf of **women** who drink
To Wives 104-5 every evidence that **women** regain their health
To Wives 106-3 Sometimes there were other **women.**
To Wives 111-19 We know **women** who are unafraid,
To Wives 114-27 We know **women** who have done it.
To Wives 114-27 If such **women** adopt a spiritual way of life
To Wives 116-28 we were pretty good **women,**
To Wives 118-19 We **women** carry with us a picture of the
The Fam Af 122-1 Our **women** folk have suggested
A Vi Fo You 160-11 companionship among **women** who knew
A Vi Fo You 160-25 expression on the faces of the **women,**
Wonderful
Bill's Story 8-24 incredibly more **wonderful** as time passes.
Th Is A So 17-11 which is indescribably **wonderful.**
Wo Wi Ot 100-12 live a new and **wonderful** world,
A Vi Fo Yo 152-32 bound to them with new and **wonderful** ties
Work
Doc's Op xxiv-28 Though we **work** out our solution
Bill's Story 14-27 They in turn might **work** with others.
Bill's Story 14-30 imperative to **work** with others
Bill's Story 15-14 **work** with another alcoholic would
Ho It Wo 70-20 We think of their needs and **work** for them.
Into Ac 84-15 materialize if we **work** for them.
Into Ac 86-2 have the proper attitude and **work** at it.
Wo Wi Ot 89-3 intensive **work** with other alcoholics.

Wo Wi Ot 98-11 we put our **work** on a service plane,

To Wives 116-31 put spiritual principles to **work** in every

To Wives 119-14 he should **work** with other people

To Wives 119-22 to dampen his enthusiasm for alcoholic **work.**

Th Fam Af 123-23 take him many seasons of hard **work**

Th Fam Af 130-15 where our **work** must be done.

To Emp 144-25 As our **work** spreads and our numbers

To Emp 146-6 They **work** hard and they play hard.

To Emp 146-10 curb his desire to **work** sixteen hours a day.

To Emp 146-15 This **work** is necessary to maintain his sobriety.

To Emp 149-31 He will **work** like the devil

A Vi Fo You 151-25 Feel better. **Work** better.

A Vi Fo You 160-9 dedicated their home to the **work.**

A Vi Fo You 162-7 it might prejudice his own **work,**

A Vi Fo You 162-9 Understanding our **work,** he can do this

Work-outs

To Wives 117-15 These **work-outs** should be regarded

Workable

A Vi Fo You 163-19 to adopt any **workable** method of

Worked

Bill's Story 14-31 as he had **worked** with me.

Th Is A Sol 25-8 we saw that ir really **worked** in others,

Mo Ab Al 35-28 occasions we **worked** with him,

Wo Wi Ot 95-13 Show him how they **worked** with you.

Wo Wi Ot 95-30 merely have an approach that **worked** with us.

To Emp 144-5 it has **worked** with us.

Worker

A Vi Fo You 163-29 So our fellow **worker** will soon have

Working

Wo Wi Ot 100-14 when **working** with a man and his family,

To Wives 119-7 you and your husband are **working** together

A Vi Fo You 153-23 In the chapter "**Working** With Others"

Workings

Th Is A Sol 26-13 of the inner **workings** of his mind

Works

Bill's Story 14-31 Faith without **works** was dead,

Bill's Story 15-18 a design for living that **works**

Into Ac 86-1 It **works,** if we have the proper attitude

Wo Wi Ot 89-3 It **works** when other activities fail.

World

Th Fam Af 128-26 everyone in the **world** but his family?

Th Fam Af 132-7 to minister to our troubled **world.**

Worldly

Th Fam Af 128-13 he is above **worldly** considerations.

Worry

Into Ac 83-20 We don't **worry** about them if we can

Into Ac 86-14 careful not to drift into **worry,**

Into Ac 88-3 excitement, fear, anger, **worry,**

To Wives 114-29 you probably **worry** over what other

To Wives 116-33 **worry** and hurt feelings

A Vi Fo You 151-3 from care, boredom, and **worry.**

A Vi Fo You 155-18 he lived in constant **worry** about

A Vi Fo You 159-25 thus relieving much **worry** and

Worse

Ho It Wo 68-10 When it made us cocky, it was **worse.**

Dr Bob Ni 175-8 so that I got rapidly **worse.**

Worshipfully

We Ag 54-11 had we not **worshipfully** beheld the sunset,

Worshipped

We Ag 54-9 Had we not variously worshipped people,

Worst

Mo Ab Al 43-5 it's best moments for the **worst** I have now.

Into Ac 73-5 hung on to some of the **worst** items in stock.

Worthwhile

To Emp 148-26 give your **worthwhile** man a chance.

Wrapped

Th Fam Aft 122-4 he is to be **wrapped** in cotton wool

Wreck

Th Fam Af 123-19 take time to clear away the **wreck.**

Wreckage

A Vi Fo You 164-23 Clear away the **wreckage** of your past.

Wrecked

A Vi Fo You 161-25 Being **wrecked** in the same vessel,

Wringer

Mo Ab Al 38-20 have been through the **wringer,**

Wrong

Bill's Story 13-18 these individuals, admitting my **wrong.**

Th Is A So 21-22 getting tight at exactly the **wrong** moment,

We Ag 56-17 religious people I have known are **wrong**?
Ho It Wo 59-28 when we were **wrong** promptly admitted
Ho It Wo 66-2 To conclude that others were **wrong** was as far
Ho It wo 66-4 that people continued to **wrong** us
Into Ac 77-12 sincere desire to set right the **wrong.**
Into Ac 80-14 a **wrong** he could not possibly make right.
Wo Wi Ot 98-4 are on the **wrong** track
Th Fam Af 129-20 on the **wrong** side of every argument,
Th Fam Af 131-2 placed him constantly in the **wrong.**
Th Fam Af 135-16 our friend was **wrong**- dead **wrong.**
Th Fam Af 135-21 was **wrong** to make a burning issue

Wrong-doing
Ho It Wo 66-28 the **wrong-doing** of others
Into Ac 80-11 used his own **wrong-doing** as a means

Wrong-doings
Ho It Wo 66-28 the **wrong-doings** of others,
Into Ac 80-11 used his own **wrong-doing** as a means of

Wronged
Ho It Wo 62-2 who thinks society has **wronged** him;
Ho It Wo 66-33 the people who **wronged** us were perhaps

Wrongs
Ho It wo 59-18 the exact nature of our **wrongs.**
Ho It Wo 67-15 the **wrongs** others had done.
Ho It Wo 67-23 We admitted our **wrongs** honestly
Into Ac 83-19 may be some **wrongs** we can never fully right.
Th Fam Af 128-25 If he means to right his past **wrongs,**

Wrought
Th fam Af 127-5 his drinking **wrought** all kinds of damage.
Th Fam Af 133-26 God has **wrought** miracles among us,

Y

Yearning
A Vi Fo Yo 151-8 **yearning** to enjoy life as we once did

Years

Th Fam Aft 122-22 **Years** of living with an alcoholic

A Vi Fo Yo 152-20 The most satisfactory **years** of your

Yield

Ho It Wo 70-21 when to **yield** would mean heartache.

Th Fam Af 131-20 each will have to **yield** here

Young

Th Fam Af 134-18 their **young** minds were impressionable

Yourself

Mo Ab Al 31-31 you can quickly diagnose **yourself.**

Mo Ab Al 32-2 if you are honest with **yourself** about it.

We Ag 45-15 a Power greater than **yourself** which will

We Ag 47-5 from honestly asking **yourself**

We Ag 55-26 search diligently within **yourself,**

Ho It Wo 71-7 some big chunks of truth about **yourself.**

Wo Wi Ot 90-12 to put **yourself** in his place,

Wo Wi Ot 90-27 never force **yourself** upon him.

To Wives 111-31 put **yourself** in his place.

To Wives 114-30 draw more and mote into **yourself**

To Wives 118-15 Show him these things in **yourself**

To Wives 119-20 more attention for **yourself.**

To Wives 120-27 If he gets drunk, don't blame **yourself.**

A Vi Fo Yo 153-2 what it means to give of **yourself**

The first 164 pages of the Big Book of Alcoholics Anonymous contain the whole plan for life without alcohol.

First step - First three chapters
Second step - Chapter four 44-57
Third step - Chapter five 58-63
Fourth step - Chapter five 64-71
Sixth and seventh step - Chap. six first half of page 76
Eighth and ninth step - Chap. Six pages 76-84
Tenth step - Chapter six pages 84-85
Eleventh step Chapter six Bottom of page 85 to 88
Twelfth step - Chapter seven page 89

Teachings From The Big Book

How To Get Sober And Stay Sober

- We have to quit playing God. 62-27
- Be willing to believe in a Power greater than yourself. 12-19
- Humbly offer yourself to God as you understand Him. 13-6
- Abandon yourself to God. 164-21
- Perfect and enlarge your spiritual life. 14-33
- We have to have a vital spiritual experience. 27-15
- Be willing to grow along spiritual lines. 60-9
- Fit ourselves to be of maximum service to God. 77-3
- Work with another alcoholic. 15-14
- Helping others is the foundation stone of your recovery. 97-4
- The leveling of our pride. 25-5
- Lay aside prejudice. 46-16
- A manner of living which demands rigorous honesty. 58-10, 145-9
- Be willing to go to any length 58-17
- Willing to go to any extreme. 142-31
- Ask God to help us be willing. 76-7
- Be fearless and thorough from the very start. 58-22
- We must have thoroughness and honesty. 65-32
- We must be rid of selfishness. 62-18
- We have to be free of anger. 66-20
- We must be willing to make amends. 69-26
- We have to learn tolerance and patience. 70-28
- We have to get a new attitude. 72-3
- Have love and tolerance of others. 84-29
- Live and let live. 118-16
- Let faith work twenty-four hours a day. 16-12
- We must be hard on ourself. 74-22
- Repair the damage done in the past. 76-21
- We trust in God and clean house. 98-22

What the Big Book Promises Us

- Spiritual principles will solve all your problems. 42-32
- They found that a new power, peace, happiness, and sense of direction flowed into them. 50-31
- We will enjoy peace of mind. 63-9
- We will discover that we can face life successfully. 63-10
- We will begin to lose our fear of today, tomorrow or the hereafter. 63-11
- Our fears fall from us. 75-15
- We commence to outgrow fear. 68-26
- We can be alone at perfect peace and ease. 75-15
- We are going to know a new freedom. 83-31
- We will know a new happiness. 83-32
- We will not regret the past nor wish to shut the door on it. 83-32
- We will comprehend the word serenity. 84-1
- We will know peace. 84-1
- We will see how our experience can benefit others. 84-2
- That feeling of uselessness will disappear. 84-3
- Self-pity will disappear. 84-4
- We will lose interest in selfish things. 84-4
- We will gain interest in our fellows. 84-5
- Sel-seeking will slip away. 84-6
- Our whole attitude and outlook upon life will change. 84-6
- Fear of people will leave us. 84-7
- Fear of economic insecurity will leave us. 84-8
- We will intuitively know how to handle situations which used to baffle us. 84-8
- We will suddenly realize that God is doing for us what we could not do for ourselves. 84-10
- Sanity will have returned. 84-31
- We react sanely and normally. 85-1
- Life will take on new meaning. 89-8
- A better way of life will emerge. 117-19
- God wants us to be happy, joyous, and free. 133-3
- Know happiness, peace, and usefulness. 8-22
- You will make lifelong friends. 152-31
- You can become happy, respected, and useful once more. 153-7
- In finding God you can find yourself. 158-21

Life Before AA

- We have recovered from a hopeless condition of mind and body 20-8
- Probably beyond human aid. 24-31
- Faced with alcoholic destruction. 48-7
- We could not manage our own lives. 60-16
- No human power could have relieved our alcoholism. 60-18
- Selfishness- self-centeredness. 62-6
- Extreme example of self-will run riot. 62-16
- A body badly burned by alcohol. 133-10
- Sick people, deranged men. 149-21
- Were drinking to overcome a craving beyond their mental control. xxviii-2

About God

- We are going to talk about God. 45-18
- God has restored us all to our right minds. 57-10
- When we drew near to Him He disclosed Himself to us. 57-14
- There is One who has all power- that One is God. 59-2
- God could relieve our alcoholism. 60-20
- We have to have God's help. 62-25
- The power of God goes deep. 114-17
- God has wrought miracles among us. 133-26
- God had done for him what he could not do for himself. 11-15

We Are Different

- We are not like other people. 30-14
- With us, to drink is to die. 66-19
- We are miracles of mental health. 133-15
- Have been saved from a living death. 150-3

What Happens When We Work The Program

- A revolutionary change in their way of living and thinking. 50-27
- Experience an entire psychic change. xxvii-8

The previous lists are not comprehensive or exhaustive by any means. But with this concordance you can find more and add to them.

A Room Full Of Miracles

Just look around and what do you see?
Love and warmth, faith and hope;
A lot of folks like you and me,
Learning to live and how to cope.

We once were full of anger,
Of this I'm sure we can agree;
And sometimes these things still appear,
But not what they used to be.

Lives were wrecked and in despair;
Some near death and no wish to live.
And peace of mind became so rare
There was little or nothing we had to give.

So we put out a trembling hand,
And asked for help from those who cared.
And asked of God to help us stand
Among the ones whose lives we've shared.

All were hopeless, no place to turn,
"Til we opened the door and let Him in.
And with His help, we began to learn;
Not wanting to go back where we've been.

He's given us our lives anew,
That we might pass it on to others.
He asks that, to ourselves we be true;
That we might help our sisters and our brothers.

Plumbers, mechanics and teachers,
All have come out of their gloom.
Housewives, laborers and preachers,
Miracles that have graced this room.

Again take a look around you here.
Look upon the face across from you.
Do you see peace instead of fear,
And thank God you're a miracle too?

Pat Mitchell - Jan. 6, 1980